FLASH of *Brilliance*

FLASH
of *Brilliance*

Inspiring Creativity
Where You Work

WILLIAM C. MILLER

PERSEUS BOOKS
Reading, Massachusetts

Library of Congress Catalog Card Number: 98-88116

ISBN 0-7382-0018-2

Perseus Books is a member of the Perseus Books Group

Jacket design by Suzanne Heiser
Text design by Faith Hague
Set in 10.7-point Sabon by Faith Hague

123456789-DOH-0201009998
First printing, December 1998

Perseus Books are available at special discounts for bulk purchases in the U.S. by corporations, institutions, and other organizations. For more information, please contact the Special Markets Department at HarperCollins Publishers, 10 East 53rd Street, New York, NY 10022, or call 212-207-7528.

Find us on the World Wide Web at
http://www.aw.com/gb/

*This book is dedicated to the divine spirit we all share,
and to a society beyond scarcity and separation,
a world that profits each person materially and spiritually.*

Contents

Appreciations

My special thanks to:

Kate, for her heartfelt love and support.

Latifah Taormina and Terry Pearce for stimulating my ideas and encouraging me to write about what is soulfully true.

Gay and Kathlyn Hendricks for revealing the possibility of greater depth and joy in all relationships.

Joe McPherson, who contributed so much to my knowledge and appreciation of the field of creativity and innovation.

Nick Philipson, my senior editor, and Julie Stillman, editor and project manager, for their enthusiastic support and skill in shaping this book.

Lawrence Akioshi, Julian Gresser, Joel Levey, John Maher, Chuck Meyer, Ian Rose, and others for their feedback on my manuscript.

Juanita Brown, Lorna Catford, Cathy DeForest, Jennifer Hammond, Dennis Jaffe, Sharon Lehrer, and Chuck McConnell, for their special ideas and contributions.

Lee Nelson for his wonderful images for the culture, and the person.

Dave Keaton and Bill Dowdy for their support at SRI.

Sue Lawson for her invaluable support in sponsoring creativity gatherings.

Hulki Aldikacti, Steve Arnold, Bruce Beron, Frank Carrubba, Claire Cohn, Dick Eppel, Joyce Francis, John Gooden, Jay Howell, Ron Jackson, Dennis Jaffe, Rick Laine, Sue Lawson, Edgar Mitchell, Antonio Nunez, Teddy Olwyler, Jerry Pierce, Linda Plott, Gretchen Price, Ron Richards, Fred Schwettman, Cynthia Scott, Carol Shaw, Alison Stevens, Tom Ucko, Pat Weedman, Diane Wexler, and others who shared their stories about creativity at work, as well as the multitude of managers who helped formulate examples for this text.

Foreword

Business has become much more interesting in recent years, because the questions we're dealing with have become subtler, deeper, and more complicated. Questions like:

- How can organizations maintain a core identity while adapting to different cultures and rapid change?
- Can we create a work environment where people can grow to their full potential, and still keep sufficient focus and coherence to function crisply?

A number of companies are starting to understand that all the "ordinary people"—the ones who are doing the business—have traditionally been functioning at a fraction of their collective potential. We know this because we see how people work together in crisis—rank is forgotten, bureaucracy put aside; people contribute, and they do it quickly; the best ideas come from unexpected places. Compare that with how we work on an average Tuesday afternoon: politics, anxiety, mistrust, procrastination, endless review, etc., etc.—all of which waste time and lead to weak, watered-down decisions. My own guess is that most large institutions operate at something less than 20 percent of their potential, if you measure potential by right decisions and right actions taken quickly and effectively, as in our best peak work experiences.

If we can figure out a better model than the traditional one, a model better suited to our times, the potential payoff is very, very large. An institution whose people give it more than just "doing the job," an institution that attracts great people and gives them the tools, the knowledge, and the authority to do great work—such an institution will simply beat the stuffing out of its traditional competitors.

The most obvious characteristic of that kind of organization would be its inexhaustible creativity, measured in a continuous outpouring of innovation: new products, new processes, new ways of making a difference in customers' lives. William Miller's *Flash of Brilliance* can not only help us imagine the new work culture, but can also help us and the people around us become wellsprings of innovation.

I grew up in an era in which successful organizations could continue to succeed by continuing to do what they had traditionally done. Companies knew what they were there to do; knew their customers, technologies, and competitors; and had evolved systems and cultures that assured consistency and reliability. Most of the rules for success could be found in a few words: accountability, cost reduction, "no surprises," control.

Consciously or not, the metaphor for business organizations was the machine. People were the parts. Or, more accurately, jobs were the parts—people were to fit into their jobs, regardless of their individual shapes or talents. And their most important job was to conform to the system.

Everything about the traditional corporation—from the design of its offices to the volumes that described its procedures—delivered a single, overpowering message: "The company is very big, and you are very small—follow orders and you won't get hurt!"

No wonder that words like "management" and "administration" described what people at the top of the standard hierarchy were supposed to do. No wonder that "control" was the watchword—because deviation from established processes posed dangers, not opportunities. No wonder that the way for people to succeed was to imitate and please their seniors. And no wonder that information was hoarded, manipulated, and controlled, as the currency of power.

Well, some companies are still that way, as *Dilbert* tells us. But whereas the traditional "machine" model of the corporation was pretty well adapted to the marketplace realities of North America, Europe, and Japan through the 1970s, it's less well adapted to the emerging realities that businesses confront today.

For example:

• As global competition starts to bite, competitive strategies based on cost leadership are under growing pressure. Rewards are increasingly going to those who can create new products and industries, do it faster than their competitors, adapt to a variety of local conditions, diffuse learning throughout the organization, anticipate the direction of changes in diverse global markets, and focus all the company's resources exactly where and when needed. Machines—and machine-based cultures—are good at turning out consistent outputs at low cost, but they're not much good at creation, change, and adaptation.

• Centralization of information, authority, and control is rapidly becoming a suicidal practice. As is a control-oriented culture. As is uniformity and conformity in senior management ranks. A bunch of middle-aged white guys in suits, sitting in privileged corporate campuses and relying on obsolete knowledge, isn't likely to be much good at figuring out what's going to happen next in Indonesia, Poland, and Brazil—or even in America and Europe. Diverse teams that bring together a range of perspectives and global experience will do better—if they have the right information, knowledge, and power.

• The authority of top management was legitimized to some degree in pyramid structures because that was the only place where all the information could come together. But now the needs of the global market and the abundance of information that can be shared through new information technologies have set the stage for a fundamental redefinition of the nature of authority and the role of top management.

• The price of control is becoming more evident: lost time, lost initiative, lost effectiveness. I ask people how long it takes them to come to the right decision. Call it "x." Then I ask how long it takes to convince their boss that it's the right decision. And their boss's boss. So a decision that was ready in May doesn't get implemented until December, when it's less effective, and maybe even wrong. Finally, I ask how often decisions are made better by the review process, and how often they're made worse. The answer is usually more of the latter than the former. Incidentally, I don't know of any company that has formal measurements of the net effectiveness of its own review and control processes.

What's the alternative to traditional controls? We know from experience that trust-based systems are a lot faster, but can anyone invent a trust-based system that's hard-nosed enough to prevent serious mistakes and assure adherence to core strategies and values? I think so, at least to a far greater extent than is now common; but such a system would require extraordinary attention to make sure that everyone in the organization is in fact trustworthy—not only in character, but in knowledge, skill, and judgment.

In the past, management worried about the unauthorized leakage of information to people who didn't "need to know." Now the emerging practice of knowledge management, with its emphasis on pooling the shared learning of the company's people, makes information hoarding and manipulation the thing to worry about.

Brilliant, highly-motivated, creative people—those who can make the difference between being first to market with the best product or third to market with a mediocre one—don't want to spend their lives being cogs in a machine. And they don't have to.

So the task for people in business today is to create that kind of model, that kind of work environment and culture. I think the most valuable question—valuable in dollars—business leaders can ask is, "How can we work better together than our competitors' people do? How can we create an environment in which people are more authentic, more truthful, more courageous, less defensive, less territorial, more commit-

> **How can we create an environment in which people are more authentic, more truthful, more courageous, less defensive, less territorial, more committed, more creative?**

ted, more creative—an environment that generates sustainable competitive advantage?"

It seems that the tendency of our age is toward "commoditizing" all sources of competitive advantage: product and technology life cycles are shortening, knowledge is quickly disseminated, and changes in the competitive environment make yesterday's advantage obsolete. But it isn't so easy to duplicate a successful corporate culture. Building a culture takes time: many elements—people, technology, systems, training, practices, values—need to fit together. So it may turn out that culture is the last, best source of competitive advantage, and deserves the kind of careful attention that we have traditionally paid to our products and strategies.

If any of this makes sense to you, if you feel as I do that the work we do matters and that the way we do it matters even more, then you're in the right frame of mind to read this book. William Miller's work is to help people and organizations become more innovative and to realize more of their best potentials. This book isn't abstract; it is about the realities of the workplace, and can help us translate our purposes, values, and talents into our life's work. William shows how people throughout the organization can help transform their work environment into a place characterized by innovation, speed, and courage.

The new rules for competitive success are likely to be found in those words—innovation, speed, and courage—and in others like authenticity, caring, learning, trust, diversity, and connection. As far as I know, there aren't any business school courses with names like those. So we're all beginners, and this book is a good place to begin. William offers valuable "answers for now."

Robert Shapiro
Chairman, Monsanto Corporation

FLASH of *Brilliance*

Introduction

Awaken the Creator Within

A new era trembles to be born, with and through our creativity. The world at large, and the spirit deep within us, call upon us to recognize and actualize—perhaps for the first time—the natural, creative brilliance of our lives. Certainly the problems we face at the dawn of a new millennium—overpopulation, economic uncertainty, environmental destruction, terrorist and nuclear threats, lifestyle stresses—demand our creative participation to "clean up the mess we're in." But even more, our souls urge us to ignite our lives with spiritual purpose, to cherish again the gift of being alive and rededicate our work to making a creative difference (not just making money) through our unique gifts and talents.

The breath of our own soul fans the slumbering embers of our inherent creativity. The Greek word for breath is *spiros*—the root for *spirit* and *spirituality*, the divine breath in each of us. Having been an asthmatic most of my life, I've experienced what works and doesn't work with breathing. As a consultant on creativity and innovation for most of my adult life, I've experienced how business thrives or dies by the *aspirations*, *inspirations*, and *expirations* of new ideas.

Our organizations are literally corporate *bodies*. Together we act as organisms, not machines. We are embodiments of our aspirations and actions, our gifts and greatness, our foibles and failures. Our collective spirituality "breathes" by learning and innovating. At work we "inhale" by taking in new knowledge, learning new skills, sharing insights—all of these the fresh air that invigorates knowledge-intensive businesses. We "exhale" by innovating with what we have learned—envisioning new ways to serve customers, generating product and process ideas, and putting the best of them into action. Both are necessary to sustain the life and "breath" of business.

Despite some early breathing problems, creativity is alive and well in many people and corporations, gaining newfound respect, appreciation, and even wonder. Over twelve years ago, I wrote *The Creative Edge* to challenge some limiting notions about creativity, namely that:

- Creativity existed only in a small minority of people.
- Creativity couldn't be taught, only inherited through genetic transmission.

- Creativity was something only certain individuals had, and these individuals were probably a bit crazy and eccentric.
- Creativity was mainly an issue of the brain—right/left *brain*, *brain*storming, "creative *think*ing."
- Creativity couldn't really be managed.

Since then, the field of creativity and innovation has greatly matured. Witness:

- The quality movement asked for creative ideas from every employee, and we saw that everyone had creative ideas to offer— some incremental, some breakthrough, but creative nonetheless.
- Courses on creativity and innovation sprouted everywhere. By the mid-nineties, over 30 percent of companies with 500 or more employees had creativity courses. Even graduate schools of business had them.
- Groups became the locus of creativity, through "quality circles," "cross-functional teams," and "communities of practice" Creativity is now seen not so much as an individual phenomenon as a collective one. (Even the brilliant scientist is stimulated by peers in "communities of practice," and it takes cross-functional teams to get a creative idea from concept to customer.)
- Product and process teams now look for the "product champions" within the company: the "intrapreneurs," with the heart, courage, and passion to invent new ideas, take risks, and make things happen.
- From quantum physics, chaos theory, biology, and the Internet, we have understood more about how self-organizing systems work, taking us beyond separate discussions of the "learning organization" and the "innovative organization."

Around the world, I have observed firsthand that four new business phenomena are taking us even further, *beyond the creative edge*:

1. *Relationships* based on authenticity and caring have become *the* fundamental basis for sustainable advantage. It's only with a radically deeper synergy that knowledge-creation and innovation can occur at the levels required for global industry leadership.
2. *Intellectual capital* is becoming *the* fundamental measure of future corporate performance. Intellectual capital is the sum of the experience we bring, the knowledge we create, the processes we design, the products and services we invent, the relationships we develop with customers, suppliers, and the community—the intangible assets that generate new wealth.

3. *Complex systems and chaos theory* have become *the* metaphors for creating and sustaining the living organisms we call companies. Quantum physics describes a level of reality that thrives on ambiguity and uncertainty at something very like "the edge of chaos." This creative edge lies at the border between order and chaos, between stability and instability, and stimulates a level of self-organization that defies the classic law of entropy.

4. *Spirituality in business* is becoming *the* fundamental next step for tapping the full potential and motivation of each human being. Spirituality springs from our soul's knowledge and experience of our inherent holiness, and our innate need to become one, integral whole. As we struggle with life-balance issues, we yearn to know how to bring our souls to work along with our minds, hearts, and hands. Fear of the conflict of religious differences is holding this at bay, but not for long—we're learning how to have dialogues focused on our common spiritual and human values, across geographies and cultures.

The intersection of corporate vision and our personal motivation has always sparked the question, "Creativity for what purpose?" Our challenge today is not just to understand how to manage our organizations at this creative edge of chaos, but to go beyond it. The key question is not, "What *can* we create?" or even, "What do we *want* to create?" Rather, for all of us it is, "What are we *called* to create?" That is, "What higher needs for serving each other will enrich and ennoble our lives? What are our values, our commitments, and our passions that move us to create a sustainable future for us all?"

Only when we answer that from our inmost human center, and dare to live our answer, does learning the skills for innovation take on any real meaning. Only when we venture deep within our spiritual selves, even beyond our religious beliefs, do we access the core of our creativity. There we touch the living flame, the source of love and creative insight, illuminating the meaning of our lives not just once but repeatedly.

People everywhere are responding to this call with surprising flashes of personal and collective brilliance. And there is a great rush to name what's coming. Peter Senge calls this the knowledge era[1]; Leif Edvinsson[2] and Tom Stewart[3] articulate the age of "Intellectual Capital," while Ikujiro Nonaka and Hirotaka Takeuchi explain the "pattern language of knowledge-creation."[4] Meg Wheatley calls it "the new story" whose time has come, the story that demands we live in creativity and give up "command and control."[5] Angeles Arrien, David Whyte, Fritjof Capra, Matthew Fox, Ralph Stacey, and Michael Talbot deftly weave the threads of the new story in conversations that take us from tribal wisdom to chaos theory, from timeless spiritual insight to physics' newest models of reality (our whole universe as a giant hologram[6]) in a fabric of extraordinary relationships.

Gifford and Elizabeth Pinchot show how this new story can utterly replace bureaucracy with its essential humanism.[7] Michael McMaster calls it "an intelligence larger than us, emerging at an ever-increasing rate that informs all structure, all organization—by design."[8] Verna Allee shows us how to build all that into an expanding organizational intelligence.[9] And even Tom Peters, who once said that putting spirituality and business together makes him " want to run," publicly heralds Dorothy Marcic's new book, which explores how the workplace might change if we admitted that spiritual values are just as important to organizations as they are to people.[10]

So what's up? What's going on here? All of the above, plus some. It's more than a knowledge era. A new, more spiritual story is informing our times, our lives, and our work, and at its heart is New Creativity—self-creating, spontaneous, intuitive, as intensely spiritual as it is human. The New Creativity is the real stuff, source *spiritus*, breath of life, that is ever becoming, an ancient journey into ourselves and toward each other. It is a celebration, a gift, a grace, a dialogue, and a fight for our lives.

We are an intimate part of this creation, and as such, we share in its creative nature. "Awakening the creator within" means discovering deep, spiritual purpose in life and bringing ourselves fully, creatively, and heartfully to everything we do. What we create in our lives gets expressed through family, interior life, and work. The work world offers a significant opportunity to get feedback on how well we create and a place to really practice what our lives are about.

We can literally co-create the evolution of creation. How well we creatively contribute to the lives of others worldwide endows our lives with spiritual purpose and meaning. Many of us may have started our careers with such noble intentions, but have stopped investing ourselves somewhere along the way, feeling "burned" or burned-out. Yet, when a flame is passed from torch to torch, the original flame still burns ever bright. Similarly, we can learn how to pass along the flame of our unique brilliance—burning in the air of our soul's aspirations on the torch of our unique gifts and talents—without fear of using ourselves up.

> **How well we creatively contribute to the lives of others worldwide endows our lives with spiritual purpose and meaning.**

Courageously, and with profound curiosity, we need to awaken the slumbering, creative genius inside ourselves. We cannot do this without embracing a kind of spiritual, creative electricity. I've known an element of my purpose for years: to bring creativity, business, and spirituality into the same arena and dialogue, and to help us to embody them as facets of the same jewel of our lives. The task for each of us is to awaken our creative spirit and breathe our most noble values into our work. Even after reading this book, you cannot adopt *my* sense of spirituality and creativity. You must discover your own, in every aspect of your life.

I offer you *Flash of Brilliance* to help you meet a challenge that is the same for all of us—to be all we can be, and to encourage everyone we work with to make the biggest difference possible. No matter how you've experienced your creativity at work, this book is intended for those of you who want a new vision of yourself and your workplace . . . who want yourself and your organizations to be more creative, productive, resourceful, motivated, responsible, profitable, alive, and growing . . . who want to experience the other side of stress and burnout— the creative side that profits everyone.

Examples and stories used in this book are not all from the "excellent" companies or the "best companies to work for." (As we shall explore, you do not need the optimum work environment to be able to assert your creativity.) This book is not an academic research treatise on creativity, nor is it a psychological profile of the creative person. It definitely is not the be-all and end-all on the subject of fostering innovation. It doesn't discuss product and innovation life cycles, funding for research and development (R&D), and a host of important topics for a wide variety of ever-changing business decisions.

Instead, *Flash of Brilliance* focuses on the environment, the context, necessary to ignite the wisdom for the most creative decisions to be made—the air, if you will, that is necessary to sustain the life and breath of a business and make it thrive!

PART I, Breathe New Life into Your Work, invites you to expand your notions and develop practical skills for expressing more of your individual creativity.

PART II, Foster Breakthrough Innovation in Groups, gives you specific models and methods for promoting a climate for creativity and leading innovation projects.

PART III, Revitalize the Soul of Corporate Creativity, provides you with new insights for being an innovative leader of corporate-wide innovation.

PART IV, Keep the Faith—Integrate Profits and Prophets, offers you a way to work in harmony with the goals of high achievement and social responsibility.

A key model that's used throughout the book is the Creative Journey (first explained in chapter 3), encompassing the entire innovation process. Otherwise, each chapter stands on its own, so feel free to jump around and read whatever chapters interest you the most.

Flash of Brilliance aims to take you beyond what you thought was your own creative edge. It offers you an introduction to the knowledge, skills, and attitudes you need throughout your organization for fostering strategically appropriate innovations. It is a practical guide to reframing your view of creativity, developing your inherent creative skills, and spurring your own and your colleagues' creative genius—no matter what your job is. As a result, you will develop a more powerful expression of your talents, your knowledge, your love, and your wisdom at work.

PART I

Breathe *New Life* Into Your Work

"Just how fresh are these insights?"

The mind is not a vessel to be filled, but a fire to be kindled.
—PLUTARCH

"There is no use trying," said Alice. "One can't believe impossible things."
"I dare say you haven't much practice," said the Queen. "When I was your age, I always did it for half-an-hour a day. Why, sometimes I've believed as many as six impossible things before breakfast."
—LEWIS CARROLL

The starting point for understanding and promoting more creativity and innovation where you work is *you* in your own work, moment by moment and task by task. If you don't know your powers to be creative, much of your potential will be wasted in an "I'm not allowed to be creative" hopelessness.

Some people may believe they *cannot* be more creative at work: "If I *were* in the right environment, *then* I could be creative; . . . In *my* company, I'm only allowed to follow rules and policy; . . . Things are so screwed up around here, *no one* could be creative."

Others may believe there *shouldn't* be more creativity at work: "Creativity means people out of control, going off in all sorts of directions. What we need is to put more productivity into how we already do things."

Your creativity comes from within you, not from without. You can be creative in your job in private ways. And you can be creative in helping others become more receptive to creative new ways of doing things.

This section takes you deeper into your potential to be more creative at work, discusses your creative process, gives you ways to think up more creative ideas, and offers you an approach to overcoming personal blocks to being more creative.

CHAPTER 1

Put Your *Creativity* and *Spirituality* to Work

The business of America is business.
—CALVIN COOLIDGE

We are created to develop the ability to create. The creature is designed to mature into the creator, the Son into the Father. The creation is the way by which God the One becomes many, and why Eternity is in love with the productions of time.
—JOSEPH CHILTON PEARCE[1]

INTEGRATING BUSINESS AND SPIRITUALITY

To some people, these opening statements are antithetical or contradictory. Certainly, their focus is different . . . or is it? Business aims to transform wishes into reality (through innovation). We shape the quality of our lives by transforming the deepest longings of the human spirit into reality. The two can become one.

A few years ago, I conducted with Du Pont a seminar called an Innovation Search. The purpose of the seminar was to develop new business opportunities for a material called Nomex that the company had developed. The first day seemed very creative—300 or so ideas—but nothing really sparked. There was no flash of brilliance, and I drove home puzzled. When I returned the next morning, I asked the participants to share with all of us one thing in the world situation that genuinely concerned them. Instantly, the room became alive as they anchored themselves in real-life, passionate issues: hunger, drugs, crime, resource depletion.

Then I said, "Now that you've heard each other's concerns, form groups with people you resonated with." As the participants brainstormed ways that Nomex might possibly contribute to solving their deep concerns, their creative energy rose exponentially. Ultimately, they produced over 1,000 ideas, which they then organized into the top fifty key concepts, of which ten later tested out with the highest technical and market feasibility. Of those, over the next two years, the first concept to achieve a significant profit and market share was only #8 on the initial top ten list: The opportunity of protecting precious art during shipment from museum to museum was made into a new business by a manager whose passion was preserving and appreciating art.

What made the difference? In brainstorming and implementing top ideas, the participants anchored their creative energy in something personal, compelling, and emotionally real. They tapped into their creative wellspring, and sparked innovative business ideas, based on deep, personal values such as caring for others and responsible action, and business success was born of these ideas. According to India's spiritual leader, Sathya Sai Baba, such fundamental human values as concern for well-being, responsibility, love, truth, and inner peace provide the foundation for every major spiritual tradition. And they directly support established business values:

- *Concern for people's well-being* fosters great service.
- *Responsibility* fosters trust and quality.
- *Caring* fosters collaboration and daring.
- *Truthfulness* fosters honest relationships.
- *Equanimity* fosters creative, wise decisions.

These values stimulate quantum leaps in innovation, process improvement, customer impact, and personal commitment. While spirituality in business might seem like a paradox or intrusion to some, spiritual values are actually the basis for sustainable, creative business success!

> **While spirituality in business might seem like a paradox or intrusion to some, spiritual values are actually the basis for sustainable, creative business success!**

Can we bring the paths of business and spiritual values together for the benefit of both business and our spiritual well-being? Many cynics say no, believing that getting ahead in this world is a matter of "survival of the fittest." But we have grossly underestimated human nature, just as we have grossly misinterpreted evolution itself. As pointed out by two Chilean biologists, Francisco Varela and Humberto Maturana,[2] life responds not to the survival of the fittest but to the greater space for experimentation of the survival of the fit. Even Darwin, whom we associate with the phrase "survival of the fittest," said, "It's not the strongest species that survive, nor the most intelligent, but the ones most responsive to change."

Therefore, we have long misunderstood the nature of evolution, and therefore the nature of business competition. Business is not governed by survival of the fittest, but rather, by "fit enough to survive, then the more the merrier!" After passing a threshold of fitness, nature encourages the play of experimentation to see just how many different species can thrive in a shared ecology. This same spirit of experimentation makes people, society, business, and whole economies thrive. To go beyond the creative edge means to go beyond notions of competitive "survival of the fittest."

Many people have been taught that mankind is fundamentally sinful or selfish, greedy at worst. We've passed laws designed to reign in this selfish nature, assuming there is no natural moral code inherent to human beings. How far this assumption is from the truth! We naturally find in ourselves the need and the inner resources for peace, love, and the other fundamental human values.[3] The Dalai Lama, spiritual leader of the exiled people of Tibet, puts it this way:

> *This peace of mind is a fact. There's no use denying it, presenting humans as the playthings of exclusively aggressive or possessive or dominating urges. Of course all these dangerous tendencies do exist in us, but beneath them, deeper and more permanent, lies peace. If we use this peace as a fact, we can truly offer humanity the possibility of something better. But first of all it has to be recognized, attained, and preserved.* [4]

I once conducted a survey of executives asking this question: What is the primary driving force behind your corporate success? Is it: Increasing shareholder value? Beating the competition? Making profits? Serving customer needs? Growing an organization? The vast majority of them had two observations:

1. Businesses at the top of their industry strive for success by "serving customers better than anyone else." Businesses closer to the bottom of their industry drive themselves to "beat the competition" or "make the most profits."
2. Perhaps "beating the competition" or "making the most profits" are mindsets that doom a business to be less successful, long term, than those "serving customers better than anyone else!"

Indeed, Bill Lambert, former Manager of Innovation Resources at Procter and Gamble, said, "If our sole goal is to maximize profits or beat the competition, we will not make the investments that are necessary in the long run to serve customers better than anyone else, and we won't end up #1 in our industry." We need to focus on the breakthrough choices that increase value for and delight our customers. It's fine if our competition does it too. We can expand the scope of opportunities rather than slice the pie up into smaller pieces.

Business in its basic form is the exhange of value(s) among people. The measure of our lives stands or falls on how well we contribute creatively to the lives of others. Work is one way we do this. We are integral parts of creation—that is, we are creative by nature and share in nature's creative powers. When we empower ourselves to be all we can be, we provide the DNA from which profitably innovative organizations are grown.

APPRECIATING THE ART OF BUSINESS

In his *Confessions*, St. Augustine states, "All the loveliness which passes through men's minds into their skillful hands comes from the supreme loveliness which is above our soul, which my soul sighs for day and night."[5] From Tolstoy's *What is Art?* we read, "Art is a human activity whose purpose is the transmission of the highest and best feelings which men have attained."[6] This chapter's opening quotations from Calvin Coolidge and Joseph Chilton Pearce merge with these from St. Augustine and Tolstoy in realizing business as a form of art. The artistry of business is the creative right of all those who desire true prosperity—economically and spiritually, personally and globally. The consummate artist demands a level of dedication and practice beyond what most people dream of for themselves and their work. Andre Previn once said, "If I miss a day of practice, I know it. If I miss two days, my manager knows it. If I miss three days, my audience knows it." Without mastery of whatever God-given talents we each have, we turn a deaf ear to a quiet voice within us that wants to be expressed, a "muscle" of creativity that wants to be exercised.

Similarly, peak-performing organizations also demand a mastery of their own collective creativity. Like artists, they are in the business of creativity. From the creative contributions of people like yourself, major corporations, grassroots nonprofits, government agencies, and small businesses grow and flourish. We innovate by taking our creative ideas and producing something with them. That's how we renew ourselves and stay healthy to serve our customers, clients, shareholders, other stakeholders, and ourselves. Whether we express our creativity in new products and services, new work processes, or new marketing methods, creativity is the prime source, the taproot, from which solutions spring. But what is the nature of creativity?

The *American Heritage Dictionary* defines creativity as the "ability or power to create things; creating, productive; characterized by originality and expressiveness; imaginative."[7] These four dimensions—creation, productivity, originality, and expressiveness—all suggest that creativity actualizes our human potential. Coaching people, constructing products, satisfying customer needs, counseling employees, or determining business strategies can all be either mechanical, lifeless routines or expressive, creative activities.

Throughout this book, when the terms *creativity* and *innovation* are both used, the former refers to conceiving of and developing new ideas, and the latter to applying and implementing them. When *creativity* is referred to by itself, it implies both idea-generation and implementation.

You can implement creative ideas for two purposes in business: to achieve greater revenues (for the "top line" on a balance sheet) and to achieve greater efficiency of work processes (affecting the "midline" areas of the balance sheet). In addition, innovation can be either revolutionary or evolutionary. A breakthrough for revenues would be a radically new invention; a breakthrough for processes would be total reengineering. Incremental innovation for revenues would be product line extensions, while incremental process enhancement is known as Kaizen quality improvement. (Kaizen is the Japanese term for quality improvement made in small, incremental steps.)

Compared with the past, people seem to fear creativity less; they use "off the wall" and "out of the box" as compliments now rather than as snide remarks. Skills in breakthrough creativity have strategic importance, affecting every facet of product development, manufacturing, marketing, and sales. Creativity dominates the corporate cultures of today's most successful organizations.

PUTTING YOUR VALUES TO WORK—CREATIVELY

A few years ago, members of the Corporate Innovation Committee of 3M Corporation asked me to make a presentation to them about innovative corporate cultures. At the end, the 3M representative who brought me in, Bob Gubrud, saw a book in my briefcase as I was packing. It had a faded gold cross on it.

"What are you reading, William?" he asked.

"Oh, it's a book about six saints from the thirteenth to sixteenth centuries." (That's all I planned to say, being reluctant to talk about spiritual matters with my clients.)

"What prompts your interest in that—religious conviction, curiosity, philosophy?"

"Well, to tell you the truth, for a few years now I've realized that a

major theme in my life and work has been, 'How are creativity, business, and spiritual values somehow facets of the same diamond rather than separate subjects?'"

"That's amazing. That's exactly what's been on my mind the past six months! Let's get a bite to eat and talk about that."

And so we did. We discussed how creativity encompassed how we expressed our unique individuality as well as how we responded to work challenges; how business included any organization involved in an "exchange of value," whether they be profit enterprises, government, education, or nonprofit institutions; how spiritual values were the same as the most fundamental human values which bring out the best in people of all cultures. We discussed all of these as issues of spiritual integrity—integrity, in this context, meaning "wholeness, oneness."

When my company was working with Walter Landor, founder of the world's premier strategic design firm[8], to plan a creativity center, he stated: "Real creativity involves the production not only of something new, but also of something emotionally appealing. Creative products are not just new solutions. They are fresh, evocative, and stimulating. Creativity seeks satisfaction from an awareness of 'wholeness.' It must appeal to the whole person."

To commit to creativity and innovation is to exercise our deepest personal values. Research by Barry Posner and W. H. Schmidt shows that clarity about our personal values is more important to our job commitment than clarity about our company's values.[9] People were asked to rate their commitment to their organization as related to their clarity about company values and their personal values. Those who were neither clear about company values nor about their own values rated themselves at 4.9 (out of 7.0) on commitment. Greater clarity about company values had no correlation with an increase in job commitment, whereas greater clarity about personal values increased commitment by 30 percent, to an average of 6.2!

Bob Galvin, chairman of the executive committee on Motorola's board of directors, and the man most responsible for leading Motorola's growth in the sixties, seventies, and eighties, recently addressed thirty of his vice presidents and officers. Their job, he said, was to become role models in creatively seeing and doing things differently—being "dazzling" thinkers. Their primary job? Building a new culture of collaboration based on inspiring acts of faith ("things are do-able that are not necessarily provable"), spreading hope, and building trust. When asked how these values relate to the "real world of business," he replied that executives must develop more than good technical or financial skills. They must develop character in themselves and others.

He concluded, "Faith, hope, and trust. . . . Theology is very practical business."

Motorola's values translate into action to build customer relationships based on trust even when cultural practices or belief systems are different. They've found their high ethical standards (absolutely no gifts, especially bribes, are ever allowed customers or suppliers) to be a competitive disadvantage in the short term but a sustainable advantage in the long term. For example, a distributor of their telecommunications products in the Asia-Pacific region once stopped carrying a competitor's products and started to carry Motorola's. The reason? The distributor was tired of unreliable relationships built on payoffs, and could count on a high-integrity relationship with Motorola.

What do you value? Look at your own life for the first clue. Do you have trusting relationships? Then it's most likely that you value authenticity in people and in relationships. Do you have conflict in your day-to-day life and in relationships? Then it's likely that you value drama, no matter what you might say to the contrary.

To further clarify your values, try listing the top ten things that are important to you. If you get stuck, list the opposite of things you just can't stand. Then select the top three. Finally, name one that you would like to see more of in your workplace. I led this exercise with a group of school bus drivers and mechanics a few years back. One person was rather resistant to this "creativity stuff," and was rather rough in his language. But when the group was reporting the top values they'd selected, everyone's head snapped in surprise when he said, "Love." He explained, "Isn't that what life is about? Loving yourself and each other the best you can."

Can you emphasize and live by such values and still run a successful business? For Dick Eppel, general manager of a communication systems division of a major electronics corporation, the answer is a resounding, "Yes!" He took the job with the assignment of turning the division around. He later told me the story of what happened:

It was definitely a division in serious trouble, a result of too much success in their marketing activities without enough forethought for how they were going to execute that successfully. Clearly, one goal had to be to satisfy the customer. And the second thing was to get the people to believe that there was a recovery possible here.

We set up a prioritization of what customers we were going to satisfy when, with the goal that we were going to satisfy all customers. We would not take on any more business whatsoever that would jeopardize satisfying our current customers. That was to convince the employees that we weren't asking impossible things of them. Everything had to be credible—

the "road map," the vision, the "how-you're going-to-get-there"—all had to be credible. I was the one who had to say, "Trust me. Once we get through this, then we are all going to win."

One time, a salesman came to Dick with a potential new customer who wanted a delivery date that Dick knew they couldn't meet. The salesman wanted an exception to their strategy so he could get the sale.

I hung tough on not accepting business that we couldn't deliver on. That was a test. I would talk to a customer, look him in the eye, and say, "Do you want me to lie to you?" I used words that had an emotional impact, but there was no ambiguity. He accepted that. It turned out that we could execute good business, deliver on that business, and manage it on a schedule, even though there were threats of customers' going someplace else or walking away from it.

After two years, things were significantly improved. Turnover was down. We got the division to breakeven, or pretty close to breakeven. Every contract got delivered on—every contract. The most important piece that we saved has represented about $13-20 million per year of cash-rich profits ever since.

What did it take for Dick and his division to succeed? He named two things besides having the right strategy:

One was a sense of positive perseverance: positive expectations, positive visualization. That had a lot to do with the result. The second thing was that the management team—the people and myself—for one reason or another, amalgamated in a way that was very unique to me. I've always felt like I had good teams to work with, but in this one, there was a bonding beyond friendship and camaraderie. There was such a sense of caring, a genuine sense of love, even though that word was never expressed verbally.

Truth telling. Love. Business. They need each other: Truth and love enrich business success, and business is a way for love to express itself, serving people's needs. Why then are we so afraid at work to call it "love," when that's what it really is?

Love and oneness sustain our souls and stimulate sustainable business success. We *are* the organizations we work for—responsible for everything that happens, and we share in every success. When we act with this level of responsibility, we carry the spirit of all creation in everything we do.

TAKING RESPONSIBILITY

We're all naturally creative. Without creative expression in our work lives, we feel a certain "flabbiness," like we haven't exercised an important muscle. ABC News's Peter Jennings once interviewed Holocaust scholar and author Elie Wiesel over breakfast in Krakow, Poland, lunch in Auschwitz, tea in London, and dinner in New York. The next day, Jennings was back anchoring the newscast. "Tired?" he was asked. He replied, "It's only the days when I haven't made a really creative contribution that I'm tired."

There is much for us to do together. Our planet, our people, need us badly, for the sake of whatever we collectively, and each of us individually, most value and cherish: better health, higher living standards, a greater sense of family and community, profitable progress, inner richness, or more regard for our environment. Our—your—creativity is in demand, not as some "nice idea" or "liberal humanistic dream," but as a hard, cold necessity and stark reality. To live successfully in a world dominated by the following eight pressing issues, we must demand creativity from each other.

• **The globalization of national economies.** We now have a truly global economy: No nation and no company is an island unto itself, unaffected by economic problems or successes elsewhere. Our communication technology links people virtually everywhere on the planet. However, our awareness of being a global family is just beginning to catch up with these developments. Our human family includes both people on the other side of our desk and people on the other side of the world—a collective consciousness that has a profound impact on all phases of our life and work. Our challenge is to develop innovative practices of economic collaboration for mutual benefit: "them vs. us" doesn't work within the global village economics.

• **The evolution to an intelligence-based economy.** As Harlan Cleveland points out,

A century ago, fewer than 10% of the American labor force were doing information work; now more than 50% are engaged in it. The actual production, extraction, and growing of things now soaks up less than a quarter of our human resources.[10]

Knowledge is a new type of resource, more like a flame than an object. With objects, like an apple, if we take some away, eventually nothing is left. With a flame, we can light a thousand candles so they all have flames, including the original. In the same way, knowledge is expandable, diffusive, transportable, and shareable—particularly with the explosive growth of the global Internet. We still often operate with a vocabulary and with management systems based on producing objects, not flames, but we must embrace knowledge as the key asset for generation of wealth. The fact is that in the last five years, knowledge-intensive companies accounted for 28 percent of the employees in U.S. corporations, but 43 percent of the employment growth. Our challenge is to learn new ways to foster creativity for flames/information, and new ways to manage and account for the products/services we produce, especially since knowledge may be considered less valuable when it is shared.

• **The pace of technological evolution.** Electronics is but one field in which rapid technological advances make products obsolete within a year or two. We live in a world impacted by developments in remote sensing from space; disease-resistant crops; gene splicing; fuel cells; medical lasers, advanced ceramics, alloys, and composites; "smart" membranes; computer-aided design, engineering, and manufacturing; expert systems and artificial intelligence; global cellular radio communications; optical computing; nutritional treatment of disease; universal Internet access; and so on. Our challenge is to be more than just reactive or even responsive, but to be proactive in *choosing* and valuing what we give birth to technologically.

• **The super-competitive environment.** Corporate globalization and the explosion of technology have changed profoundly the nature of competition. Speed rules in an era of hyper-competition, which ironically has also spawned "the death of competition": Competitors are finding more and more ways to collaborate to build the strength of their industry and even inventing new industries together. Rather than competing for a piece of the pie, they're busy expanding the pie itself. The strategy of regaining profitability by downsizing won't go away, but we've discovered its limits: Downsizing does little to spur innovation and revenue growth, the sustainable path to corporate health.

• **New and shifting social values and demographics.** Since the 1960s we have been in a period in which seemingly sudden discontinuities with past trends continue to emerge. Examples of these discontinuities include: the 1973 oil embargo; the opening of United States–China relations; the movement to self-responsibility and preventive medicine; the political, social protests that ended the Cold War; and so on. Each shift alters the field of business opportunities, government policy, and social lifestyle. Our challenge is to develop flexible, innovative plans and responses across a variety of possible future scenarios.

• **Changes in labor force values.** That today's work force has a different mix of personal and work values is not news. Many have cheered the fact; many have bemoaned it. Our challenge is to develop appropriate ways of leading, more than just "managing," the gold-collar (professional), white-collar, and blue-collar work forces—and perhaps to challenge the notion that there is any difference.

• **Health, lifestyle, and stress awareness.** In 1900, only 4 percent of the American population was over sixty-five, and the top four causes of death were the acute, infectious diseases (diphtheria, cholera, small-pox, and typhoid). In 1990, 15 percent of the population was over sixty-five and the top four causes of death were vascular (heart attack, etc.), cancer, diabetes, and cirrhosis of the liver. The most noteworthy aspect of this second list is that, according to the U.S. Centers for Disease Control and Prevention (CDC) in Atlanta, 75 percent of the incidence of these diseases is brought about by our lifestyles. This self-destructive approach to life is intricately linked with our work climates, our technologies, our attitudes toward stress, and our values. Our challenge is to develop the willingness and ability to use our talents collectively, in harmony with ourselves and with each other. With the renewed exercise of our creative powers, the current lack of harmony *can* be healed for the benefit and profit of all.

• **Prosperity versus human survival.** In 1960, countries located north of the equator were about 20 times richer than those south of the equator. By 1990 in the Northern Hemisphere, countries were 50 times richer despite vast amounts of economic aid, trade, loans, and catch-up industrialization in countries in the Southern Hemisphere. The wealthiest 20 percent of the world's population now earns approximately 83 percent of total world income, while the poorest 20 percent earns only about 1.4 percent. This growing disparity cannot and should not be sustained. It threatens both economic and social stability and the basic tenets of morality that support that stability. The imbalance is compounded by the resource-consuming lifestyles of the richest, which lead to global depletion of resources, and by the exponentially expanding population, especially in Southern Hemisphere countries. Even with the end of the Cold War, worldwide weaponry sales continue to siphon essential financial resources away from measures to alleviate the impoverished conditions that afflict half the planet.

In 1953, President Dwight D. Eisenhower said:

Every gun that is made, every warship launched, every rocket fired signifies, in the final sense, a theft from those who hunger and are not fed, those who are cold and are not clothed. This world in arms is not spending money alone. It is spending the sweat of its laborers, the genius of its scientists, the hopes of its children. . .This is not a way of life at all in any true sense. Under the cloud of threatening war, it is humanity hanging from a cross of iron.[11]

The cross of iron has yet to be brought down. It's a matter of our will—of living up to our spiritual values.

These are the issues that move me, and concern me deeply. Global problems are local problems that have reproduced too many times. Whether it's my job or yours, it's *what* we create and *how* we create it that makes our lives meaningful or not.

You and I can respond to these issues in three ways: We can reach back for "the ways things were," "plan" reactively to and for a future that seems out of control, or work to create a future we want for ourselves and for our children's children. Business plays a key role in transforming society and our quality of life. Determined *innovation* is what it will take—the creation and actualization of breakthroughs and incremental improvements in products, services, processes, and management methods. The creative challenge for corporations is to develop business models of value-exchange that resonate with hearts, not just pocketbooks, with goodness, not just goods.

> **Business plays a key role in transforming society and our quality of life. Determined *innovation* is what it will take.**

Willis Harman, in *Global Mind Change*, points out the opportunities and the responsibilities that business leaders and managers (at all levels) face as we approach the early days of the twenty-first century.

Leaders in world business are the first true planetary citizens. They have worldwide capability and responsibility; their domains transcend national boundaries. Their decisions affect not just economies, but societies; and not just direct concerns of business, but world problems of poverty, environment, and security. World business will be a key factor in the ultimate resolution of the macro-problem. It crosses national boundaries with much more ease than do political institutions and the business corporation is a far more flexible and adaptive organization than the bureaucratic structures of government. Up to now, there has been no guiding ethic . . . (but) such a new ethos for business may be in the process of forming. [12]

Can a major corporation be both socially responsible and profitable? Unequivocally, yes. If corporations can contribute responsibly to solving problems such as these, the world will gladly support them. If we choose to, we can spawn a future that profits each of us. But only when we make our workplaces more creative, more productive, and more alive will we know how to achieve true, sustainable (and sustaining) material and spiritual prosperity.

IN CLOSING . . .

You can develop your deepest values as well as your talents. As you face big and little challenges, you can ennoble your work by responding from the deepest part of your purpose and values. Whether you are coordinating projects as a manager, constructing a product, satisfying a customer's needs, writing letters, counseling a student, or determining business strategy . . . you *can* create a nurturing environment for growing your soul where you work. Commit yourself wholeheartedly to your organization's becoming the best it can be. Don't wait for the organization to prove itself to you; the proof of the worth of your commitment will come *after* the commitment, not before!

Become aware of your organization's external environment and internal climate. Learn new ways to explore problems and entertain new possibilities. Learn more about being a visionary leader, taking the initiative, and building coalitions. Get others involved in your vision, get involved in theirs, and persist until, collectively, you are successful. Learn how organizational *systems* work to reinforce your values and ease the innovative process. Learn to embrace the changing world—and the world of change—and master the art of managing change.

Develop yourself. Assist others in their development. In the world of life and organisms, if you're not growing, you're dead. Your organization can suffer the same fate. And if you *are* growing, you're celebrating. Life at its fullest is a spiritual, creative celebration. Life at work is no exception.

CHAPTER 2

Develop Yourself as a *Creative* Spirit

*About two years ago I had absolutely the worst day of my life. Every-
thing went wrong . . . projects didn't work, people didn't respond the
way I wanted, and I was real depressed at the end of the day. I went
off to a coffee shop and I wrote on the top of a piece of paper
"Lessons Learned and Relearned." I went into some kind of altered
state and came out of it hours later with twenty-seven lessons learned.*

*At the end of that (first) session, I felt totally contented, joyful, and
successful, and realized that I had just had one of the best days of my
life. And ever since then, it was like a total attitude shift on the dimension of what is failure, what are problems. Now, very often, at the moment of something not working out, I say, "Ah, it's going to be great
this evening when I write the lessons learned."*

*So in the context of creativity, this attitude is: Every moment is a
creative wellspring for growth—including, and maybe especially, the
ones that don't work out quite the way you thought. (With) the ones
that work out the way you thought, there's probably not that much to
learn . . .The ones that are surprising are the ones that can be milked.*

—Ron, MARKETING CONSULTANT AND PROFESSIONAL SPEAKER

CLARIFYING YOUR CREATIVE PURPOSE

So, you believe that maybe, just maybe, you want to be more creative,
or you want to lead others to bring out their creativity. But you don't
even know if it's possible to "learn creativity." Besides, you're so very
busy with organizational brainteasers (called "jobs"), you have little time
to think, and less to think creatively. You might muse, "Besides, with so
much to get done, creativity just might mess things up even more."

The more issues that compound your life and your work, the more
you need to be creative, and the more you need to inspire everyone
around you to exercise their creative talent as well. The quality programs of the last decade proved that every employee has the potential

to contribute creative ideas when the issues are focused enough. Where do you begin?

Let's start with what moves *you*—what motivates *you* to make a difference. Then we'll explore how you express your creativity day to day, in ways you probably don't even give yourself credit for. Finally, we'll move on to what qualities you can recognize more clearly in yourself that define *your* unique version of a creative person.

Author Brian Swimme says,

> *Precisely because you are aware of the limits of life, you are compelled to bring forth what is within you; this is the only time you have to show yourself. You can't waste away in a meaningless job, cramming you life with trivia. The supreme insistence of life is that you enter the adventure of creating yourself.*[1]

And Kahlil Gibran adds,

> *Work is love made visible. When you work with love, you bind yourself to yourself, and to one another, and to God.*[2]

We typically spend around 2,000 hours per year at work, sometimes more. This represents perhaps 40 percent or more of our waking lives. Many of the joys and dramas of life occur during these work hours. If we wish to contribute to making society a place where each person can express his or her best, we can start with our organizations.

What do you want to create with your limited time on earth? We are by nature creative engines, running twenty-four hours per day. What do we do with this creative power? Many of us let it idle, or we power up without consciously knowing where we want to head, what we want to create with our life energy. At worst, we run our creativity based on limiting beliefs and then are surprised by our own unwanted creations.

What's the alternative? It is to navigate your life with a clear sense of personal values as your compass. What do you value? Your personal purpose reveals what you value the most. We all have goals in life, from taking care of our family to having a certain career, but what is the thread of continuity—the purpose— that runs through these goals and gives them unity and continuity?

You can state your purpose in six different ways. There may be some overlap in your answers, but start from the top and work down:

1. What possessions or social status do I wish to acquire?
   I want a comfortable retirement and a home in the Caribbean.
2. What milestones do I wish to achieve?

I want to be part of growing this business by 25 percent each year over the next five years.

3. What type of experiences do I wish to have?
   I want to work with people of different cultures from all seven continents.
4. What gifts and talents do I want to express?
   I want to use my natural enthusiasm, my analytical abilities, and my determination to do things right . . . to help groups perform at their best.
5. What difference do I wish to make to others?
   I want to provide my children and the people who work with me the best opportunity to fulfill their career aspirations.
6. What type of person do I wish to become?
   I want to become an everyday example of a person who is loving, trustworthy, and truthful.

As you can see, your purpose becomes more and more basic to your soul as you move to increasing depth:

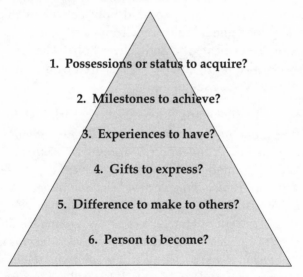

1. Possessions or status to acquire?

2. Milestones to achieve?

3. Experiences to have?

4. Gifts to express?

5. Difference to make to others?

6. Person to become?

Examine honestly all your key ambitions and activities at work, and see which statement(s) you find most enduring across all of them. That's the basis of your real-time, not-just-nice-sounding personal purpose. Notice how your values show up in your purpose.

Your search for personal purpose and meaning must ultimately go beyond how you acquire things and experiences to a deeper, more resonant meaning. You can find this meaning amidst the creative expression of your mind, heart, and soul. With a tremendous amount of courage—literally, "heartfulness"—you may lead the way to a new story about success in business. Fred Schwettman, as head of Hewlett-Packard's Circuit Technology Division, once related to me:

We had a discussion about values and beliefs in our staff meeting to really articulate what the personal purpose of each of us was—what each of us was doing to grow. An example could be: "To know God or to find love associated with God and to practice that in whatever I do." If you're not accomplishing something here that's really important to your basic reason for existence, perhaps you haven't really thought about it a lot.

As time goes on, my purpose turns more and more spiritual. What can I contribute to people's lives? I also have to spend my time trying to figure out how we'll survive within this industry. You can practice honesty, integrity, and caring, and all of those things, but at the same time, this is a tremendously competitive environment. But overall, when the time comes to check out, you better feel really good about what you accomplished— and making a little profit here and there is probably not going to cut it.

We all face serious planetary issues. The population increase, and the subsequent demands on food and water supply, is just one. At Monsanto Corporation, people deeply believe in their mission of "abundant food and a healthy environment." Can a life sciences company really be dedicated to and deliver both? The top executive team recently clarified for themselves, and shared with each other, their personal purposes. As a sampling . . .

- Sector President and Senior Scientist, Kish Kishore: *I inspire myself and my colleagues to solve the problem of hunger and provide health and vitality through better nutrition.*
- Chief Information Officer, Pat Fortune: *I exploit technology to define and solve difficult problems that impact hunger and well-being worldwide, especially among children.*
- Vice President of Human Resources, Donna Kindl: *I bring energy, excitement, and passion to my relationships with others and inspire them to see what is great about themselves.*
- Corporate President, Hendrick Verfaillie: *I inspire and connect people, capabilities, and strategies to feed the world and make it a better place to live.*
- Sector President, Jan Novak: *I nurture and am nurtured by the extraordinary potential of people and the magnificence of nature.*

These people have personally dedicated themselves to a cause. They've come together, in the form and "body" of their corporation, to combine their personal purpose and talents and make a difference in the world. You can do the same in your own realm. Your personal purpose is the driving force for expanding and investing your creativity, where the payoff for you is greater meaning, satisfaction, even enthusiasm and fun. The payoff for others is the benefit of the unique difference only you can make in their lives.

LOOKING INTO THE MIRROR: THE CREATIVE YOU

Still, when asked, "Are you creative?" many of us answer, "Sometimes . . . It depends on what I'm doing." If asked, "Are you creative at work?" our answers may sound more like, "Here and there," or "Rarely," or "Sometimes I have my moments."

It seems to me that where I'm creative in my work right now is really insignificant—things like the way I dress. I simply don't want to slide into being a regular librarian. I find we get very bogged down—we're understaffed and underbudgeted—and nothing gets done. Sometimes I feel a little outrageous and do some very small things a little differently. I had an outrageous little party to celebrate the finishing of a project. I think in this particular setting, such things aren't usually done.

—Teddy, librarian

I know that some of the time I do not recognize when I'm really being creative, and I overlook opportunities to be creative. As a result, I experience a whole range of feelings—excitement, frustration, joy, disappointment, enthusiasm, anger—and my productivity at work is often mirrored by these feelings.

I have produced more and enjoyed myself more at work as I have come to understand all the different times when I've been creative or could be creative. For myself, I've identified seven arenas for my creativity. Think back to different moments in your life, and see if you've experienced them as well. In what ways have you been creative?

Thinking Up a New Idea

The world may remember Leonardo da Vinci for Mona Lisa's smile, but most of us don't know that he was the first person to come up with the idea for contact lenses. Back in the 1500s, he figured out the best way to correct poor vision was to put a "short water-filled tube sealed at the end of flat lens" against the eye. Since then, millions of dollars have been spent perfecting this idea; it's only in the past forty years that we have finally developed the technology to make Leonardo's idea

> **Your personal purpose is the driving force for expanding and investing your creativity**

work. Coming up with new ideas or improving on old ones is a common way we focus our personal creativity.

Can you recall a time when you had an insight into or a solution for a problem? Understood a problem in a new way? Developed the concept for a public relations campaign? Came up with the idea for a new product? Developed a recipe? Put various thoughts together for the first time? Phrased a thought in your own terms? This realm of new *ideas and concepts,* all involving intuitive or logical thinking, is an important arena for creativity. Creativity has often been considered the domain of profound thinkers with a string of degrees after their names, especially in the disciplines of science, technology, and philosophy, but even a new understanding of the source of a disagreement or a child's discovery of how to stack toy rings belong in this category of creativity.

Somebody came to me recently with the problem of making silicon nitride powders. We can make silicon nitride fibers, but could we make very fine powders? We came up with some solutions that we thought could do it, but neither of us were satisfied with them.

About a month later an idea popped into my head which I believed would solve the entire problem, but I don't know how I reached that conclusion . . . Instead of making polymers beforehand and spraying them and heating them, (the idea is) to create the polymers as you spray them.
—Rick, lab director in organo-metallic chemistry

Making Something Tangible

"If nobody else is going to invent a dishwashing machine, I'll do it myself," proclaimed Josephine Cochrane of Shelbyville, Illinois in 1886. She proceeded to go into her back yard and build the first dishwashing machine. Although her first model was crude compared to today's standards, she is credited for inventing a major kitchen appliance. Inventing and building tangible objects is another application of our creativity.

Can you recall a time when you wrote a report or book or paper that you especially liked? Designed or produced an advertisement? Engineered a piece of machinery or electronics? Took a photograph? Composed a piece of music? Drew or painted a picture? Designed a costume or other piece of clothing? All of these involve creating and producing something in the *material, sensory world.* Creativity has often been applied to material works of art and various new consumer products, which fall in this category. Whether engineering a product or a report at work, these involve expressing yourself by making something concrete and real for other people to share *repeatedly* and appreciate by seeing, hearing, touching, smelling, or tasting.

*When I'm being creative, I feel like I'm in a flow, and the results I'm pro-
ducing are superior—for instance, in writing a business report. Sometimes
I sit down and think, "Oh, this is not only a logical way of looking at this,
but it's also a way I haven't thought of before—a new perspective" or, "This
is a way to present this in the best possible way." And then when I get finished it doesn't look like just another business report.*

*The report comes more from my heart than my head, but it's full of
facts: very cost-conscious and bottom line, with benefits and costs involved.
Otherwise, even though it could be technically well put together, with excellent grammar, it still wouldn't have that spark to it.*

—Sue, project manager of computer systems in a bank

Doing Something Spontaneous

The next time you are sitting on the beach enjoying the cool taste
of an ice cream cone, think about who came up with this spontaneous
idea. In 1904, Arnold Fornachou, an ice cream vendor at the St. Louis
World's Fair, ran out of paper dishes. Fortunately, his stand was right
next to a Syrian baker who was selling *zalabias,* a thin Persian waffle.
Legend has it that Fornachou bought a waffle, twisted it into a cone,
scooped in some ice cream, and a great treat was born. Acting in a
spontaneous way is another outlet for our personal creativity. Using
our wit to spice up the dinner conversation, making up a new game to
entertain our children, or figuring out a quick and easy way to settle a
dispute, are all examples of how we spontaneously generate new and
unique ways to deal with everyday situations.

Can you recall a time when you gave a speech "off the cuff"? Sang
a song in a new way or improvised music "ad lib"? Made an inspiring
play in sports (a special move while running with a football or adjust-
ing to the bounce of a tennis ball, for example)? Responded spontaneously in a meeting or a work conversation with a sincere plea or
justification for an idea? All of these situations involve a sense of spontaneity, a moment not to be repeated easily. *Spontaneous* creativity is
often experienced as being at our best, purposefully expressing our
competence and confidence in the moment.

*I really trust spontaneity to carry some creativity. I'll do things on the
spur of the moment knowing that the thing that makes it is the creativity.
At first, that's pretty terrifying. At the same time, once you begin to love
that process, you become committed to it.*

*For example, I did a lot of sales work, and you certainly can play a
sales presentation very safely. I've had times when I've said to a prospect,
"This isn't touching you, is it? Something, some way that I'm presenting this
isn't speaking to you. So let's talk about that, instead of what I'm selling."*

That is an example of being willing to risk and see what happens. More times than not, it works because people are dying for that real stuff. In risk is creativity.

—Jay, community relations director for a college

Producing an Event

People had been thanking the gods with harvest feasts for thousands of years before the Pilgrims decided to celebrate the first American Thanksgiving. But it was the idea of a Pawtuxet Indian named Squanto to use the celebration as a way to solidify the friendship between the early English settlers and the Native Americans. Producing an event is a great opportunity to exercise our personal creativity.

Can you recall a time when you directed a meeting at work? Developed new procedures for getting work done? Planned a wedding or holiday dinner? Devised a way to gain consensus in a strategy discussion? Organized a picnic? Sometimes creativity has been applied to *events* or *processes* that have been uplifting or moving experiences. The fluid mixture and flow of decor, people, sequence of happenings, and background are part of the process of creating events, whether just for yourself or for others, too.

Or perhaps you once said, "I want such and such in my life," and you eventually got it. *Circumstances* that we wish for and find ways to fulfill make up another aspect of this type of creativity.

I had the idea for the conference and let it sit awhile. The process took two months from the time we said it was a "go." Picking the speakers was more intuitive. We worked the two months on the specialty sessions, calling people, getting leads—kind of like a detective story, running into people and asking, 'Who would be good for that kind of session?' And I visited or called or wrote almost every chief executive officer, and also sold the blocks of tickets. I would say half the conference registration came from that. It's one of those things where you do it once in a certain way, and then if you have to do a different one next year, you do it in a different way.

—Carol, assistant dean of engineering at a university

Organizing People or Projects

While serving as a British soldier in the Boer War, Colonel Robert Baden-Powell became concerned that young men from England lacked the strength of character and resourcefulness required to inherit the responsibilities of managing the British Empire. So he decided to form a club for boys that would imbue them with the attributes of loyalty, courage, and leadership. This club, founded in 1908, grew into the Scouting Movement, which provides education and direction for boys and girls all over the world. Organizing people or projects is another common outlet for our personal creativity.

Can you recall a time when you put together a new project or work team? Started your own business? Joined a political party or a church? Changed the policies and rules of a work group? Developed a new system for getting things done? As human beings and social animals, we create organizations and social movements—purposeful "families" and groups. This arena also involves creating "structures" and rules to guide social interactions and tasks over a sustained period of time.

One of the biggest challenges and creative moments I've had was in the sixties. A bunch of us were working in a mental health center and just decided we were going to start our own facility. My whole life was marked by the fact that these challenges were so immense. We realized, "Gee, we don't know anything about managing and how to organize. How do we make people do things? How do we get results? How do we set things up? What do we do with the money? How do we do books?"

The way in which we learned showed how quickly twenty-two-year-olds can learn. We were all supposed to be just case workers, at the lowest level you could possibly be in the mental health system.
—Dennis, clinical psychologist and consultant

Building a Relationship

In 1530 the famous Dutch philosopher and educator, Erasmus, came up with the bright idea that children should learn manners. In order to spread the word, he wrote the treatise *On Civility in Children*, which was responsible for developing the traditions of western culture for the education of young children. How we build relationships with others is another way we manifest our creativity every day.

Can you recall a time when you said to someone (or yourself), "I like the way you handled that situation. You dealt with that person very well"? A time when you resolved a difficult conflict by trying a new approach with the person? A time when you had a romantic evening? A time when you really felt that a co-worker was also your supporter and friend? *Relationship* creativity focuses on how you develop collaboration, cooperation, and "win-win" relationships (i.e., those in which both parties feel good about the interactions). Whether in our jobs or in our homes, what we make of our relationships is a true signal of the values that underlie our creativity. We have many degrees of freedom in how we relate to others in any given circumstance. How we finally express ourselves—in words, actions, and even feelings—is a creative act.

You might not think that a person in real estate management, dealing mostly with tenants and money, is creative. It's a hard business! After thinking about it, my creativity is relational—working out conflicts and problems where no previous pat answers existed. My process is to let conflicts arise, not smother them. They're hard at first to deal with—usually unpleasant—but out of expressions of feelings, a compromise can always be found.

In our business, and with a small staff, it is not cost-effective to spend a lot of time on a problem and find the perfect solution. You find something that works, do it, and keep moving on. You'll find out soon enough if it doesn't work, and then you try something else.

—Linda, real estate manager

Changing Your "Inner Self"

Jean Nidetich was fat. She had tried lots of fad diets that didn't work. She was frustrated. But in the early seventies she figured out the best way to lose weight and keep it off was to change her attitude toward herself and food. She just decided that "Nothing tastes as good as being thin feels," and the key idea behind Weight Watcher's Inc. was born. This group has helped thousands and thousands of people lose weight by helping them develop a new belief about themselves. Being open to new approaches to how we live our lives and think about ourselves is another way we can use our creativity to make our lives richer and more fulfilling.

How often have you experienced, or witnessed, a "change of heart"—a change of perspective, of feeling, or of attitude where the situation didn't change, but the person's point of view did? Have you ever heard someone say, "Cheer up. Don't be so sad" or "Cool down that hot temper of yours"?

Statements like these point out that we can change our inner emotions even while the outer situation remains the same. We can create different *"inner" experiences* of events. This type of creativity can be nurtured in ways that encourage inner strength and openness rather than a control or suppression of feelings.

The term *creativity* has not often been applied to this arena of inner experience, perhaps because our perceptions so often focus on external objects (for example, the creativity of a sculpture) or because to many, the act of creativity implies some sense of will and control, whereas feelings and thoughts often seem to come to us without control ("If I could stop feeling sad, I would!").

If ideas and insights are internal happenings that are considered creative, then other inner experiences can likewise be considered creative. I think of both thoughts and feelings as "content" or "internal products" that we can eventually create, so that a new inner experience spontaneously occurs without a change in situation.

Our inner experience is the most fundamental arena of creativity. Opening ourselves to acting creatively through generating new ideas, producing something in the material world, spontaneously expressing ourselves, shaping events and circumstances, organizing group life, and developing relationships is enhanced by exercising our inner creativity.

Even managing stress and preventing burnout depend greatly on exercising creativity at this level. Seeing our own creativity in a new light—reframing how we perceive our creativity and expressiveness—is an experience of inner creativity.

I've been a president of a company, and I feel rapport and kinship with the executive world, but I used to have quite a lot of anxiety preparing to speak to groups of executives. I would put in mammoth amounts of preparation, yet my ratings were mediocre.

Then I was asked to give an important speech. And I began working on that speech, and I did a lot of things I had never done before. I resolved that I would have absolutely no limits. As I faced the audience of 200 people, I smiled at them, they smiled at me, and I could literally feel the remnants of low-level anxiety draining out through my legs. I felt nothing but excitement, confidence, delight at being there.

Rather than being stiff, tense, lacking animation, lacking variety, no drama . . . there I was, audience with me, live interaction, a lot of humor, a lot of pauses, a lot of drama. I said to myself, intellectually, "Hey, the body-felt sense of excitement and anxiety are just about indistinguishable. It's your interpretation."

—Ron, marketing consultant and professional speaker

Creativity, therefore, expresses itself in richly varied ways. How do these actually show up in the workplace? We once posed this question to the brand managers, staff, and division executives of a retail consumer products firm. They coordinated everything from advertising to distribution of new and existing products, and they wanted assistance in improving their corporate climate for innovation. They pinpointed a variety of new ideas that corresponded to the seven arenas for creativity we have just discussed.

TYPE OF CREATIVITY	EXAMPLE
Thinking up new ideas	Looking 5 to 10 years ahead to avert threats to the company
	Defining new market segments and their needs
	Linking new technology development to market needs
Making something tangible	Producing products with higher quality
	Improving current products
	Packaging products more innovatively
Producing an event	Promoting the company's products at events with greater flair
Organizing people or projects	Reducing cycle time of production processes
	Speeding up the process of pushing through good ideas to implementation
Doing something spontaneous	Expediting responses to urgent customer requests
Building relationships	Getting people inside and outside the company to give input to new product development
	Getting customer opinions and counteracting complaints
	Stimulating and rewarding everyone to accept responsibility for innovation
Changing your "inner self"	Gaining new confidence, and feeling an appropriate level of urgency rather than being too comfortable with the status quo

What does it mean to be creative and innovative where you work? What would the list look like for your organization? What would you add or subtract to this list? What about for your job?

The ultimate definition of creativity in your life is your personal one. "Working creatively" might simply evolve for you over time. Although you may wish to add other arenas where you are creative, these seven—*ideas* and concepts, *material* world, *spontaneous* actions, *events* and circumstances, *organization* of systems and purposeful groups, *relationships* , and *inner experience*—are a place to start in further developing your creativity.

BECOMING A "SPIRITED" CREATOR

Who do you think of as a "creative person?" Albert Einstein? Jonas Salk? George Lucas? Michelangelo? John Lennon? Picasso? Gandhi? How about yourself? Your manager? Your next door neighbor?

In our everyday language and experience, we may describe a friend or co-worker as being "creative." And we might easily look back in history at the best known inventors, scientists, writers, artists, and musicians and label them "creative" . . . at least in comparison with others.

Such comparisons leave the impression that the general population is uncreative and perhaps unable to be creative. Rumors abound that "Once you're past a certain age, you're no longer as creative." Who or what is the "creative person"?

Before the seventeenth century, people did not consider creativity a human attribute. Greek mythology tells the tales of nine Muses—goddesses who presided over creative endeavors—who would bestow creative ideas for humans to implement. Today we still use the phrase, "when the muse visits" to describe flashes of creative insight. Later, the poet John Donne stated that "art is counterfeit creation," meaning that real creativity came only from the supreme being. Starting with Isaac Newton and the scientific revolution, a new paradigm emerged—that a few geniuses were born with special creative talents: extraordinary people like Leonardo da Vinci, Rafael, Thomas Edison, and Vincent Van Gogh.

In the mid-twentieth century, researchers discovered that scores on IQ tests had little correlation with scores on creativity tests. With that, creativity left the realm of the genius and entered the world of everyman. We began to see that while people varied in both levels of creativity and styles of creativity, virtually everyone exercises novelty in solving challenges they've never faced. We tread into dangerous territory if we try to generalize about "what creative people are like." We gain a significant payoff for this risk if we open our minds to new notions of our own creative power and how to exercise it, however.

I have long investigated "original thinkers," great artists, and pioneers in business. Abraham Maslow shed considerable light on their common qualities when he described the human drive toward self-actualization (which is a form of inner creativity[3]). Dr. Joseph McPherson, my former mentor in the Innovation Program at SRI International, identified certain internal habits that support and develop our inherent creative talents. He grouped these into five categories: self-orientation, motivation, attitude toward others, attitude toward time, and intellect. Maslow's and McPherson's work, in conjunction with my own, can be combined into a model that sharpens our view of ourselves and how we can bring our own creativity—our own brilliance—to work.

People who fully express their creative potential are SPIRITED people. Your creativity is based on key strengths in a few of the following personal qualities. Which do you see in yourself?

S = SELF-AWARE

Open to new ways of doing
    things
Actively develops own intuition
Willing to feel emotions
Seeks insights about self and
    others
Knows own personal purpose
    and values
Maintains confidence in tough
    situations

P = PURPOSEFUL

Sees the big picture
Envisions what's important
Commits wholeheartedly
Likes challenge and self-ex-
    pression
Links goals to personal values
Promotes highest benefit for
    everyone concerned

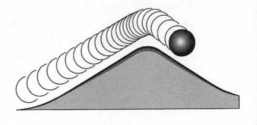

I = INCISIVE

Looks for input from others
Seeks opposing points of view
Assesses situations systemi-
    cally, holistically
Shows curiosity
Discerns objectively
Gains clear insights in com-
    plex situations

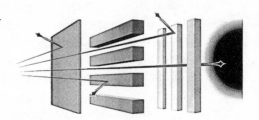

R = REWARDING

Shares credit
Seeks to see positive
    performance in others
Expresses appreciation
    easily
Values intrinsic motivations
Affirms diverse viewpoints
Celebrates completions

I = INVENTIVE

Generates many options

Switches easily between logic and imagination

Promotes "Beginner's Mind"

Plays spontaneously

Looks at problems in new ways

Envisions what might be possible

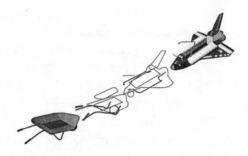

T = TRANSFORMING

Takes persistent action

Moves people to action

Energizes self and others

Values and respects people

Acts with integrity to keep agreements

Chooses growth over fear

E = EVALUATIVE

Makes decisions based on personal values

Seeks long term as well as short term benefits

Looks beyond "the numbers"

Seeks consensus when possible

Judges at appropriate times

Anticipates consequences

D = DAUNTLESS

Takes initiative

Comfortable with ambiguity

Takes prudent risks

Intuitively foresees future patterns and trends

Asserts self courageously

Acts independently if necessary

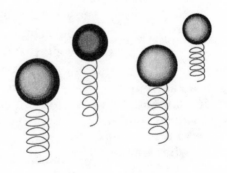

Nolan Bushnell, founder of Atari and Axlon Toys, has said he would rather be a person with twenty ideas, of which five might work well, than a person with two ideas that both work well. That way, he figures, he's three ideas ahead of the other person. "Unless you're willing to accept failure," Bushnell suggests, " you're not really willing to push yourself to the edge."[4]

Whether you know it or not, you are a creative, adventurous, peaceful, loving, productive human being. The characteristics we've just discussed are like items on a menu. We can pick and choose those that represent our strengths and a way of being that we would like to actualize in ourselves. We do not have to be—in fact almost cannot be—everything at once. We can, and do, exercise different aspects of ourselves at different times and in different ways.

DEVELOPING YOUR CREATIVITY

If we are all naturally creative, why does it seem that only a few people fully exercise their creativity? Primarily, we may underdevelop or "misplace" personal habits for being creative, often from fear of "bucking the system," our culture and society's norms. For example, Erich Fromm says that the key to creativity is our capacity to be open, curious, even puzzled.[5] Yet schools and companies reward "having the right answer," so we hesitate to say "I don't know" or "I wonder . . ."

Start now by perceiving the characteristics of the SPIRITED person in yourself. The previous list of qualities by itself gives only interesting information that is likely to be soon forgotten. If you commit to becoming more creative and purposeful in your work, you'll actively spend time seeing yourself as creative and put your creativity into action.

At most advertising agencies there is a "creative" department. Imagine a research scientist at a cocktail party asking someone from the advertising agency, "What do you do?" and getting the reply, "I 'do' creativity." The scientist could easily answer, "I do creativity also." As you might guess, we could all answer the same way about whatever work we're in.

> **Creativity is fundamentally an expression of who we are, not what we do or have.**

Yet, creativity is fundamentally an expression of *who we are,* not what we do or have. The true force of creativity is first to "be" (for example, seeing yourself as a doctor), then to "do" (going to medical school, conducting examinations), and finally to "have" (a diploma and a practice). In the natural scheme of creativity "being" comes before "doing," which comes before having."

Unfortunately, many people try to "have" (the diploma) so they can "do" (conduct examinations) so they can "be" (a doctor). All along, these people are trying to create from a sense of *not* being something, and it's therefore difficult to form a positive mental picture of finally being, doing, and having what they want.

Start with a vision of who you are and who you want to be, rather than what you want to do or have. Then build in the "doing" and "having" to fill out the vision. A focus on doing or having simply doesn't pack the power or follow-through. "Losing weight" or "giving up smoking" or "having a Mercedes Benz" usually becomes a dead resolution—and sometimes, a source of guilty feelings—unless such a goal is directly consistent with a desire from deep inside to "be" all you can be.

Take the time to imagine yourself as the creative person you want to be. This is an important step in your developing a creative edge—an internal edge as well as an advantage in your work. Your imagination is a tremendously powerful tool in bringing about the skills and attitudes to support your creativity.

By analogy, consider the example of a famous study of visualization used to improve basketball players' free-throw shooting. Three groups were tested and judged to be equal in their abilities to shoot free throws, as measured by the percentage of successful free throws. Then one group was allowed to practice more; the second group was allowed to stand at the free-throw line and imagine making successful free throws; the third group was given time off and didn't appear on the court. When the three groups were tested again, the group that had actually practiced with the basketball had improved, as you might expect. However, the group that had only visualized shooting improved almost as much. The third group showed no improvement.

Athletes have shown us much about the power of mental rehearsal under "relaxed attention" states. The method can affect even our unconscious body movements. In the same way, rehearsal with models of ourselves as creative can help us awaken the expression of our creativity more and more.

To help you see in yourself the characteristics of creative people, a personal exercise may prove quite valuable to you. Read through it first, and then please *take the time* to close the book and actually do the exercise. The insights that occur to you during the first reading are important, of course, but there is more to find in the exercise to get its full benefit.

Let things happen as you would wish them to. Don't inhibit your creative dreaming with thoughts like, "That could never happen," or "He (or she) would never go for that." Create the vision, then update it later. That way, you let yourself stretch and grow while still staying "realistic."

With that said, here's the exercise:

1. On a separate piece of paper, write down two or three moments in which you observed someone else in his or her moments of creative expression. These should be moments you've witnessed, as much as possible, rather than just recalling that, say, Michelangelo had some inspiring moments painting the Sistine Chapel. The creative moments can involve ideas, tangible creations, spontaneous moments, events, organizing, relationships, or inner change. How was this person SPIRITED?

2. Now write down two or three more moments in your *own* life when you experienced the more inspired, creative moments . . . not just in coming up with innovative insights, but actually carrying them through and fulfilling them. How were you SPIRITED?

3. Pick a current situation in your life in which you would like to be more creative or in which you want to find a creative solution to a problem. For a moment, imagine yourself to be one of the other creative people you described in the first part of this exercise: close your eyes and really pretend you are this other person. Vividly imagine this person's feelings and beliefs about himself or herself. Feel the motivation, think the thoughts, act the actions of that person. Be SPIRITED.

4. As this person, imagine being creative in the current situation you described. How is the person—or how are you as the person—being creative this time? Carry the fantasy through as far as you can, even if you don't come up with a solution you like.

5. Now, close your eyes again and recall how you felt, thought, and acted when being personally creative. Really bring moments alive for yourself. Now, while living that creative experience, imagine being creative in the actual current situation you thought of. How are you going about being creative this time? Be SPIRITED.

6. Carry the fantasy through as far as you can.

7. Now that you've completed the exercise, please try it once again. Again close your eyes and follow the directions using your powers of imagination and intuition.

The more carefully we focus on who we are deep inside and what we want to create, the more likely we are to act creatively at work. We become that which we dwell on, that which we give our attention to. Our thoughts and our words become real. That is our creative power.

If we dwell on the very things we fear or don't want, such as negative habits, we help attract them to our lives like a magnet. But by focusing our attention on ourselves in our most creative moments—or by "borrowing" the creative experiences of others to try on for a while—we can evoke and tap into our maximal creativity in any situation, for any problem.

IN CLOSING . . .

For many, there is a peculiar source of tension that arises from within us. It is the tension of not exercising our talents, not expressing our creativity and aliveness. We can become numb to this, like the apathetic workers who have already retired mentally but who still have ten or thirty years to go before qualifying for retirement benefits. This tension for growth can only be released by awakening our creative expression perhaps first at work, and then elsewhere in life.

The source of your creativity is in you, not in your environment. Even the inspiration to set up your environment to support your growth comes from within. By analogy, Kabir, the fifteenth century Indian poet says

> The jewel is lost in the mud, and all are seeking for it;
> Some look for it in the east, and some in the west; some in the water and some amongst stones.
> But the servant Kabir has appraised it at its true value, and has wrapped it with care in the end of the mantle of his heart.[6]

CHAPTER 3

Embark on Your
Creative Journey

Today I facilitated a meeting with the head of clinic nursing and her seven nursing supervisors. The purpose of the meeting was to start moving these nursing supervisors toward becoming real managers rather than "hands-on" lead nurses.

We opened up by talking about the purpose of the meeting and then about their reservations and concerns. These concerns took at least fifty minutes instead of the twenty I planned. It was time enormously well spent. I could actually see a difference in the room. They had been sitting there, scared. Some specific fears were responded to in the moment by the clinic director. In other cases it was simply acknowledged that this was something we would take into account while going through this process.

What we did, essentially, was legitimize the fears—and just listen to them. It just does wonders when you do that . . .

—TOM, ORGANIZATION CONSULTANT FOR AN ACCOUNTING FIRM

CREATING WITH COURAGE

Back in September 1973, when Watergate was constantly in the news and the oil crisis had yet to strike, I was co-teaching a college course called "The Year 2000" with Newt Gingrich, now Speaker of the House. The first exercise we gave to the students—and ourselves, since we had never done it—was to write an essay describing a plausible picture of our own lives and life in general twenty-seven years in the future. Then we each wrote an "autobiography'" of how our life progressed up to the year 2000.

Thus, we jumped ahead to create a vision of ourselves and our world and then looked back to detail how that vision might come about. This is a wonderful technique for making what we want of our lives. I, for example, already felt strongly about becoming an international business consultant, though I didn't anticipate the winding path it took for me to become one.

When we went around the class and had each person read his or her autobiography, a chilling realization dawned on us. At least half the stories had the theme: "It's the year 2000, and the world is falling apart. I'm living on my twelve-acre farm in northern Canada, and I just hope I die before it falls apart up here, too."

We explored how our present assumptions about the future would have a great negative effect on the energy and determination we put into living our present lives. We saw quite clearly that self-fulfilling prophecies *do* happen. With strongly held assumptions of gloom and doom, we would be very apathetic to the notion of social and work responsibility. The chances would be increased for the doomful future to come about in ideas, material forms, spontaneous happenings, events, organizations, relationships, and inner experiences.

Furthermore, we realized that without any vision at all, we operate reactively in the world, letting external events dictate our alternatives. We saw that having a personal vision of the future is not a luxury but a necessity. With a vision we operate proactively, shaping our world to our positive or negative vision of the future.

Is there a repeatable process for this creative shaping? I believe there is, and it lies within each of us, and is found in our own stories and experience. With any difficult challenge, we face the unknown, unwritten tale of how to find a creative solution. There are emotional downs and ups—times of uncertainty and anxiety, adrenaline rushes in response to challenges, self-doubt, fear of failing, excitement for new ideas, frustration over impediments to implementation of our ideas, joy of celebration. We've all ridden the roller coaster and made it through tough times, calling on something we might not have known was within us to secure the courage and creativity we needed to make it. That "something" we call on is our creativity, and the road we take to make it through is the Creative Journey.

The Creative Journey can be traveled in both extraordinary and everyday ways and events. As a dramatic example, Edgar Mitchell, a member of the Apollo XIV crew in 1971, is one of those rare people who has had the privilege of walking on the moon's surface. He once related his adventure to me, including how his experience in space led to the spiritualization of his personal values and his return to Earth as a very different person.[1]

How Edgar Mitchell Defined His Twofold Challenge

The idea of an opportunity to explore this new environment and then go to the moon was virtually an irresistible challenge. I characterize the space flight—of getting off the planet—as being an event as significant as when the first sea creatures crawled out onto land. For many years, since childhood, my passion has been to find out how the universe really works. Early on, I found disagreement between my scientific training and my religious training. I have been pursuing a resolution to the conflicts in cosmology ever since.

How He Focused on His Mission

I recognized very early in life that fear is to be overcome: If it is physical danger, by being skillful; if it's a psychological fear, by getting into yourself and rooting it out. Preparation for the Apollo flight involved many skills. Piloting skills were important, as were the muscle coordination and know-how to navigate on the lunar surface. In addition, there was all the academic work—geology, orbital mechanics, rocket fuels, computer systems. All that knowledge and skill had to be practiced to a point where it was automatic. To deal with unexpected events, however, our judgment would come into play.

How He Solved a Creative Crisis

There was always an opportunity for creativity, because almost never did the spacecraft fail in the ways that we had trained for. The problem that posed the most potential for creativity was before we went down to the lunar surface. The automatic abort system had somehow failed . . . in such a way that if we tried to descend to the surface, it would automatically switch on and take us back into orbit. This was less than two hours before we were to supposed to start down to the surface. Most of the time, the spacecraft was behind the moon and out of communication with Earth. We finally reprogrammed the computer, with just a few seconds to spare minutes before the engines were to be ignited.

How He Completed His Journey

Looking at the Earth, the moon and the sun—this powerful experience of seeing Earth and our whole solar system against the background of the cosmos—had a very profound effect . . . an overwhelming sense of being connected with the universe, of feeling connected to all things, to the most distant galaxies, to Earth, to self, to sun. The recognition was then, and still is, that our scientific description of the way the universe is put together was at best incomplete and perhaps in some ways inaccurate. The universe is more of a living organism than a set of discrete things. I had to shed and reevaluate much of my prior learning.

What did come out of that experience was an enormous sense of responsibility that goes with the power of creativity. We are creative individuals, and we each have to accept, along with our creative potential, the responsibility that goes with it. The word responsibility *means to accept*

*one's choices and the consequences of those choices, and to become proac-
tive rather than just reactive.*

*And that means letting go of fear. Love is letting go of fear. That is pre-
cisely the experience when you leave fear behind. And with that comes the
sense of responsiveness, or responsibility, that you take charge of your own
life, let go of your fears. Automatically that brings this deeper sense of love
and responsibility for one's self, surroundings, environment, and planet.*

He summed up his transformation, and that of many fellow space
travelers, by saying, "We went to the moon as technicians. We returned
as humanitarians." That same kind of profound shift is possible for
each of us in augmenting our work from "getting our jobs done" to
"getting our hearts won."

LIVING THE CREATIVE JOURNEY AT WORK

Every one of us, from clerical worker to executive, has personal stories
of taking on challenges that we've never faced before and finding ways
to meet them. Every new job presents such opportunities. Not every
story is as dramatic as Edgar Mitchell's, but each one of us can be as creative. Take, for example, the Brunswick Corporation, which came to me
when I headed up SRI International's innovation program. That project
unfolded in four stages, each with two steps. Here are the questions I led
the corporation's managers through and a summary of their answers:

The Challenge

Establish the Goal: What is your initial goal?
> *We want to develop a new bowling pinsetter to replace the one
> we've been making for twenty-five years. And we want to reju-
> venate the industry as well as our sales.*

Assess the Risks: What's at stake—what makes it a difficult challenge?
> *Sales are down due to a flood of used pinsetters on the market.
> In addition, we are used to the old technology and don't have
> in-house expertise for newer electronics and software.*

The Focus

Tap into Character: What about *you*—your values, your experience,
your character—gives you confidence you can somehow do it?
> *We are open to bringing in totally new technologies that we
> have no internal capabilities for. We are dedicated to the enter-
> tainment value and sport of bowling, and are determined to re-
> juvenate interest in it.*

Analyze Priority Issues: What are the most important issues that you need to resolve with some creative ideas?

Meeting customers' ongoing wishes for automated feedback on their bowling performance (to understand a run of hits or misses) and to improve scores.

The Creative Solutions

Generate Options: What are some of the options you can generate, even if you don't use them?

A pinsetter that sets whatever pins a bowler wants set for practice purposes.

A "smart card" that "remembers" who a bowler is, his averages, and how he did on different pin combinations, etc.

A computer system that analyzes a bowler's performance and recommends ways to improve technique, depending on what mistakes were being made.

Feedback on speed, accuracy, and so on as the ball travels down the bowling lane.

A method to "bet" one's pins on the odds of an opponent picking up on a particular spare, etc. (changing scoring methods).

Decide on Solution: What options do you choose?

A pinsetter that sets whatever pins a bowler wants set for practice purposes.

A computer system that analyzes a bowler's performance and recommends ways to improve technique, depending on what mistakes were being made.

Feedback on speed, accuracy, and so on, as the ball travels down the bowling lane.

The Completion

Implement Change: What will you do to implement that solution?

We contracted for a market and technical feasibility study on the various ideas, to determine priorities for development. We used company-owned bowling centers within a few hundred miles of headquarters to first install and test the ideas.

Celebrate Results: What are the results, and the satisfaction gained from them?

All three concepts were a hit with the bowling patrons and within the industry. We celebrated the renewal of our leadership in the industry as top innovator.

This set of four stages, each with two steps, represents the entire innovation process—widely applicable, for example, to projects that take two to six months or meetings that take two to six hours.

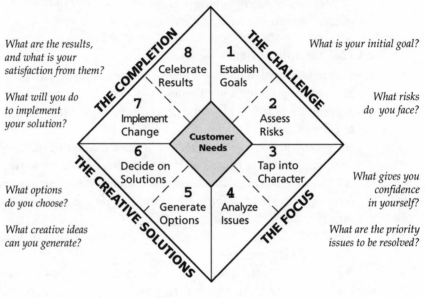

The Creative Journey

Every challenge we face goes through the very same stages, and at each stage, we have the opportunity to put our deepest values to work and take a Creative Journey.

The following questions will help you take your own Creative Journey at the deepest, most creative levels. The first question in bold is the basic query; the others (and ones you invent) can give you deeper, more profound answers.

The Challenge

Establish the Goal
- **What is your initial goal?**
- What makes this an adventure, or could?
- Who do you want to serve, and how?
- What goal are you most passionate about?
- What would make any hardship worthwhile?
- What goal allows you to best exercise your talents?
- What do you really, really, really want?
- What are you afraid to wish for?
- How can you best express your life's purpose here?

Assess the Risks
- **What risks do you face?**
- What's at stake? What makes it a difficult challenge?
- What do you fear in this situation?
- What important knowledge is missing?
- What could be the negative consequences of success?
- What past failures do you most want to avoid recreating?
- What could get in the way of your motivation to succeed?
- What are you afraid others will think of you if you fail? If you succeed?
- What prejudices might keep you from seeing the situation objectively?

The Focus

Tap into Character
- **What gives *you* confidence in yourself?**
- What did you draw upon to handle similar challenges in the past?
- How can you handle the pressures you're going to face?
- What gives you the courage to succeed?
- Where does your faith in yourself and others come from?
- What skills do you have for drawing out the best in others?
- What personal values are most important for you to act upon?
- What is the opportunity here for personal and professional growth?

Analyze Priority Issues
What are the priority issues to be resolved?
- What would other stakeholders say are their key concerns?
- What are the primary barriers to overcome?
- What is the hidden truth about this situation?
- Where does your intuition tell you to focus your attention?
- What truth is the hardest to accept?
- What new knowledge is needed to understand this situation?
- How can you keep from (a) oversimplifying the situation or (b) getting bogged down in its complexity?

The Creative Solutions

Generate Options
- **What creative ideas can you generate?**
- What ideas give an ideal solution?
- What ideas start with totally new assumptions?

- What ideas build upon what you've done?
- What ideas combine different elements?
- What are the obvious solutions?
- What ideas want to emerge on their own?
- How can you expand on ideas that have "juice"?
- What are some unique, unusual, or absurd ideas?
- What are some ideas that are exciting, satisfying, surprising, or humorous?

Decide on Solution
- **What options do you choose?**
- What are your criteria for a wise choice?
- Intuitively, what is most likely to work?
- How do your personal values enter into the decision?
- What is a sustainable, long-term solution?
- What are some quick wins?
- What's the hidden gem, whose advantages are not obvious?
- What are the advantages of others' favorite ideas?
- If you were to flip a coin, which ideas would you want to win?
- What ideas are you willing to fight for?
- What solution "stands for" the values you most cherish?
- What solutions would build the legacy or reputation you want?
- What solution are you most afraid of?

The Completion

Implement Change
- **What will you do to implement your solution?**
- How detailed a plan do you need?
- How do you gain buy-in and cooperation?
- What is the hidden wisdom in the objections that people raise?
- What has to be "let go of" to succeed?
- What is the right timing for action?
- Where will you need to push hard—or be flexible—for successful implementation?
- What commitments are you, or others, likely to miss if you aren't impeccable in keeping agreements?
- What shift is needed for people to embrace the solution?

Celebrate Results
- **What are the results, and your satisfaction from them?**
- What achievements are you most proud of?
- What are the benefits to stakeholders?

- What rewards and satisfactions do you want?
- How can you share the credit with those who deserve it?
- Whose contribution are you overlooking?
- How are you richer as a person from what you have learned about life?
- What would you have done differently?
- What important new knowledge can be gained?
- How can you bring others "up to speed" on new knowledge, information, and insights?
- When will you know it's time to celebrate? Time to move on?

Confronting these questions can open up surprising levels of creativity. One time I was working with computer software salespeople in New York City—a rather aggressive group. I asked them to state a goal we could journey on together. "That's easy," one person said. "How to make more money—more sales and profits." I replied, "Great start—and could you restate that in terms of a customer benefit?" The group paused a bit, stunned by the question and by the task. I was asking them to focus on what they would *give*—what they would provide—rather than what they wanted to *get*. Eventually they came up with, "How to provide customized solutions to individual customers at a mutually beneficial price." Defining the goal as how to serve, rather than what to get, opened up so much more creativity and energy, than the first statement. It also showed the power of the spiritual value of giving as well as receiving, focusing on the reciprocal nature of sustainable business growth and value-exchange.

> **Defining the goal as how to serve, rather than what to get, opened up so much more creativity and energy**

In retrospect, the journey may appear to have been rather linear, or step by step. However, in setting forth on the Creative Journey, the creative spark is more like a map than it is a step-by-step guide—helping you see where you are in the field of essential questions, and offering possible routes to take to reach the destination, You may set a goal, immediately think of some possible solutions, and jump forward on your journey. Or you may implement ideas you have had and see you forgot to analyze something fully, so you jump back. The important thing is to feel free to follow your instincts. Just make sure that you eventually cover all the steps and confront all questions that form in your mind. You may be tempted to bypass questions related to assessing risks, tapping into character, and celebrating results because they're more emotion-laden. Yet these questions free up the energy needed for high-level creativity!

RELIVING AN ANCIENT TALE

What makes the Creative Journey model different from normal problem-solving processes? After years spent examining corporate, scientific, and academic models of innovation, I noted that something was missing. Most creative problem-solving processes limit their focus to only the mental side of innovation, such as setting a goal, performing analysis, eliciting ideas, making a decision, and implementing it. Yet innovation takes more than good left-brains and right-brains! It's often the plunge from confidence to darkness that grabs our attention the most and makes us search our souls for the answer—and that calls upon our deepest human values, from which springs the empowerment we need. We have the opportunity, indeed the need, to apply personal values and engage our souls throughout the *entire* process of meeting not just personal challenges, but work challenges.

A breakthrough in my understanding of the emotional cycles of the creative process occurred in 1982, after I read *The Way to Shambhala* by Edwin Bernbaum.[2] I realized that virtually all stories about spiritual quests across all cultures—from the Tibetans' spiritual quest for Shambhala to the mythical quest of Odysseus—have the following plot-line (the formula for spiritual soap operas):

- You're on a quest, and you come to an impassable river (or some other obstacle), guarded by a demon.
- The instructions are clear: Withdraw to gather strength— identify with a power (the divine) so its energies merge in you; then call forth the demon to see exactly what you have to deal with.
- Do battle until you are victorious in defeating, befriending, or taming the demon.
- Engage the subdued/tamed demon as an ally to get you across the impassable river; on the other side, take an account, with gratitude, of what you've gained to assist you on the next stage of your journey.

Then, in 1987, Lorna Catford and I co-taught a course called "Creativity in Business" at Stanford University's Graduate School of Business. She helped me see the link between this heroic model and the innovation process itself, as shown in the following table.

Stage	Journey	Steps
Challenge	*Begin on a quest and come to impassable river and demon*	Establish goal and assess the risks.
Focus	*Take on inner power and call forth the demon*	Tap into character and analyze priority issues.
Creative solution	*Do battle and defeat/tame demon*	Generate options and decide on solution.
Completion	*Cross impassable river and take account of gains*	Implement change and celebrate results.

The most powerful insight for me was my new understanding of the stage of personal empowerment for facing the river and demon, and its parallel in the innovation process—that this tapping into character, including spiritual values, enables us to put our values to work. Suddenly, the basic "confidence curve" of the innovation process became clear, and I saw the power of including the emotional and spiritual as well as the mental steps in a model of innovation.[3]

The Creative Journey — The Innovation Process

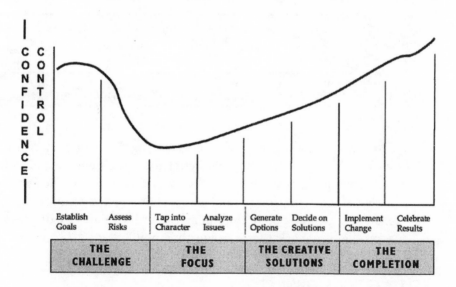

When we've seen the challenge and felt the fears associated with its risks and uncertainty, we need to gain confidence. The word confidence comes from the Latin, *con* + *fides*, which means "with faith"; by tapping into our character, we find in ourselves the inner source of acting with faith and courage. If we don't, our creative minds shrink and we come up with only the meekest, most ordinary ideas. When our confidence expands, our minds expand, giving room for the boldest, most breakthrough ideas.

Immersion into a state of fear and uncertainty isn't all bad. In fact, it's part and parcel of the process that produces the best innovations. In workshops at DowElanco and Exxon Chemical, we explored the "scientific discovery process" version of the Creative Journey . . .

The Creative Journey — The Scientific Discovery Process

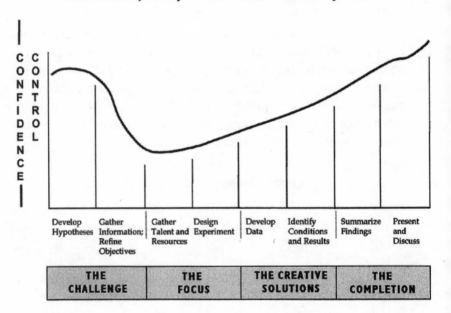

Many participants noted that by managing the emotional ups and downs of this process, they could better focus their energy and intuition . . . and perhaps speed up the discovery process itself. The benefits of a faster invention process can be huge: For a pharmaceutical that is expected to generate $350 million a year, every single day of getting new products to market faster is worth $1 million!

TELLING YOUR OWN STORY

In chapter 2, we explored how you might embody the eight qualities of a creative SPIRITED person: being self-aware, purposeful, incisive, rewarding, inventive, transforming, evaluative, and dauntless. You can use these qualities in yourself to support your creative journeys, step by step.

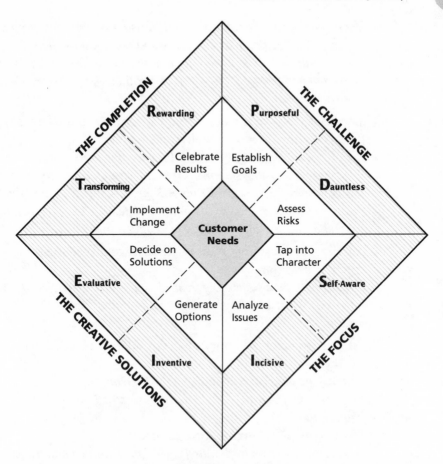

**"SPIRITED" Qualities
Support the Creative Journey**

The empowerment that fuels the Creative Journey can be found in everyday experiences of every person we work with. Think back to a challenge you've faced at work that required a new, perhaps creative, solution and you didn't quite know how you were going to find it. What story can you tell? To relive your quest to find a solution, answer the following questions. The italicized material is an example of a specific quest—that of a woman named Mary Nelson who, as President of Bethel New Life in West Side Chicago, helped pioneer the early "sweat equity" approach to rejuvenating housing in run-down communities.

What was your initial goal?
We wanted to create a low-income housing alternative to the welfare system.

What was at stake? What made it a difficult challenge?

We needed to do something about housing in our community. In ten years, we had lost 200 housing units per year in a square-mile area. Soon there would be no community left. Our church was a congregation of poor people. The governor's office and bureaucrats said, "It's not possible."

What about *you*—your values, your experience, your character—gave you confidence you could somehow do it?

People said, "We've got to do it, because this is going to be a visible symbol, a visible statement that the church cares, that this is our community. As Martin Luther King Jr. said, 'We know finite disappointment but we know infinite hope.' We have a sense that what we do, with God's help, makes a difference."

What were the most important issues that would require some creative ideas to resolve?

Financing housing was a big issue. So was getting people involved. We also needed the right skills, and a "can-do" attitude.

What were some of the options you considered, even if you didn't use them?

Having the government sponsor the housing.

Doing "sweat equity" in which people gained ownership by helping to build.

Mortgaging the church to gain capital.

Asking contractors to donate funds, labor, and/or materials.

What were the options you chose?

Mortgaging the church to gain capital.

Doing "sweat equity."

What did you do to implement those solutions?

We mortgaged the buildings five times—it gave the bankers comfort that we would do everything in our power to ensure the project wouldn't go belly-up.

We enlisted people who wanted to be homeowners rather than tenants, even if they didn't think they had leadership or building skills.

We had meetings to hash out issues like "who gets what apartment" and used these as occasions to practice communication skills that would help people continue to manage "their" property in the future.

What were the results, and the satisfaction you gained from them?

It not only made affordable housing available to people who didn't have any cash, it was a great leadership development

*tool: People found out they were listened to and had skills they
didn't know about.*

*A building is so visible. It was a positive accomplishment that
bolstered everyone's self-image and "can-do" spirit. So when it
comes to the drug pusher down the street, they say, "Wow, we
did this building, then why can't we get rid of the drug pusher?
We can do it."*

RENEWING CREATIVE ENERGY

Most creative processes end with getting feedback on results. This feedback can be mentally satisfying, but we have an emotional need for it
as well. I used to teach seminars on stress and burnout, and the most
frequent cause of burnout identified by participants was, "I've put my
heart and soul into this work and feel like I've gotten nothing back. My
work is a black hole sucking up my energy."

Without an emotional sense of completion, we keep taking on new
challenges without ever filling up our energy tanks. We get more and
more run down until we burn out. Many people shy away from having performance measured—they've been "burned" by evaluations that
primarily point out faults. Yet, without appraisals we can't celebrate
our successes.

Celebration

Celebration, rather than simply feedback, completes an innovation
process. By celebration, I don't mean big hurrahs and
pats on the back, although those are just fine. Celebration provides the moment to gain a deep sense
of satisfaction, often accompanied by sincere
feelings of gratitude, and to express those feelings from the heart. Celebration also allows the
opportunity to acknowledge any negative emotions associated with not achieving a key goal,
or leaving a stimulating project or group behind,
or ending a phase of your career. You can even express your sadness at the ending of a precious experience with colleagues as you celebrate the life and creativity that you
shared together.

> **Celebration,
> rather than
> simply feedback,
> completes
> an innovation
> process.**

Conscious celebration—at milestones throughout the Creative
Journey as well as at the end—revitalizes our human spirit and pre-
pares us for our next round of challenges. More than ever, in the hyper-
pressure of minimal time and maximum workloads, we must pay

attention to this vital act. Missing it is like missing food and sleep. It's that essential.

Conscious celebrations incorporate five key features[4]:

- Specific values (authenticity, humor, play, empowerment, elegance, spontaneity, and creativity)
- Symbols (such as a globe to symbolize the worldwide launch of a successful new product)
- Ritual (fresh rather than stifling)
- Storytelling
- Special role of leadership in the event's design and implementation.

Celebration—as a learning point, a renewal of energy, and a bonding—can become the focal point for any culture, no matter what specific values and rituals make up that culture. In fact, celebration can be the ultimate key to transforming our organizations. For example, to help turn around two failing divisions of a major housing company, a vice-president sponsored celebration as part of the company philosophy:

WE VALUE CELEBRATION AND BELIEVE THAT IT ENHANCES WORK
We publicly recognize achievements.
We encourage spontaneous celebrations.
We know that if we're having fun, we will work harder, smarter, and longer.
We evaluate managers on their enthusiasm and ability to create an environment in which it is a pleasure to work.
Employees who spread gloom will be asked to leave.[5]

It worked so well to inspire work teams that management had to issue a policy requiring employees to take at least one day off per week!

Terry Deal and M.K. Key have identified seven distinct reasons for celebration[6]:

1. *Cyclical gatherings:* to build a sense of ongoing identity in a group.
2. *Recognition:* to celebrate heroes and heroines, focus energy, share values, and provide motivation.
3. *Triumph:* to spark creative energy, spawn stories, and build affiliation.
4. *Comfort and letting go:* to heal sadness, create continuity from past to future, and help the group move on.
5. *Succession:* to bring closure, help departing people move on, and help replacements to ease in.
6. *Altruism:* to bring people together and give back to the community.

7. *Play:* to release tension, foster creativity, and generally delight everyone.

We can make ritual and symbols important in everyday events as well as major transitions. Ron Green, an internal consultant at Alcoa Aluminum creates celebrations at the end of corporate training programs.[7]

During (graduation) dinners, which are light, playful, fun-filled occasions, we present symbols to each participant to help celebrate the most important awareness of skill that he or she gained during the program—giant ears for listening skills, a clown's nose for appreciating the less serious side of themselves. . . .

These rituals . . . serve to bond the group together, and help them become part of the corporate culture, as well as serve as a reminder that each member has begun a journey toward greater effectiveness.

IN CLOSING . . .

Traditionally, we develop ourselves at work in order to deliver better results. That's one direction on a two-way street. The other is to see work as one of the main arenas where we can consciously develop ourselves. A woman I once knew worked as a customer service representative at Blue Cross, answering questions and expediting claims. She would often have to deal with very upset people—people who had simultaneously just faced their own mortality and the largest medical bills of their lives. As a spiritual practice, and to keep her own peace of mind, she used those moments to silently chant her name for God and perhaps to help the other person to regain equanimity through her silent prayer—all the while doing her best to resolve the problem quickly. She spiritualized her work.

Adults learn primarily by hearing stories of others' journeys through life and by telling our own stories. Even a project debriefing is telling a story about what just happened. Stories give the context we need to make decisions and take action. Warren Bennis says, "Effective leaders put words to the formless longings and deeply felt needs of others. They create communities out of words. They tell stories that capture minds and win hearts."[8]

When we innovate, we make up the story of the future rather than relive the past. Either way, these are the creative journeys we enact in real time at work. As the poet Alexander Pope reminds us, the creative journey takes persistence and commitment:

Fired at first sight with what the Muse imparts,
In fearless youth we tempt the heights of Arts,
While from the bounded level of our mind
Short views we take, nor see the lengths behind.
But more advanced behold with strange surprise
New distant scenes of endless science arise!
We tremble to survey
The growing labors of lengthened way,
The increasing prospects tire our wandering eyes
Hills peep o'er hills, and Alps on Alps arise!
True ease in writing comes from art, not change,
As those move easiest who have learned to dance.[9]

True innovation also comes "from art, not chance." With every creative challenge we take on, we have the opportunity to experience in a microcosm the spiritual quest of ancient times . . . growing while we achieve our goals, creating stories not only of achievement and adventure, but of personal, spiritual growth.

CHAPTER 4

Employ *Innovation Styles* as Your Compass

I don't know how or where my ideas come from. It's almost an uncomfortable feeling, but I'm comfortable now with discomfort. The creative feeling is, "I didn't really do this."

I believe that everything that can be already is. All you are is a facility for creativity. What we create already exists but not in solid form. I conceive a product instantly as a whole thing, not in bits and pieces. The moment I've got it, I've got it; I know where every piece goes.

To stimulate others, I feed the environment with tons of information. I pin up articles with comments like, "Critical development in plastics technology." Someone invariably comes up and asks why. One of my roles is to question why we are doing things. To satisfy our own ego needs? Client-dictated needs? Simply because it can be done?

—JOHN, DIRECTOR OF DESIGN FOR A PRODUCTS DESIGN FIRM

THINKING CREATIVELY FROM FOUR DIRECTIONS

At American Express Travel Related Services, I worked with Asia-Pacific managers from countries as diverse as Korea, India, Australia, and Thailand. They wanted to develop a growth strategy for their region, but they struggled at first about whether that was possible, given the vast differences in the travel needs among the countries. The breakthrough came when one person stood up and said,

As country managers, we're limiting our thinking by our history of advancing our own careers by getting people to spend more and more money in the country we're responsible for. Instead of worrying about how much money we can "import," by getting people to visit our individual countries, what if we thought about how to "export" people and money out of our countries?

Everyone was puzzled. He went on,

If I'm trying to get people to leave my country, where will they go? To your countries, most likely! You'll then be getting their travel revenue. If we *each tried to get a lot of movement out of our countries, we'd all prosper. That should be the core of our strategy!*

Their future success grew from such a radically different way of thinking about their business and careers.

When I was still head of the innovation management practice at SRI International (formerly Stanford Research Institute), I spent much of my time facilitating multi-day, idea-generation sessions with scientists, engineers, and marketing specialists. Sometimes an exercise would provoke lots of excitement and new ideas in one group, but the same technique would flop in the next group; or half the people would be engaged while the other half wondered when we'd get on to the next topic. I could have arrogantly chalked it up to "they're just resistant," but I knew better.

I seriously wondered, "Of the hundred or more idea-generation techniques available through books and my own imagination, how can I know which ones will work with different people and in different situations?" I most wanted to be able to predict what exercises would work with which people, to cut the "miss rate" from trial and error use of different techniques. I began by investigating the pioneering research of Michael Kirton[1], who has clearly shown that people might have equal levels of creativity—measured by the number and uniqueness of ideas generated—yet have totally different approaches to getting their ideas. He identified two styles: Adaptors, who are best at taking what's given and working with it in new ways, and Innovators, who are best at challenging assumptions and developing new paradigms.

Still, Kirton's work didn't quite give me the answers I sought, and when I combined it with proprietary databases at SRI about different lifestyle groups in the United States, the statistics clearly proved the breakthrough: We use a mixture of *four*, not just two, distinct strategies for coming up with creative ideas[2]. I've called these four approaches *Visioning, Modifying, Experimenting,* and *Exploring,* in a model named *Innovation Styles*. Research with people in Southeast Asia, Japan, China, Europe, the United States, and Canada has validated this model and its self-scoring survey, the *Innovation Styles Profile*.[3]

Visioning

With Visioning, you seek to see the ideal, long-term solution—you *envision* and *idealize*. You might prefer this style because you like to imagine an ideal future and then let long-term goals be your guide. Using this style means letting yourself have your dreams and realistically imagining what it would be like if those dreams came true. Visioning helps to provide direction, inspiration, and momentum to creative projects.

As an example, when Stephen Arnold was General Manager of the Education and Games Division at LucasFilms Limited, he used the Visioning style to meet his immediate business needs, to lead his industry, and to set the goals that could change the face of education. He was one of many people who shared their stories with me.

As a production organization, we're trying to design and develop exciting and successful entertainment and education products using interactive technology. Our bigger business purpose is actually to evolve the state of the art in interactive media. I do in fact go out into the future and figure out what it ought to be like. Then I turn around and look back to see what the pathway from the present to that future is.

And the pathway to get from here to there has got to stay flexible. Even though I go out there and envision sort of what I want, I turn around and say, "Ah, that's the pathway. Maybe I'll get there." But when I'm actually down in the jungle trying to get there, I see lots of other pathways, sometimes better ones that I didn't see at first. So I've got to learn to be flexible.

With your career, you might ask yourself, "What would I ideally like to be doing ten years from now, even if I've never done it before?" To develop a new product, you might ask, "What would represent the ideal wishes of our customers?"

Great Visioning Moments in History

In 1213, a group of English barons banded together with a common vision: to limit the absolute power of the king and to promise justice to all free men in the kingdom. They presented a document to King John, who refused to sign it. It took two years and the force of an army to convince the king to sign this cornerstone of English liberty and democracy, the Magna Carta in 1215.

In 1961, John Fitzgerald Kennedy shared his vision with the nation. He had a dream that within the next ten years, the United States would send a man to the moon. The nation rallied around the president's vision, and people worked hard to make it happen. By the time Neil Armstrong finally took his "giant leap for mankind," Kennedy's vision had become the vision of the nation.

Modifying

With Modifying, you seek to expand and build on what you've already done—you *build* and *optimize*. You might prefer this style because you like to modify and improve on what someone has already initiated—like an existing technology or work method. Using this style often means looking to previous situations and adapting solutions and expert opinion to fit a new purpose. Modifying helps provide stability and thoroughness to creative endeavors by ensuring that the full potential of an idea gets developed.

Gretchen Price, Director of Finance for the Health and Beauty Aids Division of Procter & Gamble, used the Modifying style to develop a new financial planning system.

The area we attacked was our profit forecasting role, which is our primary financial planning vehicle. It all comes together in this forecast, and there are literally hundreds and hundreds of people that provide a piece of information. What we've been able to do is really streamline the process, allowing some simplification in functional areas. We even took what, for this particular area in our company culture, are radical steps—like eliminating the frequency of our forecasts. So we're providing better information to the company for decision-making purposes. And people feel a lot better about it.

With your career, you might ask, "How can I build on the interests and experiences I've developed so far?" To develop a new product, you might ask, "What could improve on or extend our current product offerings?"

Great Modifying Moments in History

Before the fifteenth century, bookmakers painstakingly printed books from inked wood block letters. But in 1440, a German man put a new twist on an old way of printing to revolutionize the world. He modified the notion of fixed carved letters by creating moveable ones. He combined his moveable type with an adaptation of a winepress and invented the printing press. His name was Johannes Gutenberg.

Back in the gold rush days of the 1850s, a seventeen-year-old immigrant tailor noticed that miners quickly went through scores of their cloth trousers. He went to work sewing overalls made of a stiff canvas that could stand up to wear and tear. Suddenly, his services were in huge demand. Several years later, he substituted the canvas material with a French fabric called *denim*, and dyed it indigo blue to minimize soil stains. Sales of his pants and overalls skyrocketed. He had invented blue jeans. His name was Levi Strauss.

Experimenting

With Experimenting, you seek to combine various elements and test out novel solutions—you *combine* and *test*. You might prefer this style because you like to test out various combinations of ideas and learn from the results. Using this style often means setting up a process such as an experimental design or a focus group methodology that produces a solution by systematically combining variables in a situation and discovering firsthand what the results look like in microcosm. Experimenting helps you to expand and troubleshoot new possibilities while building a consensus for a solution.

Jerry Pierce was head of the Electronics Technology Laboratory for SRI International when he used the Experimenting style in the invention of an improved computer disk.

I had worked with optical disks for a long time and had had magnetic disks for a long time. But this was not a planned invention. It was a case of starting to use an optical disk and beginning to store information on it. Then I found out how much space was being used up on it and how slow it was. And I said, to myself "This isn't going to work." Then I had a meeting with a client, and I began to invent as I went. And in that process, I said, "Well, why don't you take the existing technology and combine it with the new technology, where the magnetic side would store the directory and current files and the optical side would store the massive archival data . . . and it's transparent to the user. So essentially you have a disk that is removable that has 400 megabytes of data on it and the speed of the hard disk.

With your career, you might ask, "How could I take the best parts of the last three or four jobs I've had and combine just those parts into a new career?" To develop a new product, you might ask, "What could be a new mix of features?"

Great Experimenting Moments in History

In 1878, thirty-one-year-old Thomas Alva Edison announced to the public that he would invent a safe and inexpensive electric light in six weeks. In fact, it turned out that Edison worked for well over a year on the invention. He experimented with countless materials as filaments, including gold, fishing line, and even hairs that he plucked from the beards of unsuspecting visitors. In the autumn of 1879, Edison discovered that a charred cotton thread would burn for thirteen and a half hours. He invented what the reporters called "a wondrous bulb that lit without a match and glowed without a flame— the electric light bulb."

In 1920, Earl Dixon was a cotton buyer for the Johnson and Johnson Company. Johnson and Johnson made large surgical dressings, and Dixon realized that they were too large to take care of the minor cuts and burns that his wife often incurred while working in the kitchen. He was determined to devise a sterile, easily applied bandage that would stay in place. After experimenting with several things, he came up with a sterile cotton ball that was placed in the center of a piece of adhesive tape. He realized that these bandages would have to be mass-produced, so he devised a way to use crinoline fabric to temporarily cover over the sticky portions of the bandage. When his boss, James Johnson, watched Dixon bandage his own finger one day, he realized they had a revolutionary new product—one that would come to be known as the Band-Aid.

Exploring

With Exploring, you seek to challenge core assumptions and discover new alternatives—you *challenge* and *discover*. You might prefer this style because you like to question every assumption and let things unfold without having in mind a long-term goal, a specific process, or even an investment in the present. Using this style often means using symbols, metaphors, and analogies to gain a totally new perspective on a creative challenge. Exploring helps you to open up the possibility for radical breakthroughs.

When John Gooden was Vice President of Design and Marketing for Design West Incorporated, he used the Exploring style to develop a new automobile seat for Pontiac.

This particular ergonomic sports seat has moving side-bolsters. These bolsters have the ability to "hug" the body, if you want that confined feeling for sports-car-like maneuvering. We were having a tremendous problem where a piece of plastic comes together with a piece of material. If that area moved, children could possibly trap their hands. We were really at our wits' end to come up with an idea. About that time, I was out in the Catalina Channel sailing, thinking about this problem—sort of laying back on the deck with a beer in hand—when a California gray whale came up beside the boat and took a big breath. That's an awesome experience. And at the time that it surfaced, I glanced over and there's the belly of this whale with this fluted structure on it, expanding and contracting. And I said to myself, "That's it!" We can have the close-out detail move in the same fashion as the belly of the whale.

With your career, you might ask yourself, "How can I challenge my assumptions about what's possible and trust what might emerge from there?" To develop a new product, you might ask, "What could break the rules of conventional wisdom in the industry?"

Great Exploring Moments in History

In 1769, a young preacher became fascinated by the gases that collected above the beer vats in the brewery next door. Not at all certain what he was out to discover, he placed a variety of substances in the nine-to-twelve-inch-high gassy area. This "fixed air" as they called it, extinguished candles, killed mice, muffled gunpowder blasts, and curiously, turned plain water effervescent when it was poured from one glass into another. The young preacher's explorations had led him to the discovery of soda water. His name was Joseph Priestly.

In 1948, during a hike in the Alps, a Swiss mountaineer became frustrated by the small, prickly burrs that clung tenaciously to his pants and socks. As he sat picking them off, an idea struck him. If he could just figure out a way to reproduce the burrs' clinging properties, he might be able to devise a fastener that could, in some cases, make the zipper obsolete. After ten years of effort, he had invented Velcro. His name was George De Maistrel.

What is your mixture of styles? Rank the following approaches to innovation from 1 to 4, with 1 being your favorite and 4 your least favorite. While this won't give the same accurate results as the entire validated self-assessment (the *Innovation Styles Profile*), you will get a first glimpse of your own preferences.

I like to find solutions by:

_____ A. Optimizing what we've already done; applying expert opinions in new ways.

_____ B. Starting with totally new assumptions; using metaphors and analogies for new insights.

_____ C. Seeking the ideal, long-term solution; imagining the best possible outcome.

_____ D. Playing with the variables operating in a situation; combining the ideas of many people.

Put your rankings here:

__ A. Modifying __ B. Exploring __ C. Visioning __ D. Experimenting

It's quite important to remember that everyone has a mixture of all four styles in their own unique blend and that each style represents a *language* of innovation and creativity, not a type of person. Even if you like to use the Modifying style more than the others, you don't have to wear the label *modifier* as if that's the only way that you're creative. One or two styles may be like your "mother tongue" that you're most comfortable speaking. The goal is to increase your fluency in all four styles; you can learn to speak all four languages without having

> **Each style represents a language of innovation and creativity, not a type of person.**

to alter your preferences. This isn't a new way to put people into creativity boxes. It's a model that helps you to be more flexible in tackling your creative challenges.

TAKING ADVANTAGE OF DIVERSITY

Diversity means more than culture or gender differences. Our distinctive talents, styles, and perspectives enrich the stew for brewing our creative ideas. In this context, each style has something to bring to the party. So does each person. When you're listening to someone else's ideas, notice whether you turn on or turn off to their ideas, depending on whether they prefer the same style as you. When you're sharing your ideas, notice if the other person is more responsive to you when you're addressing long-term goals (*Visioning*), building on the present (*Modifying*), testing new possibilities (*Experimenting*), or challenging assumptions (*Exploring*).

Each style has its drawbacks if you use it in isolation. If you use only the Visioning style, you might become so goal focused you don't see other points of view. If you use only the Modifying style, you might become too tied to present circumstances and not recognize far-reaching opportunities. If you use only the Experimenting style, you might become bureaucratic, lost in the process, having forgotten the ultimate goal. And if you use only the Exploring style, you might become too preoccupied with "blue sky" possibilities and ignore practical details.

Many times, people discount each other's ideas more for the *style* of idea than the content. People who favor a particular style often favor particular idea-killers as well:

- People who like to Modify might judge others' ideas as "too crazy" or "not worthy of consideration."
- People who Explore might criticize ideas as "too conventional" or "too inside the box."
- People who Envision might shoot down ideas as "too timid" or "not bold enough."
- People who Experiment might evaluate ideas as "too idealistic" or "not workable."

Instead of fighting over the "right" strategy for generation of ideas, remember to think of each style as a language of creativity. You can recognize what styles other people are using (without giving them a questionnaire) just by listening for the type of questions that each individual uses to stimulate new ideas. For instance, the Visioning person asks, "What ideas would give us an ideal future?" The Modifying person asks, "What ideas could adapt or modify what we've done?" The Experimenting person asks, "What ideas could combine different elements?" And the Exploring person asks, "What ideas could start with totally new assumptions?"

A division of Baxter International asked us for assistance in bringing together two different multinational sessions to explore new strategies for their line of medical products that offer an alternative to normal blood dialysis. In Europe, and again in Japan, we used the Innovation Styles to help people think in multiple perspectives, bringing respect to their different points of view and producing surprisingly new ideas among "seasoned professionals."

Antonio Nunez and Joyce Francis each use very different Innovation Styles. They were co-instructors at the California Institute of Integral Studies. They once discussed how they found a way to come together and build on their diversities.

JF: Each time I develop a new program, it draws on what I did before. Then I just try to look at where I have some excitement for re-doing or changing something that's there.

AN: What I first do is go inside to a quiet space and really check into what is true, what's alive, what has passion and heart for me. And that's usually how the course that I do gets developed.

JF: I tend to often look behind me and see the road that I have taken, as well as look around me and see the roads that others have taken. I don't think Antonio tends to look back. I think that he tends to think that each moment is a fresh new opportunity not limited by a previous experience— more so than I do.

AN: I always also think of you, Joyce, as a person who gets our feet on the ground, who does reality testing, and who allows us to structure some of our wild ideas. I find that working together is very complementary. The practical, content-oriented material is as important as the visionary, intuitive risk-taking. And in that sense, I really enjoy working with you.

JF: I think almost on a more personal level, some of Antonio's style has rubbed off on me and I've become more trusting of myself to do more instruction and fly freer. In a lot of ways he has honored my style to the extent that it's made me feel more confident just to be who I am and to be expressive. And there are times when I think my style rubs off on Antonio.

This example from Antonio and Joyce points out that one of the primary benefits of Innovation Styles is to expand the creative fluency of people working in groups. This expansion begins by honoring the "creativity culture differences" that exist between individuals, even if they are from the same country. You can employ Innovation Styles cross-culturally to:

- Gain greater participation in idea-generation and knowledge-creation (by people of different styles).
- Develop a more comprehensive, creative set of options.
- Optimize synergy in a diverse group (rather than argue over which approach is best).
- Apply easily to variety of issues (strategy, new products, quality, organizational change, and so on).

While there are some differences in the average personal profiles among people from different countries (for example, Singapore versus the United States), the more important differences can be found within most any team.

Today, right after reading this chapter, you can apply the Innovation Styles, even with people who have never heard of this model. It's simple, using a valuable tool known as the *Compass* exercise. Each style is like a point on a compass, giving you four different directions for approaching a creative challenge.

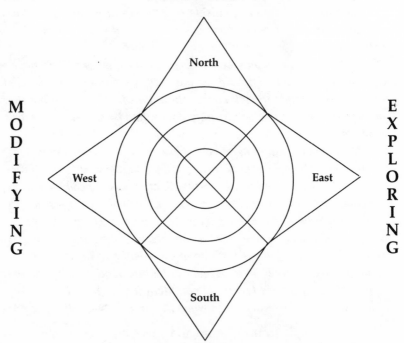

When you're ready, generate ideas by approaching the challenge from all four directions:

- *Visioning (north)*: "What ideas would give us an ideal future?"

- *Modifying (west)*: "What ideas could adapt or modify what we've done?"
- *Experimenting (south)*: "What ideas could combine different elements?"
- *Exploring (east)*: "What ideas could start with totally new assumptions?"

By asking all four questions separately and filling up a flip-chart pad with ideas for each one, you ensure that you'll get a more comprehensive set of options to choose from than if you had used just one or two styles. The Compass questions can help you solve a problem or challenge by reframing it: They change your starting points and perspectives and break your typical patterns of creative thinking. When we did that at a workshop with 3M's Industrial Tape Division, one person stood up to facilitate his "favorite" question, then turned the facilitation over to someone else for the next question. Similarly, you can improve group participation by making sure everyone's favorite Compass question is deliberately used.

For a more sophisticated use of the Compass, change the wording of the general questions to fit your specific application:

	Modifying	Exploring	Visioning	Experimenting
Basic "Compass" questions	*What ideas could adapt or modify what we've done?*	*What ideas could start with totally new assumptions?*	*What ideas could give us an ideal future?*	*What ideas could combine different elements?*
Strategic planning	How can we build on our core strengths and capabilities?	How can we rewrite the rules of competition?	How can we be ideally positioned within the industry?	How can we synergize different technologies, partnerships, etc.?
Getting ideas from customers	What could add to what you already have in place?	What could revolutionize the way things are done?	What could meet your long-term goals and strategy?	What could be tested under trial circumstances?
Promoting change in the organization	What could improve on the best of what we've done?	What could shake up or unfreeze things, to see what emerges?	What could give us a world class organization (or process)?	What could give us the best synergy among our different units?

By understanding the four Innovation Styles, you'll be able to predict which approaches will work best for a particular group and tailor both the wording and the sequence for introducing each style to the group, thus helping assure everyone's full participation and the generation of a more comprehensive as well as creative set of solutions.

TAPPING INTO YOUR INTUITION

Innovation Style addresses the *strategy*, not the *level* of creative thinking. Richness of ideas comes from the diversity of people's experience. *But where do the ideas themselves come from?*

A wealth of literature over the past twenty-five years has described the functions of the two sides of the human brain. The left side has more to do with our linear, logical, mathematical, and verbal abilities. The right side has more to do with our intuitive, spatial, emotional, and musical abilities.

Both logical and intuitive thinking are necessary for optimum creativity. Most, and perhaps all, of the great scientific discoveries have occurred with the logical providing fertile ground for the intuitive to produce insights. For example, the German chemist Friedrich Kekule worked for years to discover the molecular structure of benzene. In experiment after experiment he gathered and analyzed information that might offer a clue. One night in 1865 he dozed in front of his fireplace:

> *Again the atoms were juggling before my eyes . . . My mind's eye, sharpened by repeated sights of a similar kind, could now distinguish larger structures of different forms and in long chains . . . Everything was moving in a snakelike and twisting manner. Suddenly, what was this? One of the snakes got hold of its own tail and the whole structure was mockingly twisting in front of my eyes. As if struck by lightning, I awoke.[4]*

He had envisioned the closed-ring structure of benzene. Following his insight and intuition, logic came into play. It would have been a barren discovery had he been unable to formulate the insight and effectively communicate it to the world.

This is a typical pattern: logic preceding and following intuitive insight. Although intuition often embodies the glamour and mystery of the creative process, logical thinking is also essential. One way to view the link between logic and intuition is as follows:

> *If someone said that marbles are like oil, you might think he had a few marbles in his head . . . (But) envision lubricating oil as millions of tiny marbles sandwiched between two surfaces. Suddenly it all makes sense.*
>
> *Most often our minds work logically . . . All creative ideas are logical when you view them in the abstract . . . Divergent ideas might not fit together very well, but take them to a higher level of abstraction and suddenly you've got a whole new concept.[5]*

Across all cultures, people describe the experience of the creative moment with words like, "The idea came to me," "I was struck by an insight," "The lightbulb went off in my head," "I heard a sound (or a voice)," "I could feel it in my bones." All of this language is receptive rather than active. The notion that "I thought of this idea," with its active-voice verb "I thought," doesn't really describe the *receptivity* of the microscopic moment of the idea *being born* in us.

So the experience of having a creative insight is not an act of doing but an act of receiving! This is the phenomenon of ideas coming from "the back burner" of our minds—"cooking away" out of our conscious awareness after we intentionally put it there until it "pops into our mind." The whole "technology" of creativity is how to produce that space in ourselves.

We've all heard (and often have difficulty following) the basic guidelines of idea-generation:

- Stretch yourself to see the big picture.
- Take the initiative to write your ideas as soon as you think of them.
- Be confident and take a risk; even half-baked ideas are OK.
- "Try on" new and different points of view.
- Generate options using both sides of your brain.
- Don't judge your ideas prematurely.
- Keep pushing to generate as many ideas as possible.
- Reward yourself for each idea by building on it.

The wisdom behind "don't judge ideas prematurely" particularly helps establish this climate of "active receptivity." Intuition plays a huge role in the generation of ideas, as does the information gathering that triggers creative thinking. The model of the four Innovation Styles provides a great deal of insight about how we use intuition and data together.

Modifying and Experimenting styles start with gathering facts, details, and other data; then they use intuitive insights to make sense of the data. The difference is that Modifying builds on what is known, while Experimenting combines the components or variables in new and unique ways. James Watson reports that while he was still searching for the structure of DNA, "Suddenly I became aware that both pairs (of DNA segments) could be flip-flopped and still have their bonds facing in the same direction." That intuitive insight triggered the discovery of the famous double helix.

Visioning and Exploring styles start with looking for an intuitive insight, hunch, or hypothesis; then they gather information to confirm and "fill out" their intuition. The difference is that Visioning looks for a literal *photographic picture* of what the future will be like; Exploring uses more *symbols and metaphors* to say what something "is like." Elias Howe's invention of the sewing machine came about through intuitive imagery. Repeatedly unable to solve the problem of connecting needle, thread, and material, he fell asleep one night and dreamed of being captured by cannibals. He saw himself in a huge kettle with the fire laid, being warned to solve his sewing machine mystery or he could be cooked alive. As the cannibals danced around the pot, Howe spotted holes in the tips of their spears. Jolted awake, he realized he could make the sewing machine work if he threaded the needle at the point.

Roy Rowan, a member of the Board of Editors of *Fortune* magazine, explains, "Intuition is knowledge gained without rational thought. It comes from a stratum of awareness just below the conscious level; it is slippery and elusive. New ideas spring from a mind that organizes experiences, facts, and relationships to discern a path that has not been taken before."[6]

On the subject of intuition (like creativity), old notions frequently fly around corporate offices: "Only a few people are really intuitive"; "Most people's 'intuitive' decisions are poor"; "You can't 'teach' it anyway"; "We don't need more people taking unnecessary risks." In reality, however, intuitive information is available to everyone, but we have a tendency to discount it or contaminate it. You discount your intuition when you say things like the following to disregard or doubt information as being unreliable or "wrong": "This doesn't make sense"; "That can't be right"; "This is foolish"; "I just made that up."

When Debbi Fields was dreaming up her cookie business, all the professional marketing people she consulted said it was a bad idea, but she didn't discount her own intuitions. "I went in totally petrified. But then I said to myself, 'If it's not meant to be, that's perfectly all right.' I knew I wouldn't be able to live with myself if I went through life thinking, 'If only I had stopped listening to everybody else and just gone out and done it'."[7]

When you contaminate your intuition, you alter your access to intuitive information and your interpretation of it. There are a number of ways you might do this:

- Lacking confidence. ("I can't do this. I'm not intuitive")
- Projecting a persona image. ("I want to look good.")
- Need to be right. ("I'm 100 percent sure this is it.")
- Wishful thinking. ("I wish it to turn out like . . .")

- Busy mind. ("I can't stop my internal chatter.")
- Misunderstanding intuition's "language." ("I don't get it.")
- Fear of being wrong. ("What if I'm wrong and we've spent . . .")
- Emotionally attached to an outcome. ("I absolutely must have . . .")

To get more intuitive ideas, you can develop "intuition fluency" in four ways:

- Enter the state of wondering.
- Understand your own "language" of intuition.
- Work with symbols.
- Practice, practice, practice.

Enter into Wondering

Intuition occurs most easily in a state of wondering—a mindset of attentive openness, curiosity, and expansion. Practitioners of Zen call this *Beginner's Mind*. In the SRI International Innovation Searches (described in ch. 11), we would often put a creative thinker who was new to the subject at hand in with all the experts. Quite often, the *Expert Mind* was closed to the breakthrough questions of our "naive outsider" who had no need to be "right" about "the way things are." If you don't feel that expansiveness—if you feel blocked or "contracted"—you are less likely to be in touch with your intuitive wisdom.

Jonas Salk once said,

In 1936, two things didn't fit together . . . whether or not you had to experience infection in order to develop immunity to a virus disease. In 1939, that idea came back to me. I asked nature the question, "Is it or is it not true that you must first be infected to become immune?" And nature said, "Go ahead and design the right experiment." I designed a series of experiments and the answer came back, "Yes it is possible to become immune without being infected." You see, the answer preexists. What people think of as the moment of discovery is really the discovery of the question.[8]

Like a lens on a camera, questions focus your intuition to allow you to get a clear picture—wide-angle or very close up. Remember that asking clear questions is the first step of the intuition process. However, the quality of the questions you ask determines the type of information you receive and the potential quality of insight. Examples of good, high-quality questions are: What information do I need? What would make sense of this data? What ideas would meet our stated needs? What are the obstacles to success?

Understand Your Intuition Language

Understanding your intuition takes the same dedication as learning a language. Intuitive cues include:

- The sense of sight: sights, visual symbols. (Do things look different to you?)
- Hearing: sounds, words, music. (Is your perception of sounds around you "changed"?)
- Tactile: goose bumps, gut feeling. (What's going on inside your body?)
- Emotion: joy, contentment, "yes" response. (How do you feel?)

Usually, we trust one of our "intuitive senses" the most and another the least. Which of the four "languages of intuition" mentioned above do you use most easily and trust most readily?

Jonas Salk adds, "Our subjective responses (intuitional) are more sensitive and more rapid than our objective responses (reasoned). This is the nature of the way the mind works. We first sense and then we reason why. Intuition must be allowed a free rein and be allowed to play."

Work with Symbols

Intuition often comes by metaphoric means, no matter what the sensory cue is: a piece of music, a visual symbol, a sensation in a particular part of the body, an unexplained emotion, even a specific word (a word is a symbol, after all). Symbols are a highly sophisticated, condensed form of information. The symbols that speak to you can be literal or figurative. Einstein struck upon his theory of relativity while riding on a train and absently watching another train pull ahead at a faster speed, giving him the sense of moving backward—relatively. Louis Pasteur concluded that bodily infection was caused by external microorganisms after observing that grapes would ferment only if their skin was broken.

Regarding scientific breakthroughs, Einstein said, "There are no logical paths to these (natural) laws. Only intuition resting on sympathetic understanding of experience can reach them." Intuition stirs new ideas and concepts through concrete symbols rather than abstract words. The difficulty for most people is "interpreting" these symbols . . . "How do I know that I understand my intuition correctly?" "How do I know it's right?" First, notice if you are discounting or contaminating the information you have received. For example, have you detached from your expectations, wishes, hopes, and fears? To gain more confidence in understanding your symbols, you should try the following:

- If in doubt about your interpretation of one symbol, "ask" your intuition for a different one.
- Give a "voice" to your symbol(s) . . . If a symbol could talk, what would it say to you?
- Don't be invested in getting it right: Just proceed in a state of open-minded, curious exploration.

Practice, Practice, Practice

The practicing intuitive insists on feedback as rigorously as the scientist, while embracing a difficult paradox: While the goal is to be more accurate in your intuitive insights, you must let go of being correct in order to allow your intuition to work. One of the biggest blocks is trying too hard, wanting too much to get it right. Therefore, to increase the efficiency and effectiveness of your practice, remember to:

- Allow intuition to happen, rather than trying to "receive" information.
- Practice on small things, like predicting which elevator will arrive first.
- Learn from the results: Which "cues" were you tuning into, and which cues stimulated correct foresight? What blocks were present when your "intuitive hits" didn't pan out?
- Simply notice the symbols, images, and impressions that are stimulated by a question.
- Don't try to figure out the answer: The impressions don't have to make sense.
- Know that it's OK to think, I'm not getting anything." If you feel you aren't getting an intuitive idea or response, make something up—you'll be amazed at the level of accuracy of your "guesses."
- Record everything, no matter what you perceive—a cramp in your foot, a song in your head, a car horn honking outside.

If you keep a record of your intuitive thoughts and ideas (relative to actual experiences), objectively noting how they turned out, you'll find that the accuracy of your intuitive foresight and predictions increases weekly.

MEDITATING FOR GREATER CREATIVITY

Creative ideas happen when we open ourselves to something bigger than our own mind, just as they are spurred by being committed to a purpose larger than ourselves. Our most original ideas emerge from the space *between* our thoughts. Most of us, however, have such a constant

Our most original ideas emerge from the space *between* our thoughts.

stream of thoughts, there is very little space between them. Creating more stillness and serenity allows greater space between thoughts and thus greater opportunities for breakthrough ideas.

A great way to access and increase the intuitive space is through meditation. Meditation induces alpha waves (8-12 cycles per second) or theta waves (4-7). (Beta is 13-30, delta is 0.5-4.) It's during these states that sudden insights spring intuitively from our subconscious. Alpha and theta patterns are tranquil and prime the mind to be more perceptive. Meditation is not intended to trigger thoughts of any kind. It simply reduces tension and anxiety, which hamper intuition.

Meditation begins with the intention of connecting to a larger whole outside ourselves (a divine oneness), which has been the focus of spiritual disciplines for over 10,000 years. So another question to explore is, "What can we learn from spiritual practices that actually enhance our own creativity?" As a part of creation, we ourselves can be co-creators. We can learn from spiritual exercises how to become more receptive to our own inner wisdom and creativity. One of the most prominent of these exercises is meditation.

In athletics the optimum state for peak performance is one of "relaxed concentration" or "playing loose." Similarly, meditation is a very effective way to bring yourself into a more focused state of relaxed attention. The term *meditation* is often regarded with suspicion in the business world; some people think it sounds too foreign, mystical, and impractical. Perhaps better terms for the corporate environment are *mind clearing* or *focused concentration*.

Meditation is not, as some might think, losing your awareness. Rather, it is a *heightening* of awareness to enter your inner source of creativity. It helps you go below the choppy, surface waves of the ocean (the external world) to explore the depths beneath the surface, where the treasure is.

One talented research biochemist, Dr. Philip Lipetz, received a startling insight into a problem of biochemical pathways while meditating. After experiencing the insight for the first time, he went to his books and found no mention of what he had envisioned. The same vision came again during another meditation. Later, he discussed his insight with an eminent scientist in the field of aging research. The second scientist was amazed at the insight; other biochemists had only just finished an experiment—as yet unpublished—that could confirm the possibility of the particular interaction Dr. Lipetz had "seen." Ultimately, Lipetz started his own company (and later his own venture capital firm) to develop this idea.

There are many types of meditation practice, for example:

- Walking with special attention to your movement.
- Sitting and watching your breath, and perhaps hearing the sound "so" on the inhale and "hum" on the exhale.
- Watching or imagining a candle flame or a mandala.
- Having a vision or fantasy (guided or not).
- Following certain types of music.

One of the principal techniques for developing the state of meditative concentration is to focus on your breathing. Try the following exercise for a few moments after reading it, even if you have already experienced something similar to this before.

1. Sit or lie down comfortably with your back straight but relaxed. Slowly close your eyes. Notice your breathing. Is it relatively shallow or deep? Does your breathing start with the upper chest or with the lower diaphragm? Just notice the way it is and do not try to change it. Let it change of its own accord as this exercise proceeds.

2. Imagine a warm, golden, glowing ball of light suspended six inches above the crown of your head. Warm, golden light is streaming from this globe down through your head. See and feel this warm, golden light flow into you, gathering up all tension as it passes through your body. *Slowly* let this light wash down through your head . . . into your neck . . . your shoulders . . . your arms . . . your hands . . . your chest . . . your back . . . your abdomen . . . your thighs . . . your calves . . . your feet . . . and out your toes into the earth. Let this wash through you and carry with it all tensions, worries, anxieties, tightness . . . all thoughts and emotions . . . leaving you soothed and relaxed.

3. Now feel your breath passing through your nostrils. Follow each breath into your lungs, and notice whether the air fills the top or bottom of your lungs first. Notice whether your exhale begins at the top or bottom. Notice the time it takes to inhale and exhale. Just notice, and do not try to make any changes. If changes occur, let them do so of their own accord, from their own wisdom.

4. Listen and imagine the sound "so" accompanying each inhale, and the sound "hum" accompanying each exhale. Listen to the "so-hum" of each breath cycle. Notice any differences in your state of relaxation and awareness. Continue following your breath in this way for as long as you wish.

When you touch your innermost intuitive self, you also touch the part we all share—the spiritual core of all humanity. In a seeming paradox, you can find oneness in your ultimate, inner uniqueness. Similarly, with meditation you can identify with a problem and yet achieve more objectivity and distance from it. Thus, you can more effectively produce the creative solutions that are directly relevant to the situations you face.

I would not say such things without having experienced the results myself. One time I was dissatisfied with my career progress, so I meditated over the weekend on, "What do I need to do differently in my career?" The following Monday I had the answer, and two days later I found out about a position at the Stanford Research Institute that I probably would have overlooked had I not asked my intuition for guidance. That began my current career.

IN CLOSING . . .

The Innovation Styles, combined with the Creative Journey, have sparked flashes of brilliance and great breakthroughs for many people. But the questions remain: Do we actually use our creative power, or do we let it atrophy? Do we waste it on trivial pursuits, or do we put our intuition and values to work creatively, striving to make a difference? We have the opportunity, and the capability, of making this creative difference, if we allow ourselves to dream and develop the creative skills to actualize it. Wordsworth ponders this creative potential and piques our awareness of it within ourselves when he writes:

> Paradise and grove
> Elysian, fortunate fields—
> Why should they be
> A history of departed things
> Or a mere fiction of what never was?
> For the discerning intellect of man
> When wedded to this goodly universe
> In love and holy passion, shall find these
> A simple produce of the common day.

The height of our accomplishments will be measured by the depth of our values and by the persistence of our efforts. Do we seek everywhere for creative solutions to the most pressing, most challenging problems facing us? Or do we delegate the responsibility to unknown others, as in "It's somebody else's problem to worry about"? When we feel "love and holy passion," we eagerly apply tools of creativity, like the four Innovation Styles, to serve people the best we can.

For many Native Americans, the North is the land of Vision; the East is the land of New Beginnings; the South is the land Experimentation and Play; the West is the land of Completion. The four Innovation Styles encompass how we think creatively from all four directions. They give us the power to shift our creative points of view and to include more diverse people and perspectives in our search for meaningful, effective, creative solutions.

This shifting from one perspective to another in response to a challenge is part of the play of creativity. Experimenting with diversity is the nature of Creation—and the nature of our creative powers. When we make this play a continuous part of our lives each day, life becomes more vivid, and learning multiplies. Speaking of his time in outer space, cosmonaut Vladimir Kovolyonok of the former Soviet Union, once said, " 'Not a day without discovery' was our motto during the mission. If we were unable to make a discovery in our experiments, then we would discover what was for lunch."[10]

Furthermore, by developing a practice of meditation or contemplation, it's as if we access deeper creative insights from the inner spirits of the four directions. When we strengthen our access to deeper creative insights, we act in partnership with the inner source of creative inspiration.

CHAPTER 5

Transform Blocks
to Your *Creativity*

Sometimes I get separated from my work. I was real worried about how a piece was going to be viewed by my peers, and I just took all that totally to heart. It just screwed the whole thing up. It became an object, and then it didn't work anymore. I didn't have any rapport with it . . . I totally gave away my power on a creative level.

It's quite different when working with somebody who has commissioned you to do a work. Working under those conditions—creating a commission for somebody and working with their ideas—now that's a really creative process because I have to be able to tune in to those people. I have to pay attention not only on a creative level, but I have to listen and pay attention to what their needs are.

—PATRICIA, ARTIST

ACKNOWLEDGING BLOCKS AND LETTING THEM GO

We are *always* being creative and it simply depends on *what* we spend our time creating that makes a difference. Einstein's theory of relativity was a more inclusive scientific principle than were Newton's laws of mechanics, without negating Newton's laws. In the same way, this broad notion of creativity is a more inclusive statement for exploring the habits that support or inhibit our inherent creative abilities.

With the broader context firmly in mind, we free ourselves to refocus our creative energies in each moment of our work lives. Our every phone call, every report, every turn of a screwdriver, every meeting, every policy implementation, every strategy formulation can be experienced in terms of our creativity. We all have times, however, when it seems that the ideas and insights just don't come, try as we might. Perhaps the true test of our creativity is finding new ways to transform those "blocked" moments. It is much easier to simply refocus our creativity on new arenas than to try to go from being "uncreative" to creative.

We each have "favorite" blocks to creativity—recurring patterns that we've learned over time. Possible blocks include:

- Limiting beliefs
- Fear (of the known and unknown)
- Other emotions (such as anger, guilt, boredom)
- Stress
- Overspecialization
- Narrow thinking
- Lack of imagination

Blocks may surface only occasionally, in periods of pressure or deadlines or even no pressure, depending on our work patterns. What's important is first to recognize what they are and then begin to transform them. Looking at such a list, you might have the impression that you could never be creative without a lot of effort. However, there are some powerful principles, similar to the Creative Journey process, that can help you develop and internalize an ability to be creative rather than blocked.

Let's review the principles of transforming blocks before looking at each type in detail. As you then read through the rest of the chapter, you can imagine how you would effortlessly dissolve a block.

The art of *transforming* our blocks is different from trying to change ourselves. To change, we must recognize our past and present and somehow make our lives different. Through transformation, your energy can be devoted to building a new, chosen "reality." Rather than fighting the present situation, you simply acknowledge what's happening and then focus on what you want to replace it.

> **The art of *transforming* our blocks is different from trying to change ourselves.**

The basic steps in transforming old habits (especially blocks) are these:

1. Assume that every experience you have can positively stimulate your personal growth.
2. Discover the fundamental truth and the fundamental illusion in the barrier(s) you face.
3. Clearly envision how you want to be (and what you want to be doing and having).
4. Evoke the situation and emotions surrounding the block, holding strongly to your vision and your inner strength.
5. Take action and/or communicate with another person.
6. Allow yourself time. Have patience and honor the seasons of creativity.

Transformation takes place when a new world view (paradigm) re-places an old one.

Assume That Every Experience You Have Can Positively Stimulate Your Personal Growth

Each of us is on a path of personal growth and integration. But some-times, or often, we make incorrect decisions about life. Indeed, we may feel like we are encountering events in life without an instruction manual on living. But as Robert Louis Stevenson once said, "To be what we are, and to become what we are capable of becoming is the only end in life." (Note: This step is not required for following the subsequent steps, but it sure helps.)

Discover Both the Fundamental Truth and the Fundamental Illusion in the Barrier(s) You Face

If we are afraid of failure, the fundamental truth may still be that we want to make total use of our talents to make a real contribution. The fundamental illusion may be a belief that we will be worth more or less as a human being if we don't make an impact. One way of dis-covering the truth is to ask yourself, "What is my highest goal for this situation?" One way of finding the illusion is to write down a fantasy of the worst that can happen, the thing that makes you think "I'd die if this happened!" (which will rarely be the truth).

Clearly Envision How You Want to Be (and What You Want to Be Doing and Having)

Use all the senses and emotions in your imagination to visualize the final result. Develop a statement of affirmation stating your goal in *present time*. For example, if you are stuck "in a rut" of seeing a problem only one way, your affirmation might be, "I am now able to see this problem in a multitude of ways, opening before me a multitude of so-lutions." If you begin arguing with yourself ("Oh, I could never be that way!"), take two pieces of paper and write the affirmation on one side, the "answering argument" on the other, then the affirmation again, the new answering argument, the affirmation, the argument, and so on. You will eventually feel a shift, a sense that you can be the way you would want to be. Very importantly, you can also call on an inner strength to empower you to fulfill your vision of yourself.

Evoke the Situation and Emotions Surrounding the Block, Holding Strongly to Your Vision and Your Inner Strength

Emotions such as sadness, pain, and anger are signals to make a shift, to be more "on the mark" rather than to "sin" (which literally means to "miss the mark"). A barrier is simply a feeling or situation to which you have given over your own personal power, leaving you feeling powerless and afraid of it. By preparing your vision of yourself, taking on your inner (higher) strength, and then commanding the barrier to come before you, you take your power back. The energy tied up in the former battle becomes available to you for your creativity: the "demon" you faced becomes your ally.

Take Action and/or Communicate with Another Person

In speaking or in taking other action, your newfound power takes root. You make it more real in your own and in others' eyes. At work this can mean demonstrating your new creative insights or your new ability to follow through on your ideas. Developing a support network of people you trust can help you explore and gather your new power and insights in a safe environment.

A useful principle in taking action is to draw the distinction between handling a situation and handling your emotions in that situation. They are entirely different matters, though it is typical to assume that the situation *causes* your feelings, and that the only way to get rid of uncomfortable feelings is to change the situation. Actually, the more you give power over your feelings to the people and situations you encounter, the less able you are to respond to them creatively and effectively.

Allow Yourself Time

Have patience and honor the seasons of creativity. None of us can keep running without rest or nutrition. Similarly, none of us can be constantly "on," with full-speed creativity and innovation. Transformation sometimes happens slowly, like winter to summer, or ice-age sea to desert. These seasons and cycles need to be honored rather than impatiently judged.

There are two workable approaches to honoring the pace of transformation. The first is to make an affirmation that is more than just "a good idea" or "something I ought to do." The commitment must be intuitively and emotionally based.

The second is what I call "the hot-stove method." Whenever we touch a hot stove and experience pain, we immediately and spontaneously pull our hand away: we naturally do what is in the best interest of our well-being. There may be many situations in your life that hurt your well-being in subtle ways, and you are numb to the hurt. As you become more conscious of the damage to your well-being, you will find yourself naturally and spontaneously making changes in your life to "pull your hand away."

The hot-stove method describes the way I have significantly changed some work habits. I used to automatically presume nonsupport for a new idea I might have. Immediately I would be in a "fight-for-what-you-want" posture—and then feel self-righteous when the resistance I expected materialized. Finally I realized I was creating much (or all) of that resistance by my attitude. It was painful and difficult to face this—as the numbness to how I was "burning" myself wore off. Slowly, over the course of a year, I found myself changing as I watched myself at first fight, and then let go of, the need to do so. I held the vision that "My work environment supports my ideas. Even when the ideas get changed, they contribute to the highest good of all."

TRANSFORMING DIFFERENT TYPES OF BLOCKS

All of the seven types of blocks to creativity mentioned earlier—limiting beliefs, fear, other emotions, stress, overspecialization, narrow thinking, and lack of imagination—can be transformed for both personal growth and improved organizational productivity. In some cases, time, practice, and/or training may be needed. Other changes may be achieved relatively quickly. Understanding more about each block can help clarify what you want to achieve.

Limiting Beliefs

When I was in graduate school, one faculty member was a woman from Thailand who had come to the United States to study psychology with Abraham Maslow. She told of her first months in the States when she had observed people scurrying about, accomplishing many things but apparently with no inner peace. This puzzled her until she realized that many Americans seemed to have been raised with the notion that, "You're not worth anything until you prove yourself. And once you have proven yourself (to society/family/community), you must continue to prove yourself over and over." Her upbringing had taught her, "You are valuable just by being part of the universe. Your value cannot be gained or lost. And the art of life is living in a way that reflects that fact about oneself and everyone."

This story continues to speak to me when I feel insecure or rebellious. I ask myself, "What am I trying to prove to myself or others? Do I really *need* to? Can I still act but without these limiting beliefs driving me?"

When we are young, we come to decisions about life that may be perfectly appropriate at the time but that may or may not fit the circumstances of later life. These decisions become fundamental life principles that shape the course of our perceptions, thoughts, feelings, actions, and visions. These fundamental principles are not *what* we think and feel; rather, they are the *context* for what we think and feel. They are the lens through which we consciously and unconsciously live our lives. They are the box we live in.

One example of a limiting belief is "I must get approval from others to feel okay." Then our entire life is lived in the box of trying to get other people's approval at any cost. Other examples are "Be careful," "You've got to win," "Always play it safe," "You've got to make it on your own," "You've got to be right," and "Be nice."

These limiting beliefs result in blocks to creativity expressed as: accepting conventional wisdom ("The experts know"); tunnel vision ("I'll define the problem in ways that I know how to answer"); and social blocks, such as those discussed later in this chapter ("I'll only do things I know will be accepted by others").

Our culture has principles that can also block creativity, including: "Fantasy and reflection are a waste of time." "Playfulness is for children only." "Reason and logic are good; feeling and intuition are bad." "Tradition is preferable to change."

From my experience, there are five categories of limiting beliefs that affect creativity. The five are:

1. *Leader/Victim.* Do you generally feel that you are directing your life or that you are the victim of outside forces? Do you have a sense of personal power?
2. *Confidence and Trust.* Do you tend to see the world as friendly or antagonistic? Do you have confidence in yourself (and/or a higher power) for having your life "turn out" okay?
3. *Talent/Contribution.* Do you feel you are exercising your talents and having a positive impact on the world around you?
4. *Strength of Expectations.* Do you feel "addicted" to having life turn out according to your expectations? Do you problem solve or do you blame when your goals aren't accomplished?
5. *Personal Value.* Do you feel you have to prove yourself continually to "earn" self-esteem and the esteem of others, or do you believe in an inherent personal worth of each person?

Once you become aware of your fundamental life principles and recognize their power to shape your interactions and communications, you can intentionally give new purpose and direction to your life and your creativity. If you merely extend yourself from the past with a few "changes," there is no transformation, only more of the same.

Fear

Fear blocks often come into play in our relationships with managers, peers, friends, and others. You may recognize some of these in yourself or others:

- Lack of confidence in personal creativity. ("Other people are creative, not me." "It's too hard." "This is too ambiguous.")
- Worry and anxiety—indulging in negative thoughts about the *future*. ("Oh, what will tomorrow bring?")
- Fear of rejection. ("What will they think of me if I'm not right?" "I'll look foolish." "Play looks too irresponsible.")
- Fear of confrontation. ("I can't hold my own with this person." "Harmony at all costs.")
- Fear of success. ("Do I really deserve success? What will people expect afterwards?")
- Fear of failure. ("What if I fail? I'll look foolish and be vulnerable.")

Fears occur when we somehow decide that we can't get an important need met or that there is only one particular way to meet it. At work, you probably observe actions that don't support people's talents or dignity. These distortions hide a positive need that is being expressed negatively. For example, when we show off, the positive need is to feel socially connected, but we fear it's only possible to feel connected by showing off (or that it's not possible at all to feel connected.) Or when we are selfish, the positive need is to feel our uniqueness. When we are overly sacrificial (to the detriment of also getting our own needs met), the positive need is to contribute.

A way to conquer these fears is to discover the positive needs and creatively find new ways to express them with others.

Other Emotions

Some of the emotional patterns that inhibit creativity and innovation include the following:

- Guilt, depression, or anger—indulging in negative thoughts about the *past*: ("Oh, if only I hadn't done that . . . " "If only he/she hadn't done that.")
- Comfort with the status quo. ("Why change? If it's not broken, don't fix it.")
- Boredom. ("This doesn't interest me.")
- Excess energy. ("I can't sleep on it; my mind's too busy.")
- Intolerance of ambiguity. ("I need an answer *now!*")
- Need for perfection. ("If I can't do it perfectly, I won't try at all.")
- Need to please management. ("I must be cautious and conform. My job and life are on the line." "Follow the rules.")

- Unwillingness to collaborate. ("Please I'd rather do it myself." "That's not my area.")
- Excessive zeal. ("I'm a great scientist. Of course this invention is great. Everyone will want one.")
- Disinterest. ("What's the use? Management won't go for it anyway.")
- Impatience and frustration. ("Why isn't this working out?!")
- Seriousness. ("Let's stop playing around. We have some serious creating to do.")

Creativity at work involves creating our immediate emotional world. Have you ever noticed how much better you feel around those who have a cheery disposition than around those who don't? Situations don't cause our feelings; our perceptions do. When our perception is that "the situation causes my feelings," then we give away our inherent power over internal experience. We can reverse the power flow by bringing our own cheeriness to the moment and letting others respond to our mood (rather than responding to theirs).

One example of emotional blocks hurting innovation is the "not invented here" (NIH) syndrome. We sometimes disregard good ideas we, personally, don't think of. Sometimes it makes good business sense to do so (proprietary technology development, perhaps), but the NIH syndrome often stems from a macho ethic: "Truly competent businesspeople don't rely on others to fulfill their responsibilities." NIH people might insecurely think, "I'm getting paid to come up with ideas and make them happen. If I use this idea, it shows that I can't do my job."

There are several guidelines to keep in mind.

- Prepare a vision of feeling differently. A good affirmation to keep in mind is, "I am affected only by my thoughts."
- Be willing to use that vision to become bigger than the inhibiting emotions. Exchange thoughts of fear for thoughts of competence, confidence, love, and so forth.
- Watch out for suppressing emotions through positive thinking. Find the truth and illusion in them and evoke them to consciousness.
- Nurture alternative inner experiences ("inner" creativity). Then, over time, you can take back your power over how you feel (and subsequently act).

And again, watch out for falling into the trap of believing that the situations you face are the causes of your negative feelings. In such cases you might feel righteously justified in hanging onto your (prejudicial) thoughts and emotions. There is a well-known story about a psychologist studying the behavior of rats in a maze.[1] The psychologist had a box with five tunnels leading away from an open area. He put some cheese at the end of the second tunnel; when he put the rat into the open area, the rat ran down the first tunnel, found no cheese, ran down the second tunnel, found the cheese and ate it, and then went down the other tunnels to see if there was more cheese.

The psychologist always placed the cheese in the second tunnel before placing the rat in the open area. He wanted to see how long it would take for the rat to figure out that the cheese would be in the second tunnel and head directly down that tunnel. After a while, the rat didn't even bother going down the other tunnels once he had gotten the cheese in the second tunnel.

One day the psychologist switched tunnels and put the cheese down the fourth tunnel. When placed in the open area, the rat went down the second tunnel, found no cheese, came back to the open area, went back down the second tunnel, found no cheese, came back out, went down the second tunnel, found no cheese, came back out, and so on. Eventually, the rat started exploring other tunnels until it found the cheese.

This story shows that there is a very important difference between that rat and many people. The rat eventually explored the other tunnels when there was no cheese in the second tunnel. Many people, however, continue going down the "second tunnel" of their lives believing that at least they are in the "right" tunnel.

Stress

There are three experiences for which we popularly use the word "stress" in our culture:

- Stress experienced as stimulation from outside of us. This can be either constructive or destructive for us.
- Stress experienced as an affliction of tension, anxiety, and physical impairment.
- Stress experienced as the internal urge for growth and expression.

Stress as stimulation is something to manage. Stress as affliction is something to reduce. Stress as the urge for growth and expression is something to be promoted (in the rhythm of stress, rest, and nutrition).

Creativity is fundamentally this last type of urge—the urge to express our aliveness, to put our

> **Creativity is the urge to express our aliveness, to put our human awareness into action.**

human awareness into action. Stress as stimulation is a subset of this urge—the part that reacts to perceived threats with a flight-or-fight response. And stress as affliction is a subset of stimulation stress, reflecting a mismanagement of the stimulation.

Creativity and innovation can be spurred, at least in the short term, by any of these three experiences of stress. But a constant push to be working at 110 percent—with continuous "urgent" projects, for example—can promote an excess of stress as outside stimulation, leading to afflictive stress and low-quality output.

Afflictive stress arises when our creativity in life is misplaced, covered up, or forgotten. Our creativity is generally enhanced if stress comes from the power of our own urge to grow, taking on challenges to be all we can be. As Maya Pines states in discussing her research on stress and psychological hardiness:

> *Stress-resistant people . . . have a specific set of attitudes towards life—an openness to change, a feeling of involvement in whatever they're doing, and a sense of control over their lives.*[2]

Internal stress arises from moving away from your zones of dependable strengths. Sometimes this moving away—this stretch—is healthy, like "pushing" in physical exercise to get stronger.

With this expanded notion of the nature of stress, you no longer face a question of "responding" to stress or "managing" your stressful situations and internal responses. You can shift your attention to creating a new harmony between your internal nature and external world. This is the harmony seen in athletes in peak performance. For example, John Brodie, former pro-football quarterback, once said:

> *Sometimes I let the ball fly before Gene [Washington] has made his final move, without a pass route exactly, it's sort of intuition and communication . . . You can get into another order of reality when you're playing that doesn't fit the grids and coordinates most people lay across life.*[3]

In this "flow" state, athletes are alert and active, yet loose and fluid. They integrate awareness and action without "talking" their way through the steps of performing.

For further ideas on overcoming stress blocks to creativity, there are numerous books and courses that give specific details and counsel on ways to reduce afflictive stress, manage stimulating stress, and actualize internally generated stress for growth.

Overspecialization

Sometimes the specialist knows too much. In one workshop on new metal materials, we had to invite some nonmetallurgists to help generate new ideas; the metallurgists knew too much about what you *couldn't* do with certain metals.

Specializing can be both freeing and confining. It is freeing in that specialization enables us to express ourselves in unique ways. Dancers who work out eight hours a day become free to move their bodies expressively and uniquely; without the practice and discipline, the freedom is lost.

Specializing can also be confining by dominating our time and restricting us from developing other viewpoints and new talents. Painters know that working in new mediums—from oils to chalks—not only gives them new modes of expression but also new insights into what they can do in their more familiar mediums. Sculptors like Rodin often painted as well, to keep their creativity free to grow.

Narrow Thinking

We may have favorite problem-solving modes, and these may keep us from working on a problem in the easiest mode. Take for example this story from James Adams's *Conceptual Blockbusting:*

> *One morning, exactly at sunrise, a Buddhist monk began to climb a tall mountain. A narrow path, no more than a foot or two wide, spiraled around the mountain to a glittering temple at the summit. The monk ascended at varying rates of speed, stopping many times along the way to rest and eat dried fruit he carried with him. He reached the temple shortly before sunset.*
>
> *After several days of fasting and meditation he began his journey back along the same path, starting at sunrise and again walking at variable speeds with many pauses along the way. His average speed descending was, of course, greater than his average climbing speed. Prove that there is a spot along the path that the monk will occupy on both trips at precisely the same time of day.[4]*

Did you solve the puzzle? More importantly, for our purposes, can you remember *what thinking processes* you used in working on the puzzle? Did you verbalize? Did you use imagery? Mathematics? Did you consciously try different strategies on the problem?

If you happened to choose visual imagery as the method of thinking to apply to this problem, you probably solved it. If you chose verbalization, you probably did not.

A simple way of solving the puzzle is to visualize the upward journey of the monk superimposed on the downward journey; if it helps, imagine two monks, one leaving the top and the other the bottom, starting at sunrise. It should be apparent that at some time and at the same point on the path, the "two monks" will meet.

Some of us like to use our intuition without previous investigation of details and data. Other people like to find the mathematical formula that expresses probabilities and proceed from there. Others like to start with verbal descriptions of the problem to be solved, while still others like more pictorial problem statements.

When looking for innovative solutions, sometimes our usual "tunnels" of problem solving just don't have the cheese. By staying in the most appropriate style of thinking for the stage of the creative process, you keep your perceptions open to the most relevant information. As you develop flexibility in trying different approaches to solving problems, you free yourself to give creative service to your organization and the world.

Lack of Imagination (*Image*-ination)

Sampson Raphaelson, screenwriter of the first talking movie and famous playwright of the 1930s and 1940s, defined imagination as "the capacity to see what is there." The lack of "image-ination" is usually merely a lack of conscious practice of our imaginative abilities. For example, we need imagination to experience fear, because fear is an emotional reaction to our imagining an unwanted future event. Even when facing a concrete, impending danger, fear arises in conjunction with an imagined, unwanted outcome of the event that perhaps will occur only a few seconds later. Fear, therefore, is successful imagination, whether or not it is appropriate or misdirected.

More often, we may simply be out of practice in consciously eliciting images with all our senses—sight, hearing, taste, smell, and touch. As an exercise, please imagine the following:

- A yellow daisy
- The voice of Frank Sinatra
- The smell of bacon
- The smoothness of glass
- The tartness of a lemon
- The sound of a trumpet
- The sweetness of pure honey
- The coldness of an ice cube
- The smell of fresh-cut grass

You may have noticed yourself being more attuned to one type of sensory imagery than another. This is common. You might even have noticed that your body reacted physically to some of the images, such as the cold ice or tart lemon.

You can also manipulate your imagination. Now, please imagine the following:

- A horse jumping on a huge trampoline
- A large glass of milk being spilled on a table and running onto the floor
- The table with milk on it moving its legs to also "run" across the floor

Your imagination can be improved by having fun with images such as these.

IN CLOSING . . .

I'm fond of an expression, "Acknowledge the dark, dwell on the light. Abundance and love for all." Our creativity is developed by recognizing the way things are, including the things we consider dark or negative, and then leaping forward to envision what we want to create. We do not have to try to change anything about ourselves. We just have to focus on creating whatever way of being that our inner wisdom advises.

When you reach barriers in your path, you can prepare and evoke a newfound strength from within. Calling forth your fears, angers, or external obstacles, you can turn the negative energy into your ally and do what you once thought was impossible. This lesson is truly applicable to facing the challenges of being creative in your work world. As you meet your challenges successfully, you will find that each situation can be a source of more power, love, and wisdom.

As you have seen, the balance that most promotes our creative self-expression is the harmony of inner peace and external action. It is difficult to develop this state if we perceive ourselves to be internally split, fighting with our blocks in a tense struggle to be creative.

Focus on some habits you might wish to nurture in yourself and plant the seeds of an affirmed vision. As with any growth, be patient. It does no good to dig up a plant every day to see if the roots are growing yet.

As the Chinese poet Lao Tsu has said,

> In the universe, the difficult things are done as if they are easy.
> In the universe, great acts are made up of small deeds.
> The wise person does not attempt anything very big, and thus achieves greatness.[5]

And, as a close friend of mine says, "There is no such thing as failure . . . only feedback."

Foster *Breakthrough Innovation* in Groups

"I didn't actually build it, but it was based on my idea."

So far we have been focusing primarily on you, the creative individual. Now comes the question. How do you take your creative actions and potential and make them work within the group for the benefit of the whole organization?

Think of this question in terms of taking a journey. You and others are the drivers supplying both the intention to travel and the will to start the engine. But you still need a destination, a vehicle, an engine, and fuel. The destination comes from the organization's sense of purpose and vision. The organization itself is the vehicle. The steps of the group innovation process constitute the engine. External events surrounding the organization—social, market, political, competitive, and so on—supply the fuel (the "externally supplied motivation").

Pretend you are taking the journey by boat. In some organizations it may seem like you're on a passenger ship with, say, 3,000 people, each using his or her own 100-horsepower outboard motor (with extended propeller shaft), who may or may not be trying to propel the liner in the same direction. Other organizations seem to have 3,000 people purposefully heading in a single direction, with a single 300,000-horsepower engine and a single rudder. Which is closer to being like your organization?

This section enables you to set the climate for creativity, stimulate more creative teamwork, run more creative meetings, and conduct your idea sessions using specific tools (related to the Innovation Styles).

CHAPTER 6

Stimulate a "CREATIVE" *Climate* for *Innovation*

> *The thing I remember most about this one major project is putting one vision out, then allowing whatever happens to happen. The only thing common to everyone working on it was some sense of what was going to be the final result. For me to look back on my corporate experience, that element was present whenever something was done effectively, though I wasn't aware of that at the time. I was aware of when I was trying to force my will on the group versus the times when I was synergetic and open to suggestions.*
>
> —TERRY, POLITICAL STRATEGIST

PLAYING A NEW GAME

Surely you've once heard someone say, "This team is a well-oiled machine." For most of the past three centuries, science conceived of the universe as a machine, and our organizations were derived from that same metaphor. At work, people were treated like parts in the machine, with little engagement of their spirit, will, passion, creativity, or intelligence. The leader had to carry 200 percent of the burden to "fill people" with vision, motivation, and knowledge. When change was introduced, people were considered the prime obstacle to getting the new machine "humming along," because of their burdensome emotions and resistance. People occupied preset roles in the system; when one person left, another took his or her place. Job descriptions remained stable as people became interchangeable parts.

That system worked fairly well so long as the company owned the primary assets of wealth production: materials and equipment. Today, the game is totally different. The primary assets used to produce wealth are intelligence and knowledge—and a large portion of those assets go home each evening in commuter traffic. With the accelerating speed and hyper-competition of global markets, the rate of knowledge-creation, information exchange, and relationship formation have likewise increased exponentially. Only a part of employees' knowledge and relationships can be institutionalized, and little of it can be controlled using the same management tools of the past. A whole new metaphor—a whole new story—has to be told to understand the dynamics of organizational learning and innovation.

Mother Nature has become our best organizational guru. From an evolutionary perspective, how could life have emerged from a primordial "random soup of chemicals?" If things are supposed to degenerate to lower forms of energy (the law of entropy), why has there been a continuous emergence of more and more complex beings over millions of years? You can simulate this problem by asking a set of computer programs with random bit strings to see if they can evolve order out of such random chaos. Amazingly, they can—and even more incredibly, the randomness is essential to the process! *Chaos* is the raw material of life's creativity!

Chaos theory has evolved itself into "complex adaptive systems" and thus become a science. The components of these adaptive systems interact and adjust according to each other's behavior—they learn, through a process of spontaneous self-organization. According to Ralph Stacey "Complex adaptive systems have an inherent order that is simply waiting to be unfolded through the experience of the system."[1] This self-organizing principle has manifested itself in, for example, the extraordinary growth of the Internet without anyone trying to manage it by some strategic plan. The same power for expansive, responsive, innovative behavior can be unleashed in any organization that masters the principles of complex, living systems. Dee Hock, who headed up VISA so masterfully, calls such organizations *"chaordic"*—they master the fine line between chaos and order![2]

In sum, the new game is radically different[3]:

ASSUMPTION	OLD GAME	NEW GAME
Physics analogy	Newtonian	Quantum
New knowledge by:	Analyzing into parts	Seeing the whole
Information is:	Objectively knowable	Relative, unbounded
Growth is:	Linear	Organic
Management by:	Control, predictable	Insight, participation
Motivation	Extrinsic	Intrinsic creativity
Organization	By design	Always emerging
Evolution by:	Competition	Cooperation
Employees are:	Units of production	Co-creative partners
Viewpoint:	One best way	Many ways
Structures:	Inflexible	Responsive

Thus, we're finally perceiving the organization as an organism! What are the implications of this shift from a mechanical model to a biological metaphor? We realize that creativity is a group phenomenon as much or more than an individual one. Projects spur spontaneous self-organization through bottom-up cooperation. Centralized, or top-down control is a ticket to disaster—shared purpose and vision, rather than tight audits, are the new "controls" for making sure that empowered people make decisions that align with global strategies. (This alone is a big challenge for people who learned to be successful as "controllers.") "Management" has diminished in importance, while "leadership" has emerged as vital in *every* member of a team. Learning and innovating are the two most fundamental competencies upon which work processes, customer satisfaction, and financial performance are built. And the prerequisite for group learning and innovating is high-integrity relationships. Ironically, the "soft stuff" of relationships has become the most fundamental capability for strategic advantage!

> **Creativity is a group phenomenon as much or more than an individual one.**

LEADING BY THE NEW "WORTH ETHIC"

The old company-employee agreement of "Work hard and we'll take care of you" has died. People now identify more with their profession than with their employer. "Managing productivity" has become a well-accepted notion, but "managing creativity" appears to some people to be a paradoxical concept. Management implies control, and control seems to be the opposite of creativity. But when "management" becomes "leadership," creativity can be managed without stifling it.

Some managers still practice the philosophy that people can be controlled or manipulated into thinking, feeling, or acting in specific motivated ways; this is mechanistic thinking that is proving less valid in today's work environment. The design of "idiot-proof" jobs—jobs that do not inspire employees and leave little room for creativity—is another consequence of this "control" mentality. Many people feel alienation, isolation, afflictive stress, and even burnout from working where this mechanistic management is still attempted.

By contrast, leaders *empower* people as well as motivate them. They supply "environmental encouragement," that is, a corporate culture where people can exercise their inherent talents for creative and productive work.

Leaders are not just a charismatic few, but people who realize that leadership can be learned and practiced. They realize that the old work ethic hasn't died, as some have feared, but is reemerging in a new, more responsible form: The popular movements for participation and involvement reflect a trend of taking *more personal responsibility* for decisions.

The newer work ethic strongly values individual responsibility over following orders, personal expression (creativity) of our unique talents over fitting in, and creativity over business as usual. Author Kate Ludeman describes this as the "worth ethic."[4]

I once attended a meeting at Sun Microsystems when it was about $450 million in size. One of the venture capitalists who helped fund the start-up also attended. We discussed why smaller, entrepreneurial firms seemed more successful than larger corporations in launching innovative new products. His thoughts surprised me. He believed it wasn't so much that smaller companies were closer to their customers or that they had more financial resources available; rather, he said, "I believe it's because people in smaller companies are more likely to feel that they individually can make an important difference."

This "worth ethic" comes at a time when flexibility is increasingly required to meet the accelerating pace of change in the economic, political, and social realms of our world. As such, it can be seen as a societal survival mechanism that offers us the highest of benefits. It is part and parcel of managing in the information age, especially with the growing body of knowledge of workers, whose brainpower has become the key corporate asset. Moreover, such heightened individual responsibility is in tune with America's entrepreneurial traditions.

The process of valuing the worth of everyone's contribution to innovation must begin with the initial hiring process. Early support for a person's professional growth, as well as potential contribution, goes a long way to building commitment and loyalty as well as high performance. For example, when Sue Lawson was an executive at a major banking software company she told me that when she offered a job to a new person, she'd tell them, "If you come to work for us, I know that someday you'll no longer be working for me, or even the company. Anticipating that, my commitment to you is that when you leave, I'll have done my best to see that you've grown professionally and, hopefully, personally."

She followed through, often marketing specific types of software projects solely because her staff needed them to continue growing. The extra commitment and loyalty she inspired turned into intellectual assets for the company and the people she hired; the company also had 50 percent lower turnover than the industry average for that type of work.

Dell Corporation is another perfect example. In three fiscal years, from FY96 to FY98, its revenues grew at a rate of over 50 percent per year (to $12.3 billion in FY98) and the number of employees has more than doubled (to over 16,000). Dell's entire business model requires a hyper-speed work pace, so much so that the employees have coined the term *"Dellocity"* to describe the velocity of their work. Not only does the company need to expand its executive ranks, but even its current managers have to grow their own skills ultra-fast just to handle the increasing complexity and span of control in their *current* jobs. The same is true everywhere in the organization.

Like so many other companies, Dell tells its employees, "When it comes to your own career development, we'll offer you new learning opportunities, but you have to take the initiative to keep ahead of our growth curve." It takes each person's intrinsic motivation to support this furious pace of performance and professional growth; there's no way a centralized career development function could do it. Extrinsic rewards such as stock ownership programs are the consequence, not the cause, of creative performance. Dell's ability to keep innovating with its products, service, and quality has gained Wall Street's attention to the tune of a *2,000 percent* increase in their stock price between FY96 and FY98.

APPRAISING AND REWARDING CREATIVITY

A company's appraisal and reward process can make or break its efforts to ensure that knowledge and innovation thrive rather than struggle to survive. Frank Douglas, former head of research at Ciba Geigy, and now head of R&D at Hoechst-Marion-Roussel, is a living example of the right way to do this. As one sterling example of "walking the walk," he once sponsored a major research effort to develop a drug which, after five years began to look like a potential blockbuster. Then a lab technician noticed something mysterious about the livers from test animals, and a lab supervisor decided to investigate the mystery. Ultimately they found that the drug, in addition to doing its wonderful healing, was leaving serious deposits of cholesterol in the liver and the damage couldn't be reversed.

The project had to be canceled, and the research team members were crestfallen. As Frank later told me, they were very anxious that management would see them as failures. He addressed them, saying,

First, I want to congratulate you that the climate on your team allowed the lowest-status person to raise an issue that could derail a blockbuster project and you listened. By listening and following through, you saved un-

told misery and substantial financial losses that would have occurred if this drug wrongly made it to market.

Second, I have three goals as head of research: (1) have a market winner that advances science; (2) if I can't have that, I at least want a market winner; and (3) if I can't have that I definitely want something that advances science. You have been eminently successful in creating the new knowledge no one had before—you discovered a mechanism new to your field that will impact other projects we have. While the program had unwanted results, you achieved a breakthrough in learning. I will make sure you have the time to write up your learning for your professional journals and get the recognition you deserve for your fine work. Then I'll reassign you to new projects.

Frank knew how to acknowledge the value of knowledge-creation, to reward it with recognition opportunities and keep the creative spirit alive and well in his people. He acted as a true sponsor of innovation.

The creative culture lives and dies by how well appraisals and rewards help stimulate risk taking, creativity, and knowledge-creation. Frank Carrubba, as head of HP Labs, once said that HP would be in big trouble if his group was always 100 percent successful in achieving their annual goals. He knew that the only way to achieve 100 percent in a given year is to set safe annual goals, and that without goals that require a "stretch," HP would not remain an industry leader. He set out to find ways to anticipate, plan for, manage, and reward some degree of failure. To signal the importance of taking high-risk goals, he coined the term, *intelligent failure.* Former CEO of Silicon Graphics, Ed McCracken, told me he called it *competent failure.* At Hoechst-Marion-Roussel Pharmaceuticals, Frank Douglas avoids the "F word" and calls the concept *high learning, unwanted results.* All of them see that stretch goals require a spirit of experimentation in which any learning is positive, even if undesired, because it adds to the company's inventory of intellectual capital.

> **New learning (knowledge-creation) takes equal importance to goal achievement in the new appraisal process.**

Therefore, *new learning* (knowledge-creation) takes equal importance to goal achievement in the new appraisal process. A vice president at a Fortune 100 telecommunications company sends her top people to various countries in emerging markets to pioneer new industries in those countries. To get her top talent to take these high-risk, entrepreneurial assignments, she tells them, "You have two objectives: (a) to find suitable partners and get the business up and running profitably and (b) to "crack the code" of building a business in this type of country, so that by your trial and error learning, we can build businesses in similar countries more efficiently. In one case, it took three years to become profitable, but that experience helped shorten the profitability point in a similar country to only nine months. The manager of the original country shared in the credit by having "cracked the code" for that type of situation.

To address this dual focus on business achievement and transferable learning, we developed with her staff the following approach to appraisals and rewards—a process applicable to most businesses.

Appraisals

The *Full Value Appraisals* assess the full value of what a person contributes in the following *ABLE* categories:

- Achievement = producing a specific business result.
- Behavior = performing with a designated skill or style.
- Learning (transferred) = showing that a new learning or insight has been either (a) communicated/published or (b) actually used by others.
- Effort = passing milestones that are on the critical path to a key achievement.

Personal learning is not the issue. *Transferable* learning, in which other people and the business benefit as well, merits the highest value. For example, in a biotech company, if a biochemist isolates a new enzyme, that's the deliverable of a project; if he or she also develops a new enzyme-isolation methodology, that's a transferable insight that could impact many different projects. If a manager supervises the development of a new product that's better than the competition's, that's an expected deliverable; if he or she also documents new ways of managing cross-functional teams, that's a bit of new knowledge that, if transferred, could benefit many project teams.

The ABLE categories can be weighted in many ways, depending on:

- Circumstances. For example, a new sales relationship may take two or three years of effort to produce a significant achievement or sale.
- Experience. For example, there might be different first-year expectations for newer or younger employees.
- Job assignment. For example, starting a new venture in a new territory.

Sometimes, different job functions can breed different goals, where what's optimal for one person in an organization may mean suboptimal results for another. By including a rating for *cross-functional team performance,* you can encourage collaboration without the stress of competing goals.

Most of us are reluctant to have our performance measured; yet without appraisals we can't get acknowledgment and recognition for our successes. No performance appraisal methodology will work for all people, in all professions, in all situations. The guidelines that best foster creativity build on four widespread principles that are often difficult to implement:

1. Individuals must be involved in setting and evaluating their performance.
2. Both formal and informal feedback are required.
3. Flexibility in evaluating results is essential.
4. Risk and failure need a degree of nonpunitive tolerance—even encouragement.

Feedback is the answer to the question, "How do we know when we're successful?" Sometimes we are afraid of failing, so we refuse to open channels of feedback. In doing so, we not only keep ourselves from knowing about failure, but also from experiencing our successes. Only with good feedback channels can we experience personal satisfaction and a sense of accomplishment.

For innovation to thrive, the feedback must be tolerant of mistakes. For example, an ad for 3M headlines: "3M has made a lot of mistakes. We're very proud of them." It goes on to say, "Everyone who is alive and moving makes mistakes. The trick is to learn from your mistakes and move on. [If venture risks are reasonable], we tend to be willing to make an investment and learn."

Rewards

At Pillsbury, I conducted research with brand managers from the U.S. foods division, asking them to rank the following rewards ("SATISFIERS") for innovativeness :

___ Self-determination—autonomy, flexibility in job assignments, etc.

___ Advancement—promotions, etc.

___ Training and development—opportunities for greater expertise, personal growth.

___ Intrinsic—doing what you love to do.

___ Social—being able to work with the people you most want to work with.

___ Financial—salary increases, bonuses, etc.

___ Impact—having an impact by achieving meaningful goals, serving customers.

___ Environment—good working conditions, hours, attractive surroundings, equipment.

___ Recognition—public or private recognition by bosses, peers, or subordinates.

___ Security—of specific job assignment, overall employment, etc.

We found that there was a correlation among intrinsic SATIS-FIERS, such as autonomy, private recognition, and personal and professional growth. There was also an inverse correlation between this group and a group of extrinsic SATISFIERS, such as promotions, financial rewards, and public recognition. About half the group were inner-directed people who needed a "maintenance" level of extrinsic rewards but were most motivated by intrinsic rewards. The other half of the group were outer-directed people who were moved to action by extrinsic rewards but needed a modicum of intrinsic satisfaction. The U.S. population is split about 50-50 between these two, but intrinsic satisfaction is moving ahead as the primary reward for the risk taking that breakthrough innovation needs. Any approach to "full value" appraisal and rewards has to take this difference into account.

For all employees, *Full Value Satisfactions* can be represented by a star configuration, with each point of the star being one of the five sources for job motivation:

Professional Development

Career Progress

Compensation

Recognition

Autonomy

Full Value Satisfactions

In our client's internal survey of key business builders, they were asked to rank the importance of these categories to their motivation and satisfaction, starting with the most important. The results were as follows: *Intrinsic, Professional Development, Career Progress, Compensation, Recognition.* Their energy and commitment to do a great job stems from their inner spirit, becoming all they can be and making a difference where they can.

FOSTERING A CREATIVE CLIMATE

But even all this isn't enough to have a climate where innovation flourishes! You need more than just leadership, creativity training, or new appraisal systems. So, how can you mobilize the creative potential of the people and resources in your organization? In such an environment, stimulating a climate for creativity and innovation is a creative act in itself. You can't rely on any generic prescriptions for fostering creativity, but you can generate a climate for innovation by paying attention to eight key issues, which just happen to spell the acronym CREATIVE:

COOPERATIVE LEARNING

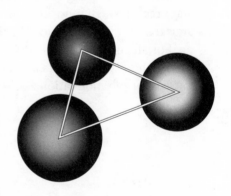

- Seeking input from people of different backgrounds and points-of-view
- Analyzing issues from a systems perspective
- Being open to personal learning and change, nondefensively
- Developing coalitions to pool information and analyze issues
- Establishing communities of practice to share learning
- Using information technology to augment personal intelligence

How well are diverse perspectives elicited? How flexibly and spontaneously do people self-organize as needs emerge? How are the capabilities of information technology leveraged for creating and sharing new knowledge?

RISK AWARENESS

- Being aware of potential risks and opportunities for the person, team, company, customers

- Defining "what's at stake"
- Sensitizing everyone to the nature and speed of change in the business
- Establishing scanning and monitoring systems
- Gathering, assessing, and distributing information

How well do you intuitively "foresee" what's coming? What trends and events reflect threats and opportunities for your organization? How well do people in your group understand this environment?

EMPOWERMENT

- Initiating "stretch" challenges that don't always have traditional solutions
- Becoming energized and courageous in tough situations
- Seeking to grow as a person through the challenge
- Acting with heart and courage for what's personally important
- Allowing others to take risks and sometimes fail
- Taking on roles commensurate with experience and potential

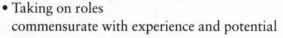

Who are the best initiators of new ideas in your group? How much "stretch" and challenge is encouraged? What are appropriate limits for risk taking?

APPRAISAL AND REWARDS

- Assessing and gaining satisfaction from (a) what was accomplished (getting results) and (b) what was learned (getting smarter)
- Developing appropriate menus of intrinsic as well as extrinsic rewards

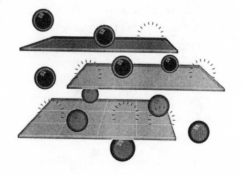

- Using peer and full 360-degree assessments for performance management
- Transferring new knowledge to other groups

How are the key learnings from your group's projects assessed and carried forward? What intrinsic satisfactions as well as extrinsic rewards does your group most desire?

TRANSITION MANAGEMENT

- Getting buy-in from those impacted by change
- Implementing change rapidly, flexibly, and systemically
- Acting responsibly and keeping time, performance, and budget commitments
- Promoting personal growth and change during periods of change
- Retaining high productivity during periods of change
- Leveraging resources for long-term health and growth

How well is the process of organizational change strategized and implemented? How do you get people involved? What does it take to make the personal adjustments to change and still stay productive?

INTUITION AND LOGIC

- Using different thinking strategies to create new knowledge and generate ideas
- Applying intuition and logic together to seek unconventional ideas
- Giving time and support for new ideas to emerge and mature without premature closure
- Entertaining a diversity of perspectives
- Challenging assumptions to see problems from new angles
- Seeking a "beginner's mind," open to new ideas

How do you challenge assumptions about "the way things are" and provoke new ideas? How well does your group avoid the twin problems of "group think" or "idea killing?"

VISION AND VALUES

- Defining the challenge to be intrinsically motivating
- Seeking a goal that makes a compelling difference
- Staying true to one's values
- Aligning with a common vision of the company's growth
- Attuning everyone's own core values with corporate values
- Establishing learning goals as well as visionary achievements

What is the purpose of your organization or group in the long run? What are the personal life purposes of members of your group? What values are most prominent in actual practice?

EXPEDITED DECISIONS

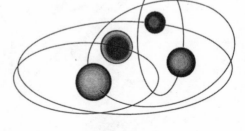

- Moving quickly to respond to urgent customer matters
- Evaluating alternatives based on intuition, experience, and facts
- Getting broad input and open discussions for decisions
- Sharing power
- Generating high debate with low emotional conflict
- Staying true to vision and values

How well are alternatives given detailed scrutiny? What role does intuition play in group decision-making? How well do you make decisions consistent with the values everyone supports?

In chapter 3, you entered into the world of the Creative Journey as a model for the innovation process. The illustration on pages 38–39 showed how your SPIRITED qualities support you in this journey.

Likewise, the attributes of a CREATIVE climate directly support you and all your teams to take the most innovative Creative Journey possible:

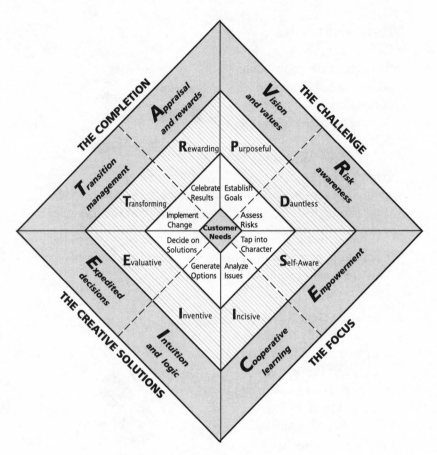

The "CREATIVE" Climate
Supports the Creative Journey

Suppose you took the pulse of the spirit of your organization. How healthy would your CREATIVE climate be? The table on page 115 evaluates the CREATIVE climate at one organization. Notice the strengths and weaknesses of this company's assessment:

What You Observe	CREATIVE Climate	Strength, Weakness
People are too busy to share information across organized boundaries; they concentrate only on meeting their own goals and objectives.	COOPERATIVE LEARNING	Weakness
People in product development proactively getting to know customers and their needs; they learn and share the latest in technology and industry developments.	RISK AWARENESS	Strength
People are not afraid to take on ambitious challenges of their own choosing; they feel eager to stretch their own boundaries.	EMPOWERMENT	Strength
People conduct performance appraisals only on what has been achieved against expectations; they do not assess the value of "new knowledge-creation" after successes and failures.	APPRAISAL AND REWARDS	Weakness
People are ill-informed and caught by surprise when changes are announced; they do not understand or buy in to the need for change.	TRANSITION MANAGEMENT	Weakness
People actively challenge the core assumptions behind a situation; they use intuition as well as logic to find breakthrough new ideas.	INTUITION AND LOGIC	Strength
People can't state their own values or the company values clearly; they don't feel a personal connection to the company's aggressive goals for financial returns.	VISION AND VALUES	Weakness
People arguing intensely about what to do, yet with high respect for each other's opinions; they attack the problem, not each other.	EXPEDITED DECISIONS	Strength

IN CLOSING . . .

As stated earlier, the opportunity exists for all of us to revive and manage our organizations through the creative, responsible, spirited expression of ourselves at work. What does it take to do this? Be willing to develop the attitudes and skills within yourself to take advantage of the conditions around you and to nurture your own unique talents and experiences as well as those of your compatriots. The eight elements of the CREATIVE climate provide some stimulation and guidelines for doing this.

This chapter and the following seven chapters will give you many ideas for building a more CREATIVE climate, as described below.

Chapter		CREATIVE Climate
PART II	**Foster Breakthrough Innovation in Groups**	
Chapter 6	Stimulate a CREATIVE Climate for Innovation	Empowerment Appraisal and rewards
Chapter 7	Align and Attune Innovative Teams	Expedited
Chapter 8	Take the Lead in Innovative Meetings	decisions
Chapter 9	Generate Ideas by Modifying and Experimenting	Intuition and logic
Chapter 10	Generate Ideas by Visioning and Exploring	
PART III	**Revitalize the Soul of Corporate Creativity**	
Chapter 11	Inspire Growth with Purpose, Vision, and Values	Vision and values
Chapter 12	Create and Manage Knowledge	Risk awareness Cooperative learning
Chapter 13	Implement Strategic Innovation Management	Transition management

Creativity is both a work style and a lifestyle. The two go together. Life is a twenty-four hour a day proposition, and creativity cannot be turned on and off like a lightbulb. Creativity implies full implementation of our potential, not just dreaming up good ideas. That implementation requires drive and determination—acting with our full sense of personal power. Ultimately, this is a test of leadership: doing what it takes to develop a CREATIVE climate flexible enough to foster peak performance for each individual, not just a few key people, and not just the common denominator of the average employee.

Your sense of personal power determines how well you'll manifest this climate for yourself and your colleagues. Realize that your power comes from within you, from your inner sense of purpose, from who you are deep inside. You *can* make a difference in your organization and in the world. Awaken the creator within you. Experience your power *before* you act, and your effectiveness will be multiplied. Don't hold back. As Somerset Maugham once put it, "You'll win some, you'll lose some. Only the mediocre are always at their best."

CHAPTER 7

Align and Attune
Innovative Teams

> *I was hired essentially to promote anything from a big event—like a "walk" for people over sixty years of age—to something like Christmas camp for seniors. Before I got the job, I was on this committee as a volunteer.*
>
> *The committee wasn't the ideal situation. Most of our meetings were very task-oriented. I facilitated the meetings but got caught up in "Let's get it done. Just got to get it done." The more process-oriented way is more involving and getting input from everyone up front. Fortunately, the walk came off successfully because we were so dedicated, I think.*
>
> *One of the creative aspects of this project was the mix of people. Serendipitously, we drew together four or five people who were very different, very unique and talented, and in very different areas. We complemented one another.*
>
> —CLAIRE, ASSOCIATE PROGRAM DIRECTOR FOR A SOCIAL SERVICE AGENCY

STRIVING FOR MORE THAN TEAMWORK

To take an idea and make it useful and appreciated in the world we need others, and others need us. If we see ourselves as operating in more isolated fashion than we would like, we *can* develop ourselves to be more than a one-man band. There's much we can do to transform territorial battles, to get a project team functioning smoothly, and to develop synergy among different people's talents.

There is an extraordinary team expedition-competition called the *Eco-Challenge*, sponsored by the Discovery Channel on TV. In 1997, it was in British Columbia (BC), Canada. Seventy teams of five people engaged in an "expedition race" over an eight-to-nine-day period. The challenge was to hike over glaciers, mountain climb (rappel, etc.), raft, mountain bike, kayak, and swim. In 1998 in Queensland, Australia, the teams will go through rain forests as well as outback desert. The teams train for a year, as much as sixty hours per week. All members of a team must finish together. In BC, only fourteen out of seventy teams finished. The rest dropped out due to heat, hypothermia, exhaustion, or injury.

Interestingly, the highest finishing teams didn't necessarily have the best athletes, but they did have the best friends. As one person put it, "Everyone has a breakdown during the journey, and the team carries that person. And every team has its moments when it is carried by some individual on the team." In BC, the two teams "racing" to finish second shifted out of the competitive mode after five days. These teams realized they were on an expedition adventure, competing against the course, not each other. They began to help each other and decided to cross the finish line together. One person said, "It turned out to be three-quarters competition and one-quarter expedition together." The shift that had occurred among the ten of them had clearly been an exhilarating experience.

Today, conventional wisdom designates *teams* as the groups led by the heroes of corporate folklore—by the leaders who are bold and decisive and lead the others on the team. All the management literature says so, and team-based management dominates many corporate cultures today. But go deeper than this conventional wisdom and you'll discover something new that can revolutionize all our notions of teamwork. In the New Story of Creativity, the depth and quality of our relationships determines our capacity for breakthrough thinking. We've entered an era of *relationship* heroism, where people who are the most successful in creating the flexibility and spaciousness of authentic and caring relationships will be the most successful in exercising extraordinary leadership.

PLAYING IN TUNE TOGETHER

There are two fundamentally different starting points for building strong teams:

- Relationship-oriented: developing teamwork by focusing on interpersonal dynamics.
- Task-oriented: developing teamwork while doing actual work.

Orchestra members can give a great performance only if they have developed great attunement (being in tune with each other) and alignment (playing on the same page at the same rhythm). If they don't tune their instruments, their music will not be pleasant, even if they start and finish the same piece together. In business, *attunement* means resonating with the individual purpose and values of each person. *Align-*

ment means agreeing to work toward the same purpose, and working in rhythm to achieve it.

Alexander Graham Bell once said, "*Great discoveries and improvements invariably involve the cooperation of many minds.*" You can promote greater collaboration, communication, and creativity on your teams by aligning and attuning people on six key issues:

Attunement on	**Alignment on**
• Personal purpose	• Purpose and vision
• Interpersonal relations	• Roles
	• Empowerment
	• Processes for working together

We often begin team development by trying to define and align with the group's purpose, but without much emphasis on "tuning in" to each other as individuals first. Time is wasted as the team struggles to collaborate like novices in a three-legged race. Relationship-oriented team building fixes this problem. If you see that your group communications are most problematic, start by focusing first on interpersonal relationships and personal purpose; only then will dialogues on aligning group purpose, roles, empowerment, and processes be productive.

If your group has previously formed close relationships with each other, or if they're extremely task-focused and "won't hold still" for this "soft attunement stuff," then jumping in to start aligning on task-oriented issues makes sense. You can leave interpersonal communications and personal purpose to the end. Under these circumstances, a task-oriented approach shines by being time- and energy-efficient.

No matter which approach you take, you might benefit from an outside facilitator. You can direct the facilitator to take any of three distinct roles:

- To lead the entire process (most involvement)
- To step in when things get rough
- To not step in unless specifically asked by the entire group (least involvement)

You and your team should choose which of these facilitator roles fits your needs best to start with. You can always adjust the role later.

TAKING A RELATIONSHIP-ORIENTED APPROACH

A few years back, the Industrial Tape Division of 3M set aggressive growth goals that their current product portfolio *and likely pipeline of products* would not meet. We worked first with their technology managers and then their entire technology and marketing organizations to create not only new technology and product ideas, but new knowledge as well. While the management group had had multiple sessions of team building (up to their eyeballs!), they required another level of breakthrough synergy to find the hidden crevices of thinking where breakthrough ideas hadn't yet seen the light of day.

We said, "There's a sea of issues and opportunities to explore, but first we must check out the boat (their teamwork)—and check it periodically during the journey." To make their diversity and differences an advantage rather than a hindrance, they developed greater appreciation of what each person could offer and how to relate to each other with greater openness. Only then did they generate new ideas and strategies for multiple scenarios of their future competitive environments. As they jelled more and more, their learning curve increased, and their collaborative creativity went through the roof. They launched themselves into a new era of growth, with new competencies to create knowledge, technologies, and *high-integrity* relationships.

By focusing first on relationships, you enhance the spirit of collaboration through potentially difficult discussions of purpose, roles, power, and processes. Your goal is to create high-integrity relationships. *Integrity* here means much more than ethics. The word integrity has the same Latin root as *integer*, and means oneness, wholeness, unity . . . and a congruency of thoughts, words, and deeds.

Clarifying Your Personal Purpose

Your personal integrity starts by living in harmony with your own personal purpose. In chapter 2, you listed increasingly more profound personal goals in response to these questions:

1. Possessions or status to acquire?

2. Milestones to achieve?

3. Experiences to have?

4. Gifts to express?

5. Difference to make to others?

6. Person to become?

To bring your group together as real people, not just faceless "corporate roles" working together, take the time to explore each person's personal life purpose and goals. (You'll also find that this produces a group purpose that is naturally more energizing and more intrinsically motivating.) Really strive to understand what your people feel is most important in life. Find out how everyone is doing with achieving it— what are their current concerns in connection with their purpose? How might this particular project give them an opportunity to implement their purpose and practice their values?

Deepening Relationships Through Basic Human Values

With this level of feeling and connection, you can begin fostering profound relationships that actually increase the likelihood of achieving breakthrough results. In 1990, when Frank Carrubba was head of HP Labs, he conducted a study to discover the key differences between unsuccessful product teams, successful ones, and the truly extraordinary teams who surprised even themselves with their breakthrough results.

The difference between unsuccessful and successful was (predictably) due to levels of talent, motivation, and vision. Yet there was no difference in talent, motivation, or vision between successful and extraordinary teams! Brainpower was necessary yet insufficient for truly extraordinary results. The finding that superior teams have a much higher level of authenticity and caring dominated the research results. The lesson learned was that individual genius counts for something but that a high degree of synergy among people allows their collective genius to achieve breakthroughs.

> **Superior teams have a much higher level of authenticity and caring**

Authenticity and caring are two of the fundamental human values that allow a group's talent, motivation, and vision to express itself without barriers. How do you consciously develop these and other human values on your own teams?

Authenticity and Truthfulness
- *Say what you mean.* Start the sometimes-difficult process of building trust by making and keeping agreements.
- *Speak unarguably in terms of facts rather than opinions.* We often disguise our personal judgments as "the truth." Get to the full truth faster, and clear up many arguments, by making a strong distinction between "Here are the objective facts that an unbiased reporter would observe" and "Here's my interpretation, assumptions, judgments, or opinions about those facts."

Caring
- *Connect to higher purpose by identifying the difference you want to make in life through serving others.* Give meaning and sustainable energy to life's daily episodes and trials by discovering a way to serve and contribute to others.
- *Connect to other people by listening generously to the content, emotions, and noble purpose that are often hidden in their communications.* Create mutual understanding by feeding back the *content* of what someone says. Show true respect for the person's distinct experience of a situation by feeding back the *emotions* and the *positive intentions* behind what was said.

Equanimity
- *See yourself as the source of your inner peace and emotional reactions, rather than the victim of another's behavior.* The basic emotions of fear, anger, and sadness are caused by an attachment (even addiction) to having things turn out a certain way. Generate more equipoise in the flow of life and more wisdom in solving problems by upgrading your attachments to preferences.

Well-being
- *Find mutually beneficial solutions to common issues and problems.* Build deep rapport by sincerely seeking win-win solutions, without taking 200 percent responsibility for feelings or actions of others. Uncover those solutions together by taking a mutual Creative Journey.

Responsibility
- *Do what you promise.* Create openness by communicating fully and honestly what you are thinking and feeling.
- *Take 100 percent responsibility for the results in your work life.* Taking 200 percent responsibility leaves you exhausted and resentful by doing other people's work for them; taking 0 percent responsibility makes you feel like a victim of other's actions. See yourself as the source of the quality of your work, and empower others to be the source of theirs, by taking 100 percent responsibility.

Taking 100% Responsibility

"Taking responsibility" carries a great deal of cultural baggage and deserves additional commentary. "Who's responsible?" can be a loaded question. It can mean: "Whose fault will it be if things don't go well?" and "Who's going to get the credit?", or it can mean "How do I make sure everyone jumps in and does their part?" and "What will I do if I see people copping out?" The first situation runs the risk of blaming others for mistakes rather than finding constructive solutions. Though it may sound good, the second can result in putting the burden of achievement totally on your shoulders, leading you to oversell or to manipulate.

Responsibility is a state of co-creation with others, rather than "it's all up to me" (burden, 200 percent responsibility) or "ain't it awful" (blame, 0 percent responsibility); 100 percent responsibility is more than ownership—it's an act of *identity*. It means "I fully identify myself with the actions, integrity, and results produced by this collective group of people. I will act, and react, as if I were the one taking any of these actions."

"What does it mean for me to take 100 percent responsibility?" is not something you "get" intellectually, but something you continually live as an ongoing internal inquiry. The question "How am I 100 percent responsible here?" challenges me, frustrates me, opens me, nourishes me, dumbfounds me, and ultimately contributes to my growth like no other question.

You can have reservations *and* be 100 percent committed. We need to express our reservations and considerations but *not* have these influence our ability to take 100 percent responsibility. This does *not* mean we should ignore concerns; in fact, we must identify our concerns and then address them from a place of commitment. Acting with 100 percent responsibility means more than just working toward an external result; it also means looking inside and growing through any personal barriers to fulfilling the external commitment—calmly and truthfully facing any reservations without blame or shame. Even when authentic reservations arise, or slippage in responsibility occurs, this is the "home base" to come back to and renew.

Some teams maximize their potential by focusing on their relationships before tackling issues such as mission, roles, and how to manage a project together. Robert Staubli, president of Swissair, said, "In a company, the estimated loss of potential performance ranges from 30-50 percent due to inter-human problems, unsettled conflicts, troubled relations, insufficient freedom, and a lack of opportunities for development. I think this estimate is cautious."[1]

When companies want to set up internal venture teams in situations in which a fast response to the marketplace is needed, this sense of responsibility is essential. For example, Signode Industries, a $700 million midwestern manufacturing company has been forming a series of new venture teams to identify new business opportunities outside the company's normal product areas. Its first team consisted of six senior managers from six different departments—marketing, engineering, manufacturing, and so on. The team's initial task was to investigate the new industry area and recommend specific business opportunities within six months.

One of the interesting aspects of this venture team was that it was purposely established without a leader. The six people were brought together as peers, and they decided to manage the group as coequals. The group's sponsor was the director of corporate development, who wasn't a member of the team itself. The team members each had potential rols as inventors, product champions, monitors, and project managers.

By choosing not to have a leader, they gave up the security of having someone around who would decide what to do next, assign tasks, and step in to resolve differences. The fact that they took such a risk says quite a bit about these managers; their careers could have been affected by the success or failure of this experimental team.

Through a demanding series of over 2,000 personal interviews, they gathered opinions from prospective users and customers in the proposed industry on what new products were wanted. By becoming very aware of the current market situation, they took the first step of the Creative Journey process. However, they sometimes felt they weren't being as innovative as they would have liked.

Near the end of their six months of identifying new opportunities, I conducted a two-day "consolidation" session with them. We clustered the opportunities they had identified and shaped them into "businesses" rather than simply a set of related ideas.

Regarding the *content* of their study, their recommendations were ultimately very well received by their company officers and board of directors, and the resulting new venture is now already in the marketplace and doing well. Looking back at the *process* of working together over the six months, team members identified three norms that had helped them work collaboratively:

1. Each person could pursue a potential opportunity even if the others weren't enthused. Each could be a "product champion."
2. Periodically a consultant was brought in to help focus the group's efforts. This helped to synthesize their findings and resolve conflicts of priorities among the group members.
3. Each person respected the input of the others. This was due

partly to the personalities involved and partly to each having an important, individual expertise: marketing, sales, manufacturing, R&D, corporate planning, and accounting.

The team members were mostly in agreement that if they had to do it again, they would remain leaderless and schedule more frequent meetings with various outside consultants. The consultants could help them: (1) develop more creative ideas from within the group itself, (2) focus on the top priorities, and (3) resolve any current disputes.

For this company, the venture team was an innovation in management practices: Setting up a venture team with managers from around the company was in itself a departure from how they typically identified new business opportunities. The team's decision to be a multileader group was also an innovation in management practice that required high levels of personal responsibility to make it work.

Working toward high-integrity relationships provides an opportunity to develop our spiritual character as well. Just like growing a plant, to grow ourselves as embodied souls, we must pay attention to five elements:

Growing a Plant	Elements of the Soul	Core Spiritual Value	Relationship Practices for Growing a Soul
Sun	Intentions	Well-being	Finding mutually beneficial solutions to issues
Air	Intellect	Authenticity truthfulness	Saying what you mean Speaking unarguable facts rather than opinions
Seed	Heart	Caring	Connecting to higher purpose by identifying what difference to make in life through serving others
			Connecting to people by listening generously to their content, emotions, and noble purpose
Water	Emotion-Mind	Equanimity	Seeing yourself as the source of your inner peace and emotional reactions, not the victim of others
Soil	Behavior	Responsibility	Doing what you promise
			Taking 100 percent responsibility for results in life

The fruit that is born of these practices—high-integrity relationships—can be *the* foundation for strategic advantage, enabling faster and better knowledge-creation, innovation, customer loyalty, responsiveness, and decision making.

TAKING A TASK-ORIENTED APPROACH

The comptrollers of Northern Telecom in Canada once asked me to help reinvent their role to empower them to help foster, rather than hinder, innovation. After aligning behind the critical need for faster and more inventive product development, they explored how they could transform their reputation as naysayers and blocks to innovation. The breakthrough came when one member stood up and asked, "Do you realize that 90 percent of the figures we give to managers to make decisions for their use in making decisions are there because our government requires them for tax purposes? Could it be that, just because we use those numbers to compute taxes, they might *not* be the best figures for making decisions by?"

They strategized how to play the role of neutral facilitators and scorekeepers for executive decisions—"Here's the potential impact of these options on the growth of intellectual capital and profits." Furthermore, they saw how they influenced people's behavior by what measures they used; for example, their sole reliance on cost-recovery measures to justify investments actually stifled innovation. They began to reinvent processes that would truly foster risk taking and innovation, in part by creating measures to justify "soft" issues such as "retaining customer loyalty."

Recall that you can promote greater collaboration, communication, and creativity on your teams by addressing six issues: attunement on personal purpose and interpersonal relations; alignment on purpose and vision, roles, empowerment, and processes for working together. To get the highest creativity and productivity from a group, you must promote both alignment and attunement. Alignment gives *single-mindedness* of purpose. Attunement gives *single-heartedness* of purpose.

> **Alignment gives single-mindedness of purpose. Attunement gives single-heartedness of purpose.**

In the relationship-oriented approach, which is used when people see that attuning their communications with each other is the biggest priority, you start by focusing first on interpersonal relationships, eventually followed by aligning on purpose, roles, empowerment, and processes. However, if your group is very task-focused and your relationships are in relatively good shape, you can start by aligning on purpose and vision. You then address the other issues in sequence, leaving attunement on the most personal issues—authenticity, truthfulness, caring, responsibility, equanimity, and well-being—to deal with last. An advantage of the task-oriented approach is that once purpose, roles, power, and processes have been resolved, truly interpersonal issues are more purely defined—that is, differences in direction, etc., are cleared up first rather than being misdiagnosed as "interpersonal" issues.

Before discussing each issue separately, here's an overview of the key questions to discuss and resolve for each issue:

ISSUE	KEY QUESTIONS
Purpose and vision	• What single statement of the team's charter (purpose, vision, scope) do people agree to? • What is our mission and authority?
Roles	• What do people expect of each person, especially in terms of responsibilities? • What does each person bring to the sector team? (Good opportunity for direct feedback on strengths, without isolating that person as the sole resource for that strength.) • Do we have the right mix of talent for what we need to do?
Empowerment	• What authority to make decisions and act does the team, and individual members, have? • When do we get involved in the course of major decisions—how early?
Processes	• What are mutually acceptable ground rules for communicating, resolving conflict, generating ideas, making decisions, getting feedback, and so on? • How do we share knowledge and connection across sectors, with fewer white spaces? • How do we make sure the best ideas rise to the top, rather than the vanilla (easy to agree on) ones?
Personal purpose	• How can we learn about each other's purpose and support each other in living it at work? • What values does each person cherish and how can we operate our group by those collective values?
Interpersonal relations	• What can people do to create truthfulness, caring, responsibility, equanimity, and well-being as the basis of their relationships with each other? • How can we apply our own best experiences in teams to build better relationships with each other?

It is often wise to have a skilled, outside facilitator to act as a catalyst, guide, and arbitrator in resolving especially sticky issues. By taking one issue at a time and negotiating the best consensus agreement on purpose and goals, roles and authority expectations, procedures, and interpersonal support, any group can develop greater teamwork.

Aligning on Purpose and Vision

Deeply held purposes drive creativity and provide the intrinsic motivation needed to champion "ideas whose time has come." How can you align with others on a single purpose? As a group, research and brainstorm your answers to four questions:

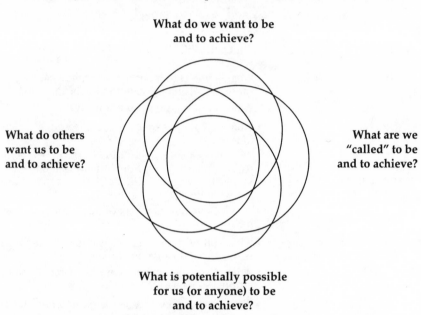

What do we want to be and to achieve?

What do others want us to be and to achieve?

What are we "called" to be and to achieve?

What is potentially possible for us (or anyone) to be and to achieve?

Aligning on Purpose and Vision

Identify the ideas in the middle zone that simultaneously most overlap all four questions *and* create the most energy. The purpose statement has to do more than just "make sense" in the situation. It must inspire your enthusiasm. Ask people to rate their enthusiasm (which in Greek means to be "filled with spirit") on a 1-7 scale, 7 being high. If anyone rates a 4 or lower, continue searching for statement of purpose that everyone can be emotionally as well as intellectually aligned with.

To maintain that enthusiasm throughout your journey together, remember to:

- State your purpose in terms of what you want for others, not just what you want to get. A focus on serving others brings more powerful, creative energy to the task.

- Create a clear picture, measurable if possible, of what it would look like to achieve it.
- Acknowledge any doubts and disbeliefs about achieving it, without holding on to them and wasting energy.
- Give your purpose positive energy and vividly imagine the feelings you'd be having right now if you had already accomplished your purpose.

Establishing Informal Innovation Roles

Individuals can play many parts in helping a group to innovate. It is usually not enough to have a great idea, boundless energy, and a committed "champion." Each of the roles may be the critical ingredient for the group's success.

There are eight informal innovation roles:

The Product Champions

These people are the energy behind ideas. They will push and shove, if necessary, to try and get their favorite ideas over the organizational hurdles, or they will operate secretively. They are the great believers in their ideas and are willing to take risks to get their ideas implemented. Sometimes their ideas are actually invented by someone else, but product champions may become excited and take them on as their own. They go beyond being the "lonely genius" to use their knowledge of company operations and the market to produce their pet innovations. More often than not, when there seem to be insufficient ideas, people probably are not aggressively championing ideas, either their own or others'.

The Sponsors

These people support and oversee the progress of the product champions. Because the product champions are sometimes likely to offend and cause waves in the organization with their zeal, the sponsor buffers the champions from unnecessary interference. This lets the product champions concentrate on the ideas rather than the politics, which may be their weak point. They may also link people in informal alliances to make better use of complementary strengths.

The Inventors

These people are the original creators of an idea, a concept, a possibility. They may also be the ones to carry the concept forward as the product champion. In many cases, however, they prefer to stay "at their bench" or in their comfortable research or staff routine. They have mixed feelings if they let someone else become product champion for "their baby," but they may do it anyway.

The Project Managers

These people are the stabilizers, the ones who know how to manage projects within the triple constraints of performance, time, and budget. They are the touchstone for the product champion to make the idea really work within the guidelines set up by the organization.

The Coaches

These people give guidance and assist the development of less experienced personnel (a mentor or big brother/sister role). Their ability to provide a role model and to communicate empathy, optimism, persistence, and a critical but trustful attitude can be invaluable to the innovation process.

The Gatekeepers

These people—and there need to be a number of them—monitor technological, social, political, market, and other emerging external trends and communicate them widely to appropriate people in the organization. This information is most often the stimulus for coming up with the innovation in the first place, as a proactive or reactive response to this input.

The Internal Monitors

Monitors also are needed to review the ongoing ideas and creative climate of the internal organization. This internal monitoring can be critical to circulating information and decisions and to determining how groups within the organization can respond creatively.

The Facilitators

These people have a high degree of skill in eliciting new ideas from groups of people and fostering more collaborative teamwork among them. They act as the neutral catalysts and change agents for more rapid, productive interactions. (See chapter 8 for a discussion of a facilitator's skills.)

Notice that this division of roles for the creative process is different from the traditional division between line authority and job expertise. In one case, a top manager may have the internal-monitor role for stimulating a project while the most junior staff member is the product champion. In another case, the monitor, inventor, and product champion may be the same person, and the sponsor might be someone outside the line organization.

Yet each role can also be formally established and rewarded. In one major corporation, for example, a vice-president officially appointed gatekeepers in letters by stating:

> *In every large organization there are a few individuals who have a special talent for knowing what is going on in a particular technical field and in keeping others informed of these advances. These have come to be known in management literature as "Gatekeepers." We have begun a program to identify and recognize these individuals. . . .*
>
> *. . . I would like you to write a two- or three-page memo on recent activities and advances in your field of interest. This should not be a primer, but should be addressed to someone already familiar with your area. During the year, as any advances are made and come to your attention, I would appreciate a short note outlining what has happened and what effects this will have on (the company) as you know it.*
>
> *Get acquainted with those others in the Corporation in your field and include them on your distribution list of documents you generate for your own divisional use.*

In some cases, different people must play different roles depending on the needs of the business. If you are producing a new product for a new market, you probably need an "intrapreneur" (product champion) heading it. If you need someone to work effectively with existing products or existing markets, you usually need a different type of leader, more of a "stabilizing manager" (à la the project manager).

During the life of a work group or the course of your career, you may be required to fill all of these roles at one time or another, especially if you are a manager. The skills and interest for fulfilling these informal responsibilities do not always, or perhaps rarely, match up with stated job-performance requirements. Therefore, this may be an important area for human resource development programs in your organization.

Each informal innovation role is important, even critical, to the overall creativity and effectiveness of your organization. Although the sponsor and gatekeeper, for example, may not be viewed as the creative ones in your group, they may be just as important to your group's creativity as the inventor or product champion. With people occupying each role and working together, the creative process can free each person to contribute in his or her best way.

Clarifying "Degrees" of Empowerment

There is no set leadership style that is best for every situation. It depends on who you are, who you are leading, and under what circumstances. Although "participation" has been widely promoted—even in this book at times—it is not always desirable. Would you want a participatory style of leadership if you were a passenger in a nose-diving airplane? There are comparable times in the life of an organization when more directive styles are appropriate.

In all, there are five major styles of leadership and influence:

- Tell: "Based on my decision, here's what I want you to do."
- Sell: "Based on my decision, here's what I want you to do because . . . (benefit for listener)."
- Consult: "Before I make a decision, I want your input."
- Participate: "We need to make a decision together."
- Delegate: "You make a decision."

Furthermore, there are three levels of delegation

- Ask: "Produce this result, and ask me before you take any action."
- Inform: "Produce this result, and keep me informed of what action you have taken."
- Do: "Produce this result, and I don't need to know what you have done."

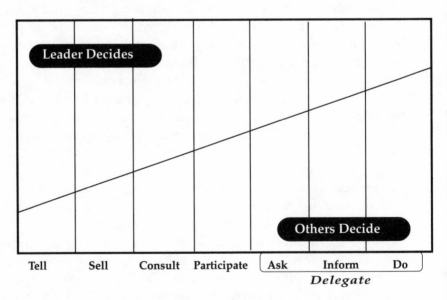

Degrees of Empowerment

In a creative climate for innovation there is an emphasis on *leadership* rather than *management/control*. At W. L. Gore and Associates, new ideas are backed only when a team appears to support them. The philosophy of team development is that "leaders are established by followers."

Leaders empower people rather than motivate them. They provide environmental encouragement within which individuals can work creatively and productively. When "management" becomes "leadership," creativity can be managed without stifling it.

Leaders specify challenging outcomes that require individuals or groups to be creative in meeting their goals. They spend time developing vision and strategy, promoting interdepartmental collaboration, leveraging their people's talents, and building trust. They are willing to invest in and take risks with individuals. They go beyond passively accepting whatever comes through the suggestion box. They actively seek to use and benefit from the unused creative potential of their employees.

IN CLOSING . . .

The new work ethic strongly values individual responsibility over following orders, creative expression over fitting in, and innovation over business as usual.

Creativity and innovation do not happen in isolation. A SPIRITED individual may have particular strengths, yet from an organizational perspective, it is equally important to emphasize collaborative roles. We must align and attune ourselves with each other if we are to have peak-performing groups (including large groups called *organizations*). Whether through informal roles, co-SPIRITEDs, leadership styles, or team building, we must also combine our talents more closely. Only then can most groups bring an idea to final achievement.

Just as creativity in general is best nurtured by fluency in your logical and intuitive processes, so also are teamwork and innovation nurtured by the harmony of head and heart. "Feel with your minds, think with your hearts" is an appropriate motto for successful, innovative work.

CHAPTER 8

Take the Lead in
Innovative Meetings

The car frame has 4,000 spot welds, which distort the frame in some way. Everyone knows this, but no one admitted it. You can distort the steel parts that must fit on the frame, and it looks reasonably good. But plastic parts are so accurate, they need a perfect body to sit on. Our design had separated the plastic body and the steel frame, but we couldn't put the two together.

We had one of those three-day-and-night, staying-in-the-office meetings and suddenly found the solution. All we had to do, first, was admit that there's no way on God's earth to put 4,000 welds on and not distort something. When we admitted it, 90 percent of our problem was solved. The solution was very simple. We had to do exactly what the casting industry does. You make the casting larger than the part: You put the part there and machine it.

—HULKI, CHIEF DESIGN ENGINEER FOR AUTOMOBILES

ESTABLISHING MEETING ROLES

Team progress will be stymied without a team process for how you meet together. Meetings take time, money, and human energy. Twenty-five percent of most personnel budgets are for people's time in meetings. Middle managers typically spend one-third of their time in meetings. Top managers usually spend two-thirds of their time that way.

Improving meetings does not require suspending all operations and going to "organizational marriage counseling." By working to improve both the output and the process of our work simultaneously, the improvements we make will have a more immediate and enduring impact. To improve the meeting process, the first step is to clarify meeting roles. The second is to agree on a process for finding innovative solutions to the team's major challenges.

Michael Doyle and David Straus wrote a classic book entitled *How to Make Meetings Work*[1] that first outlined the need for separate meeting roles for the following individuals:

- The person with authority, in charge of calling the meeting—the *chairperson.*
- The person in charge of conducting the meeting—the *facilitator.*
- The person keeping a written record of the discussions in full view of everyone—the *recorder.*
- The participants with vested interests in the discussion—the *group members.*

These meeting roles enhance group collaboration no matter what informal innovation roles people have (see pp. 129–131).

Chairperson

The chairperson is responsible for the group performing its duties and is there to give the group direction in setting goals and plans, to provide expertise, to be the leader by authority, and to delegate. She is also responsible for participating in the discussions but not for guiding the process itself (see "facilitator" below).

Before a meeting it is important for the chairperson to specify what style of decision making is intended for the problem at hand: tell, sell, consult, participate, or delegate.

With the consulting style, the chairperson can also specify to what level in the Creative Journey process she wants input: Only a definition of the problem? Analysis too? Alternative solutions? Evaluation of alternatives?

Trust in your group will be undermined if people believe the style is participative ("We decide") when the chairperson really intends it to be consulting ("I'll decide after your input") or selling ("Here's what I want to convince you to do").

Facilitator

A neutral facilitator only guides and monitors the process of participation by the chairperson and group members. Through the facilitator the climate is freed for more adventurous and productive interaction. The facilitator's role is much like that of an orchestra conductor: He doesn't play any of the music but keeps everyone working together effectively. In idea-generation sessions, he is usually most effective assuming a low-key yet catalytic role.

Being a facilitator takes quite a bit of skill in problem-solving processes and group interaction, but playing the role is enormously worthwhile and rewarding. This is even more true the higher up you go in an organization. At higher levels the amount of time spent in meetings and the impact of decisions made there are higher.

Critical tasks of the facilitator are to:

- Identify how the meeting fits into the overall plan for dealing with an issue.
- Get agreement on a clear, achievable agenda.
- Ensure that the right participants attend (number, involvement, expertise).
- Set up a way for everyone to be properly prepared (especially the facilitator!).
- Plan the *process* for the meeting as carefully as the *content* to be discussed.
- Be specific about what decisions need to be made and summarize progress along the way.
- Follow problem-solving processes (such as the Creative Journey) in a disciplined manner.
- Stay on one subject at a time (but make sure the off-the-subject comments are retained somewhere to ensure getting back to them).
- Use visual aids such as a "group memory" (to be discussed).
- Ensure that each person has a free and safe climate to present ideas without being attacked but without taking over the floor.

Recorder

The recorder provides a collective memory of a meeting by recording, on easel pads or newsprint, the main discussion and decision points. Through the recorder, the group memory:

- Focuses the group on problems and tasks (as displayed concretely on paper) rather than on personalities.
- Holds ideas to prevent information overload.
- Gives a psychological release point for participants, who then don't have to hold onto their own ideas.
- Prevents repetition and wheel spinning.
- Helps demonstrate and ensure that participants have been fully understood.
- Provides an instant record of the meeting's content, decisions, and delegated actions.
- Allows newcomers to the meeting to catch up quickly.
- Reduces status differential by giving equal weight to all participants' ideas.

Group Members

The group members are responsible for participating and facilitating as much as possible. They are the ones who have to implement and live with the outcomes. (Nonparticipation is also a choice, an exercise of personal power, albeit an abdication.)

When a meeting is over, the most important and helpful way to improve meeting effectiveness is to take five to ten minutes and say, "Now that the meeting is over, how did it go?" Critique both the content and the process of the meeting. A simple way to do this is to discuss the following issues:

- Listening. Did people listen carefully to each other's views?
- Openness. Were ideas expressed with candor? Were differences thrashed out?
- Task orientation. Did the discussion stay on track to get the task accomplished?
- Participation. Was there lively interplay, with many members contributing and no one person dominating the conversation?
- Atmosphere. Was the atmosphere satisfying, challenging, and stimulating?
- Mutual support. Was there genuine concern for others?
- Leadership. Was the style of leadership appropriate? Was it concentrated or shared appropriately?
- Task accomplishment. How well was the task accomplished?

TAKING A CREATIVE JOURNEY TOGETHER

Challenges are simply situations we want to change and problems we want to solve. Problems are OK. With time so precious, an urgent question to answer is, "How do we rise to the challenge *together*, as one?"

When you're in a meeting, nothing tears down the will and creativity of a group faster than unproductive "bitch sessions" disguised as problem solving. When you need to develop an innovative solution to a major challenge, the Creative Journey provides a robust, flexible process—whether you're managing a two-year project or conducting a two-hour meeting. In my experience, you can get twice as much done, twice as effectively, in half the time (or close to it), by going through each step of the journey together.

Recall the four stages of the Creative Journey, each with two steps:

> **To develop an innovative solution to a major challenge, the Creative Journey provides a robust, flexible process**

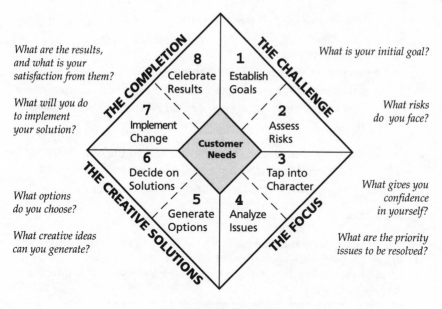

The Creative Journey

For example, imagine that your company has gone through a reorganization and downsizing, to be able to respond faster to rapid fluctuations in customer needs and market demands (is this too hard to imagine?). You're part of a team with representatives from all over the organization to figure out how to improve morale. You're meeting together to get started. How do you begin tackling this challenge?

The Challenge

Your first meeting may be devoted solely to defining your challenge. Begin with any first statement, from anyone, about your goal. As a group, play with expanding or narrowing the scope until everyone agrees it is both big enough to be meaningful yet small and manageable enough to empower your group to achieve the goal or influence it. For example, you might come up with:

Key Question #1: "What's our initial goal?"
• Formulate an initial goal statement.
 To ensure positive morale in an entirely different work environment.
• Restate your initial goal in broader terms.
 To create a work environment where employees are very content and loyal to the company.

- Restate your initial goal in more narrow terms.
  To ensure clear communication and high satisfaction throughout the organization.
- Formulate your final goal statement.
  To ensure clear communication and high satisfaction among employees and management in an entirely different work environment.

In defining your goal it is important not to make it so narrow that it limits your imagination. This usually happens when you define your problem in terms of a specific solution. For example:

Instead of . . .	Say . . .
"How can we get that department to write the new procedures?"	"How can the new procedures best be communicated?
"How can we build a better mousetrap?"	"How can we respond to our "mice" overpopulation?"

To persist toward solving this challenge and meeting your goal, remember to make the goal measurable, focus on it often, and believe in its importance. Then, brainstorm what's really at stake—the risks and opportunities presented by the challenge.

Key Question #2: "What risks do we face?"
List of barriers, unanswered questions, etc.:
- Not communicating
- Different jobs, managers, agendas
- Not physically together (geography)
- "How do we measure and reward performance in the new job environment?"

John's gospel begins with, "In the beginning was the Word . . . and the Word was made flesh." Your goal is your participation in "speaking the word" so it can be made real, for the highest good of all concerned.

The Focus

As you look over your list of risks, you might feel overwhelmed, anxious, dispirited . . . or perhaps excited and pleased at the challenge. The mood of your meeting could be pretty low. If you plunge ahead to analyze the problem or generate ideas without addressing this problem, you'll likely end up with even more tension and wheel-spinning. If people's hearts aren't in it, you'll be going through the motions while people secretly don't believe you can really be successful. Every innovation process has its "dark nights" of low confidence, which must be accepted as just a natural part of the process—it's OK. After Einstein had described some previously mysterious orbit behavior of Mercury using his gravitational field equations, he said,

> *In the light of knowledge attained, the happy achievement seems almost a matter of course. But the years of anxious searching in the dark, with their intense longing, their alternations of confidence and exhaustion, and the final emergence into light—only those who have themselves experienced it can understand that I was beside myself with ecstasy for days.*[2]

To focus on what your group "brings to the party" to handle the challenge with confidence, spend some valuable meeting time identifying the strengths of each individual, the team as a whole, and the company. For example:

Key Question #3: "What gives us confidence in ourselves?"
Belief in ourselves:
- High skills, energy, positive attitude
- Work well together, have single purpose, motivated
- Recognize that "this is the way to go," executive support, financial backing

No one person in your meeting has all the information or all the ideas. Your focus will get sharper when you involve people with diverse backgrounds in analyzing the most significant issues that need to be resolved (by creative solutions in the next stage), even if it causes some tension and disagreement of perspectives. As one of the many, many ways of analyzing, you might examine the challenge from the points of view of different stakeholders. For example:

Key Question #4: "What are the priority issues to be resolved?"

Stakeholders	Key Issues
Employees	How to communicate new goals, mission
Team leaders	How to gain support from the executive team
Customers	How to service me and my priorities with fewer people
Executives	How to make the numbers and make sure the overall organization process works

Although this level of "digging in the facts" may seem tedious to some of your group, meeting together to air different viewpoints builds trust and confidence that everyone's key issues will be addressed. No one will hold back afterward, feeling that their ideas are not wanted or respected or nurse a "hidden agenda" that might emerge in the form of premature idea-killers.

The Creative Solutions

Your most stimulating, even humorous, experiences as a team can occur at meetings where you dream up creative ideas to solve your challenge. In chapters 9 and 10, you'll discover many advanced tools for stimulating more and more ideas together. At this point, however, focus on the basics of how to keep your ideas flowing and well documented.

On the wall of your meeting room, place these reminders so everyone "catches the spirit" for idea-generation:

- Stretch yourself to see the big picture.
- Take the initiative to write your ideas as soon as you think of them.
- Be confident and take a risk. Even half-baked ideas are OK.
- Try on new and different points of view.
- Generate options, using both sides of your brain.
- Don't judge your ideas prematurely.
- Keep pushing to generate as many ideas as possible.
- Reward yourself for each idea by building on it.

The difference between idea-generation and evaluation is the same as setting up a buffet dinner versus choosing items off the buffet. Evaluating ideas too early limits the range of delicacies you could eventually choose from. Be aware of how often you stop yourselves with idea-killers. Idea-killers are the thoughts we think or hear from others that awaken our fears of being impractical, stupid, unsuccessful, and on and on. These idea-killers are the statements we make to ourselves or others, like:

- "Oh, that will never work."
- "That's a crazy (or dumb) idea."
- "Top management will never go for it."
- "That's already been tried."
- "That idea is ahead of its time." (Sounds like a compliment, doesn't it?)
- _____ (silence)

We must eventually evaluate the alternatives, of course. However, the creative process works best when we separate the evaluation step from the alternative-generation step. Keeping them separate not only opens us to generate alternatives more freely, it also helps us to avoid rushing to a solution by judging too hastily, "That's the perfect solution!"

No one I've met has gone through a brainstorming session without thinking some of these idea-killers. You can use this fact to your creative advantage. Imagine a diving board. When someone jumps on the end, the board first goes down before springing the person higher into the air. An idea-killer depresses the board, and you can use it to launch into another creative idea that would solve that objection. For example, "That would be too costly" can launch new ideas by turning that statement into the question, "How can we make this idea more cost-effective?"

To capture your ideas, you might have one person write them all on flip-chart paper. Or each person might write their own ideas on Post-it pads—which is a convenient way to cluster ideas into similar concepts (something that is harder to do from flip charts). Another approach is to tape a large sheet of paper on the wall and write down the ideas as a "mind map" or "idea tree," which starts with a central topic (a product, market need, technology, or work process) and branches out into ideas. For example, suppose you want to build a new product line around your great water softener product. Your "tree" might begin something like this:

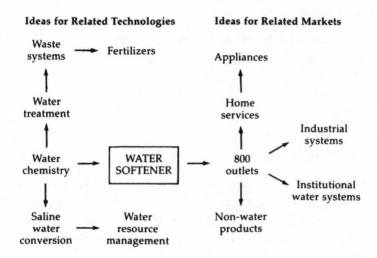

Notice that the tree in this example is a mapping of ideas that occur to people based on related technologies and markets. With other types of problems, the branches may be based on personnel, production, or other considerations. As you can see, the drawing can look confusing to an outsider, and the relationships between ideas may not be obvious. However, your intuitive mind can go to work to see relationships and patterns hidden in normal lists of ideas. By duplicating how meeting participants' minds are intuitively working, these types of maps can get you away from pat, quick-fix solutions and onto potential breakthroughs.

In our ongoing example, idea-generation looked like this:

Key Question #5: "What creative ideas can we generate?"
How to communicate new goals, mission?
• Staff meetings with managers, leaders, employees
• Newsletters

- E-mail
- Posters, plaques, banners
- "Idea fairs"
- Employee-of-the-Month awards
- Performance and idea awards
- Audiotapes
- Fifteen-minute videos for staff meetings
- Advisory Council memos

When your meeting process turns to decision making, you might start by declaring, "Each person automatically gets their favorite concept accepted into a first-draft, 'collage' solution. We'll figure out inconsistencies and missing elements from there." This usually energizes the eventual debate while keeping minds open to others' ideas. The collage solution from our example was:

Key Question #6: "What options do we choose?"
Collage of each person's top idea
- Newsletter
- Audiotapes
- Idea fair

Whether or not you take this first step, there are then many ways to assess your alternatives to make the best decision, including the following:

- *Criteria checkerboards.* Each alternative is listed on one axis of a matrix, and each criterion is listed on the other. Each alternative is rated on a specified scale (1–10, high/low/medium, +/0/-, etc.) for each criterion, and the checkerboard shows you the relative merits of the alternatives.
- *Rank ordering.* For each criterion, each alternative is compared to each other one. Each time, the "winner" gets a point. Then the scores are totalled.
- *Sorting by category.* Alternatives are grouped into categories and evaluated as synergistic "clumps" of solutions, according to a criteria checkerboard, rank ordering, or other means.

There are also many ways to then select among your alternatives, including the following:

- Choosing combinations of solutions
- Building a solution starting with one acceptable component
- Eliminating unacceptable alternatives until an acceptable solution is left
- Backing off and *not* deciding

Whatever evaluation methods your team uses, there are two keys to successful assessment and selection:

- *Letting the best solution emerge.* "Letting go" of our ego or will, and surrendering to a higher will can ultimately bring us more satisfying and productive decision making. The solutions tend to be more easily and effectively implemented.

    Sometimes we might have a pet solution, a hidden agenda, an important self-interest (financial or otherwise), or a desire for a "convenient" solution. Or we might take persistence to the point of narrowly focused stubbornness. These can hinder us in objectively seeing the highest good of all.
- *Using intuition and emotions.* At times, facts and figures can be manipulated to support all sorts of ideas, sometimes at odds with what seems intuitively correct. Whether dealing with a new customer or a new idea, getting a feel for the situation and acting with that extra "data" can make or break a decision.

If a meeting ends up with ideas that "make logical sense" but don't inspire intuitive or emotional commitment, the solution or decision that comes out of that meeting will be mediocre at best. Use the enthusiasm test (see page 128) again to ensure that the decision matches what people stand for—their own values and purpose.

The Completion

For your team to be successful, you must act on the decision(s) made. Some people love the meetings where you come up with ideas but quickly get disinterested when the time comes to act. Just because a great idea has been generated doesn't mean the work is done. Action takes courage. Even an Einstein must *write* his formulas and *document* and *defend* his data and insights to get them accepted. You have to document, support, even fight for your ideas with passion, at least to a strategic handoff point where others can take it further.

> For your team to be successful, you must act on the decision(s) made.

Base realistic action on commitments that align with your personal purpose and values. True commitment frees rather than restricts you. For example, dancers with commitment learn skills that allow them to express movements that most of us can't; through their commitment, which involves *action* (practice), they develop and earn a freedom of movement most of us do not enjoy. Meeting together, you must by all means be totally honest about what you feel authentically enthused about and what your team can count on you for. Only then do you have true commitments, ones that free you to *act* and make midcourse corrections rather than restrict you through ongoing disappointments and problems.

To provide sustainable energy for completing your work, meet together to plan how to meet both short- and long-term achievements, as our continuing example demonstrates:

Key Question #7: "What will we do to implement our solution?"

Solution	Short Term	Long Term
Newsletter	Ideas for content and format	Staffing and first issue
Audiotapes	Record old speech texts and memos	Record scripted messages; full distribution
Idea Fair	Buy-in by management and employees	Logistics planned and date set

Setting a short- and long-term action plan might be easy, but the meetings where you have to actually follow up can be the most difficult meetings you'll face. Have commitments been kept fully? Have they been met on time and on budget? Are we each doing our part towards achieving our goal?

During any plane flight, there is a constant interaction between the piloting and navigation, whether done automatically or in person. With all the variations of winds, pressure areas, and other factors, a plane must constantly make midcourse corrections. For even as much as 95 percent of the flight, the plane is off course to some degree! Yet the sum of all the midcourse corrections results in a successful landing. Your meetings provide the forum for this process of self-correction, using a set of success measures you define together. Our model team generated these ultimate measures of success, along with a set of satisfactions and rewards they and others would find fulfilling:

Key Question #8: "What are the results and our satisfactions from them?"

Measures of Success	Satisfactions/Rewards
Understand mission	More time—less stress
High energy and spirit	Recognition
High survey scores	More enjoyment
Higher productivity	Higher appraisal ratings

Your team needs more than just feedback in this stage of completion. The former CEO of Intel Corporation, Andrew Grove, has stated that we prevent work satisfaction for some people by divorcing them from the output of their work; then they usually play unproductive games. Others have had jobs where the work seemed endless—a constant flow of projects with no ending points to appreciate. And how many times have you heard the complaint, "I never hear about the good work I do, but make one mistake and I never hear the end of it."

What happens to creativity in either situation? For most of us, the creative process needs a point of completion where we truly experience our results, even if they are not what we expected and/or wanted. You renew your energy for the next challenge by talking together about what you did or didn't achieve, and what you have learned that can make a difference to you and others in the future. Debrief the entire process, meeting after meeting. For each stage of the Creative Journey discuss how well you fostered an open, questioning "CREATIVE" climate for experimenting with new ideas, and how well you personally brought out the "SPIRITED" qualities in yourself and each other.

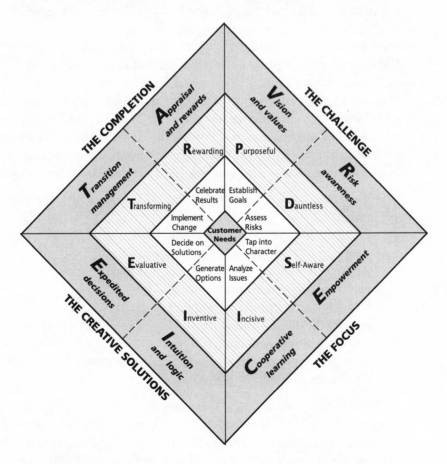

The "CREATIVE" Climate Supports the Creative Journey

Link your outcomes back with your individual purposes and values, and see how your own, personal journey in life has been enhanced. Taking the time to express gratitude for what you experience together—not just at the end, but through all your meetings—replenishes your spirits and gives you greater soul-satisfaction.

REFINING THE CORPORATE INNOVATION PROCESS

The Creative Journey takes individuals and teams on a robust (exhausting but invigorating) course down the road to resolving problems and meeting challenges. But how does it fare as a model for corporate innovation? After all, the process of business innovation is highly uncertain and unpredictable. James Brian Quinn, a Dartmouth College business professor, and others have researched this matter and found that less than 25 percent of major business innovation results from highly structured planning systems. The artistry of managing innovation requires a delicate balance between the evolutionary stages and the "disorganized" process of innovation.

Parallel to this unpredictability, an idea for a new product must be subjected to various phases of evaluation and development, must survive key decision points, and must reach certain milestones to be implemented and be successful. You might think, it's a wonder that any novel idea ever gets introduced or acted on! The Creative Journey provides a simple way to map this complexity. For example, a consumer products company identified the following needs for improving their innovation process and shortening the new-product development cycle:

- Institute a more formal process for identifying and evaluating ideas.
- Focus on long-term issues and problems.
- Respond faster to changing market conditions.
- Appreciate and value intuition, not just logic.
- Develop a system for transmitting ideas.
- Develop better criteria for judging ideas.
- Prevent "killing" of good ideas.
- Reduce management approval time.
- Give higher priority to ideas with very high potential return on investment.

Management designed a team-oriented product development process (page 149) that included ongoing consultation between the team and its executive sponsors. The simplicity of this process—this map—made it much more likely that people would collaborate to ensure rapid and creative new product development.

Targeted Activites to Facilitate the Creative Journey

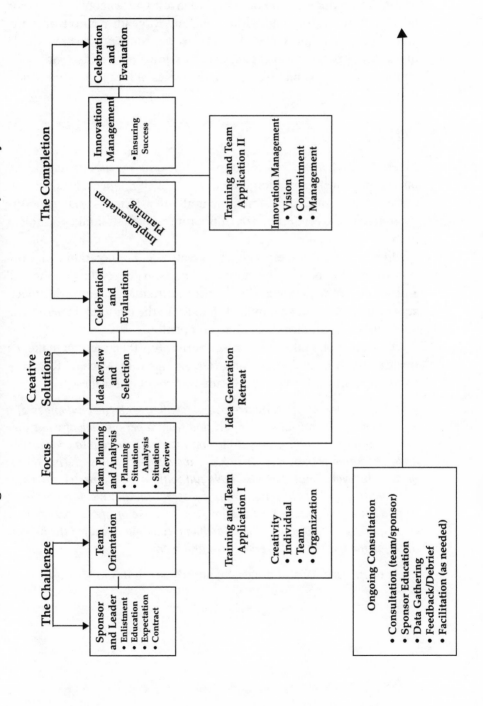

How well do you know the steps required to carry an idea through your organization? Is the process flexible or cumbersome? Is it simple enough to encourage you and others to invest your energy to champion an idea? Is it rigorous enough to hone and forge ideas into truly valuable concepts? If not, you and others need to aim your creative thinking at the process itself. The Creative Journey stands ready as a template to assist you in remapping the stages of idea generation where you work.

IN CLOSING . . .

Meetings have an incredible impact, not only on *what* gets accomplished in your organization, but also on *how* it happens. Productivity, morale, teamwork, and commitment all are affected. Usually it takes much longer to recuperate from a poor meeting than it takes to hold it in the first place.

Effective meetings, especially for creative idea-generation and problem solving, can be a real pain or a real pleasure, depending on the skill and sensitivity with which they are conducted. Managing your meetings properly can make a huge difference in the emotional energy you invest in seeing an idea through to completion.

As your group takes a Creative Journey together, you can make it a spiritual quest of the *group* character. As stated by Michael Ray, professor at Stanford University's Graduate School of Business,

> *The real heroes of today are people dealing with the challenges of a world in chaotic transition . . . operating from a perspective of what they can do in service, competing yet moving more and more into cooperation and co-creation with others. They know the difficulty and suffering that is part of this world. But they also have full faith in their inner creativity or spirit with its infinite intuition, will, joy, strength, and most importantly, compassion. They know that the joy and promise of life is taking these inner qualities and bringing them forth in a constant quest for the highest good for themselves and everyone around them.[3]*

It takes practice and diligence, but it's worth it. Go for it.

CHAPTER 9

Generate Ideas
by Modifying and Experimenting

I almost overanalyze a problem from a logical, structural perspective—
What are the pieces, what are the implications of this and that, what
are the relationships? It's a very three-dimensional puzzle. The most
creative example was a market research study I did for an amusement
park on how many people might visit a new attraction. The problem in
doing the project was that you can use any given fraction of visitors
you want, and "whoopee" you have any answer you want.

We tried to figure out a way to structure it so that you couldn't give
the "right" answer. I came up with a way involving the fraction of the
people going to attractions, the average number of attractions that
people visit, and people's ranking of attractions. I just sat down and
played with the equations and it all fell in place. The result was within
one percentage point of eventual, actual statistics.

—BRUCE, LITIGATION ANALYSIS CONSULTANT

BECOMING "FLUENT"

Often the hardest part of generating new solutions is knowing where
and how to begin looking for them. Whether you're seeking to create
new material artifacts, new concepts, new spontaneous happenings,
new events, new organizing principles, new modes of relationship, or
new inner experiences, it's often useful to have structured ways of jour-
neying to discovery.

In chapter 4, you discovered that each person employs a mixture
of four distinct Innovation Styles, each with its own unique question
to stimulate new ideas:

- Visioning: What ideas gives us an ideal future?
- Modifying: What ideas optimize what we've done?
- Experimenting: What ideas combine different elements?
- Exploring: What ideas start with totally new assumptions?

You can study hundreds of different idea-generation tools in books today, but these techniques are all variations of the four basic styles. For example, you could write a "wish list" of everything you wished could happen to resolve a challenge. Or you could close your eyes and vividly imagine having everything you wanted. Those are different techniques, but both represent the same basic style: They ask you for an ideal, Visioning solution.

You can become more "fluent" in all four styles by learning more detailed techniques for thinking creatively in each style. In this chapter and the next, you'll learn a total of fifteen idea-generation tools—three to five techniques for each of the four styles, as shown below.

VISIONING

- Wish List
- Future Annual Report
- Visualization

M O D I F Y I N G

- Force-Field
- Attribute Listing
- "S C A M P E R"

- Guided Imagery
- Analogy
- Forced Association
- Dreaming
- Drawing

E X P L O R I N G

- Matrix Analysis
- Morphological Analysis
- Nature of the Business
- Alternate Scenarios

EXPERIMENTING

Whenever you're facilitating idea-generation, you'll benefit greatly by knowing which techniques belong to which style. You can better select the techniques that will work for a particular mix of people, or which tools to introduce first and last. For example, a group of people who strongly prefer Modifying will not start well with Exploring techniques, but could warm up to their value if they were used later. And you'll be less likely to load a session with all Visioning techniques just because that's *your* favorite style.

This chapter contains Modifying and Experimenting tools, which are presented together because both styles begin with gathering facts, details, and other data. Modifying builds on what is known, while Experimenting combines the components in new and novel ways. In a sense, both of these styles are more "linear" than intuitive, in their approach to generating ideas. They take advantage of different ways of organizing known information to help you approach problems from new and more comprehensive angles. Using a logical pattern or a sequence of steps, they help focus your attention on *where* to look for innovations. When you finally see your solutions, you might almost nonchalantly think, "Of course . . . there's the solution."

> **Modifying builds on what is known, while Experimenting combines the components in new and novel ways.**

USING MODIFYING TECHNIQUES

Modifying techniques all embody the basic compass question (see page 73): "What ideas could adapt or modify what we've done?"

Force-Field Analysis

This method was first developed by Kurt Lewin, a social psychologist. Its name comes from its ability to identify forces contributing to or hindering a solution to a problem, and it can stimulate your creative thinking in three ways: (1) to define what you are working toward (your vision), (2) to identify strengths you can maximize, and (3) to identify weaknesses you can minimize. The method is quite simple.

Using a format like the one that follows, pick a situation you would like to see changed—for example, your product line, work conditions, or relationship with your boss.

1. Write a brief statement of the problem you wish to solve (write objectively, as if you were a newspaper reporter).
2. Now describe what the situation would be like if everything fell apart—absolute catastrophe.
3. Now describe what the situation would be like if it were ideal.

4. Presume the center line represents your current situation. "Catastrophe" and "ideal" are playing tug-of-war. Fill in what forces are tugging *right now* at your situation to help make it more ideal and what forces are trying *right now* to make it more catastrophic.

Suppose you want to explore how to foster a better climate for innovation and creativity in your organization? Using observations from the example in chapter 6, your force field would include the elements in this analysis:

FORCE-FIELD ANALYSIS

(1) Problem: How to foster a better climate
for innovation *and* creativity.

(2) Catastrophe: No innovation in products or marketing	(3) Optimum: High innovation with responsible risk

(4) Forces

−	+
A person with a new product idea not knowing where to take the idea if his/her supervisor doesn't like it	A new product succeeding in the market because of up-to-date information on consumer values and lifestyles
A brainstorming meeting producing uninspired or impractical ideas or ideas that don't get acted on	An individual finding time to incubate a problem, literally "dreaming up" a solution
Performance appraisals and rewards that encourage short-term profits and status quo operations at the expense of long-term investment in needed innovations	Senior management clearly stating a vision of the organization's future and the requirements for market-oriented, innovative new products and services

The primary function of the force field in idea-generation is to present three different stimuli for thinking of new options or solutions. Because the field represents a kind of tug-of-war, there are three ways to move the center line in the direction of the more desirable future:

1. Strengthen an already present positive force
2. Weaken an already present negative force
3. Add a new positive force

Therefore, the force field presents you with focuses for exploring possible solutions. You can then employ matrix analysis or other idea-generation techniques. The primary benefit of the force field is that it identifies strong points in a situation as well as problem areas. These strong points can be the foundation of the most effective solutions, which might have been overlooked otherwise.

Attribute Listing

Whether you have a procedure, product, or process you wish to improve, one method of getting ideas is to write down all the attributes or components and see how you can improve upon any one or all of them.

For example, a bicycle has these attributes among others:

- Frame
- Pedals
- Drive sprocket
- Chain
- Rear sprocket and chain guide
- Brakes
- Tires
- Handlebars

Each attribute has seen dramatic improvements and innovations in the last thirty years, including:

- Much lighter-weight frames based on new, lightweight materials
- Pedal grips and straps to secure feet better
- Double-drive sprocket for ten gear capabilities
- Stronger chains with special clamps for easier changing
- Improved derailleur gears for rear sprocket
- Hand brakes that grip tires to replace rear axle brakes
- Racing handlebars for more effective racing position

Attribute listing is similar to force-field analysis. The force field provides specific negative and positive aspects of the problem, whereas attribute listing provides neutral aspects. Both identify categories in which improvements might be found.

SCAMPER

Alex Osborn, a pioneer in creativity facilitation, developed a list of "idea-spurring questions" that were later arranged by Bob Eberle as the mnemonic SCAMPER:[1]

S = Substitute? (other ingredients, material, power, place . . .)
C = Combine? (blend, alloy; combine purposes, appeals . . .)
A = Adapt?
M = Modify? (color, shape, motion . . .)
  Magnify? (stronger, larger, thicker, extra value . . .)

P = Put to other uses?
E = Eliminate?
R = Reverse? (roles; try opposites, upside down . . .)
      Rearrange? (pattern, sequence, pace, components . . .)

Apply these questions to your situation and see what ideas emerge. If you wanted to develop a new office procedure or work flow, you could first identify all the steps currently being taken. Looking at your list, use SCAMPER as a mind jogger to imagine many different ways to do the same work.

Many new products have been developed using *opposites*, or the reverse. King-sized cigarettes came from "short-long"; sidewall tires from "black-white"; powered car windows from "manual-powered"; and so on. Substitution has also been important. Milk cartons substituted paper for glass. Fiber-reinforced composite materials have been used in tennis rackets and airplanes as substitutes for materials with inferior strength-to-weight ratios.

USING EXPERIMENTING TECHNIQUES

Experimenting techniques are all variations on the theme "What ideas could combine different elements?" They start with understanding all the key variables for analyzing a situation, and then generate ideas for each combination, or intersection, of those variables.

Matrix Analysis

Imagine you want to develop some new product ideas. After having identified various market needs, available technologies, and product functions (what the product *does*) you might develop a two- or three-dimensional matrix to identify where to explore for new ideas. For example, you might use a market-technology matrix, as shown below.

TECHNOLOGIES	MARKETS			
	A	B	C	D
1				
2			x	
3				
4				
5				

Every intersection (x) represents a place to look for new innovations that apply a particular technology to a particular market. For example, to develop a packaging product for a plastics firm, your matrix might be very similar to this:

TECHNOLOGIES	**MARKETS**			
	Transport	Medical	Beverage	Industrial
Co-extrusion				
Resin blend		*x*		
Laminates				
Adhesives				
Thermoform				

Perhaps you would use a market-functions matrix instead. For the purposes of idea stimulation, you would assume that you could develop or find any technology needed. Your market-functions matrix might resemble this:

FUNCTIONS	**MARKETS**			
	Transport	Medical	Beverage	Industrial
Damage resistance				
Moisture barrier		*x*		
Reusable				
Lightweight				
High temperature range				

Within each matrix you could explore new packaging ideas and even fill in the possible technologies to be applied, thus making a "working" three-dimensional matrix.

Morphological Analysis

This is a fancy title for a very simple and convenient way of generating solutions to problems that have many variables to consider. For example, suppose you want to invent a new mode of transporting people and things. You must take into account:

- The driving force
- The mode of movement
- The material used in construction
- The primary purpose

Within each of these issues there are many alternatives to be considered. For example, under "driving force" you could list these possibilities: diesel, gas turbine, steam, pedal, electric motor, squirrels in a cage, horse, and wind. And under "mode of movement" you could list: rail, wheel, rollers, coasters, air cushion, water, and so on.

If you make a similar list underneath each of the issues, you get a table similar to this:

DRIVING FORCE	MODE OF MOVEMENT	MATERIAL	PURPOSE
diesel	rail	plastic	people
gas turbine	wheel	metals	animals
steam	rollers	wood	heavy freight
pedal	coasters	stone	baggage
electric	air cushion	cloth	foods and spices
squirrels in a cage	water	glass	plants
horse			
wind			

You can develop new ideas by combining anything from the first column with anything from the second plus anything from the third and fourth. For example, how about a steam-driven vehicle that rides on coasters, is made of stone, and is used for carrying heavy freight? Or how about a squirrel-driven vehicle that floats on an air cushion, is made of plastic, and is used to transport spices?

The ideas that emerge from this method can range from the very practical to the very outlandish. Although some of the ideas from this method will be eliminated after the first evaluation, they certainly open up the alternatives to consider—alternatives that might otherwise be overlooked. And even if the particular option isn't the correct solution, it may provide the stimulus for someone to devise the winning idea.

This method can work with any number of issues or variables. For example, imagine you wanted to find new opportunities in the food industry. You would deal with many food issues, including forms, kinds, properties, processes, and packages. Some of the particulars of these issues might include those in the table on page 159.

Pick one or two items from each list to make a complete idea. How about a soup made of fruit and spices with medicinal properties (antihistamines?), packaged as a freeze-dried product in small sacks?

FORMS	KINDS	PROPERTIES	PROCESSES	PACKAGES
preserves	meat	cost	ferment	bottle
drink	vegetable	convenience	freeze dry	can
chips	fish	nutrition	compact	pouch
flake	fruit	taste	blend	foil/paper
stew	dairy	texture	form	aerosol
roll	grains	odor	fried	box
soup	nuts	viscosity	bake	cup
topping	spices	medicinal	stir	sack
snack				

A primary benefit of this method is that it conveniently structures the search for creative solutions of complex problems in a logical way that is easy to follow. Besides, it can be a lot of fun.

Nature of the Business

How the people in an organization define the nature of their business can have a tremendous impact on what they do and how they do it. When the Southland Corporation realized that their 7-11 stores were not really in the "grocery" business but rather the "convenience" business, it led them to an entirely different marketing strategy and inventory for their stores.

Businesses can define and organize themselves in many different ways, according to:

- Their products or services ("a steel strapping company")
- The markets they serve ("products for the transportation industry")
- The functions they serve ("products for shipping stabilization")
- Their technologies ("products based on steel and polymer technologies")

For example, a bank could be defined as being in the financial business, the management-assistance business, (with financial resources to help implement management decisions), an information-processing business, or the achievement-and-experience-development business (with resources that enable a person to achieve his/her own entrepreneurial firm or to experience world travel).

If you were to work in a bank, its business definition might give you very different ideas for products and services. For instance, as a financial business you might offer loan packages and trust investment services. As a management-assistance business, you might offer software packages for a client's financial decision making or management consulting on corporate acquisitions. As an information-processing business, you might offer market-analysis services tailored to a specific company's target markets. As an achievement-and-experience-development firm, you might operate a travel agency in the banking offices or develop small business education packages (perhaps as computer-aided instruction).

Virtually all companies are going through some redefinition of their business during this decade. For example, is a company that pays for health-related expenses in the *insurance* business or in the *health-care coverage* business? Depending on the answers, organizations in the health care industries—from insurers to hospitals to pharmaceutical firms—are supporting or fighting different payment schemes, trends for self-insuring businesses, expansion of health maintenance organizations (HMOs), proposals for government involvement, and so on. The stakes are high and getting higher as health costs escalate.

Building on this technique and using the morphological analysis method just described, you could explore the nature of your business by combining individual opportunity ideas in multiple ways. For example, you might want new plastics packaging products, but what really is your business? Your variables would be markets, functions, technologies, products, services, and process equipment. You could first make a *key-word* index as seen below.

MARKETS	FUNCTIONS	TECHNOLOGIES
beverage	damage resistance	adhesives
medical	moisture barrier	laminates
industrial	reusable	coextrusion
transportation	lightweight	thermoform
toys	high temperature	resin blend

PRODUCTS	SERVICES	PROCESS EQUIPMENT
cans	leasing	case opener
cups	manufacturing supply	lidding machine
trays	repair	wrap machine
pouches	training whole systems	depalletizer
cartons		conveyor

Every new idea could then be expressed in terms of these key words. One idea, for example, might be a damage-resistant, thermo-formed can for the toy industry, with case operation equipment and manufacturing supply services also provided.

With all ideas expressed in terms of key words, a computer can sort all the ideas for a given item, for example, a business built around the beverage market or damage-resistant functions or adhesive technologies. This type of ordering makes it easy to cluster the opportunities to show overlaps in market penetration, to demonstrate the viability of technology investments, and so on. From these insights you can examine the possible primary definitions of the type of business that would take advantage of your best opportunities.

Alternative Scenarios

There are two primary ways to explore the range of possibilities for the future: hypothetical situations and alternative scenarios. Both are excellent in generating new approaches to business by breaking habitual ways of perceiving the environment.

With hypothetical situations you make up something and solve it: "If a particular set of conditions prevailed in my industry ten years from now, what would I do—then and now? To what conditions is my organization most vulnerable? What can we do in response to these vulnerabilities?"

Alternate scenarios are a more comprehensive way of asking these same questions. Scenarios are qualitatively different descriptions of plausible futures. They give you a deeper understanding of potential environments in which you might have to operate and what you may need to do in the present.[2]

When managers do long-range planning based on a single forecast of trends—a single notion of what their market and business will be like in two, five, or ten years—they are actually taking the risk of "betting the company" on that single forecast. Even with "high, low, and probable" projections, the first question usually asked about a forecast is, "Given its assumptions, how far off can it be?" Besides being risky, this practice can also prompt people to avoid action during uncertain times, paralyzing management decision making. Scenarios help you to identify what environmental factors to monitor over time, so that when the environment shifts, you can recognize where it is shifting *to*.

Thinking through several scenarios is a less risky, more conservative approach to planning than relying on single forecasts and trend analyses. It can thus free up management to take more innovative actions. (Curiously, many Japanese and European firms seem very open to using alternate scenarios. American companies often think that planning more than three to five years ahead is somewhat impractical and that forecasts are suitable for such time periods.)

Rather than being general "future histories," scenarios are developed specifically for a particular problem. To begin developing scenarios, first state the specific decision that needs to be made. Then identify the major environmental forces that impact the decision. For example, suppose you need to decide how to invest R&D funds in order to be positioned for opportunities that might emerge by the year 2000. The major environmental forces might include social values, economic growth worldwide, and international trade access (tariffs, and so on).

Now, actually build four scenarios based on the principal forces. To do this use information available to you to identify four plausible and qualitatively different possibilities for each force. Assemble the al-

DRIVING FORCES	SCENARIOS
	BUSINESS TODAY
ECONOMIC	
Interest rates	Moderate-high, 8–10%
Economic health	Relatively slow growth
U.S. foreign trade	Deficit
Third World debt	Confidence in Third World
U.S. budget	Deficit/no panic
Protectionist legislation	No legislation/none of significance
TECHNOLOGICAL	
Imaging/internal process	Read only
Cable/satellite	80%
Home computers	60% affluent/30% general
"Pacing" technology	No major breakthroughs
COMPETITOR	
Consolidation of industry	High
Intensity	Very intense
Options (relative)	Many
Technical usage	Not significant

ternatives for each force into internally consistent "stories," with both a narrative and a table of forces and scenarios: Build your scenarios around these forces. Each scenario will have a story line.

A midwestern bank used scenarios to stimulate new ideas for maintaining a strong consumer-lending business in the face of heated competition with brokerage firms, insurance companies, and other financial services providers. Scenario story lines emerged for "Business Today," "Heated," "Belt Tightening," and "Isolation." The following chart details each of the bank's scenarios (some driving forces have been omitted):[3]

With the scenarios in hand, identify business opportunities within each scenario. Then examine the links and synergies of opportunities across the range of scenarios. This will help you to formulate a more realistic strategy for investment.

Using these scenarios helps identify what environmental factors to monitor over time. When the environment shifts, you can recognize where it is shifting *to*.

HEATED	BELT TIGHTENING	ISOLATION
High, 10–12%	Moderate-low, 6–9%	Low, 5–7%
Rapid growth, inflation	No recession/less disposable income	Recession
Balanced	Deficit	Deficit
Confidence in Third	Third World okay, with restrictions	Concern high
Deficit	Balanced	Deficit
Mutual trade	Low–moderate legislation	Moderate-high legislation
Interactive/read	Interactive	Read only
90% (20% 2 way)	70%	50%
70%/35%	50%/25%	40%/20%
Breakthroughs	Breakthroughs	No major breakthroughs
Moderate	High	Moderate (federal controls); moderate number of failures
Intense	Intense	Less intense
Many	Some	Few
Major applications widespread	Few applications in a concentrated number of companies	No major advantages

IN CLOSING . . .

There are many other Modifying and Experimenting techniques to stimulate your creative problem solving and to give you a clearer path for your follow-up actions: Kepner-Tregoe, value engineering, Delphi, and mathematical analyses of data, just to name a few. All of these can be employed by you individually or as part of a group.

Either way, these techniques are very powerful in showing you *where* to look for innovations. They are complemented by the power of the intuitive techniques to tap your inner source of creative insight. That is the subject of the next chapter.

CHAPTER 10

Generate Ideas by *Visioning* and *Exploring*

I'm valuing more and more the whole area of visualization, or imagery techniques. When I'm talking with a person about her skills, values, and interests, sometimes I will get an image, a picture of something. Often, I feed this back to her and ask, "What do you think? Does this make sense?" It will clarify something she wasn't able to put into words.

I recently was working with an incredibly brilliant woman who is getting to be nationally famous in her field. She could out-logic anybody in the world. In career counseling we went through skill analysis and values, all this analytical stuff. She came back and said, "Well, so, I'm still not clear about what it all means."

I said, "Well, let's take all that analytical stuff and put it away. Just close your eyes and reflect a bit." It worked into a visualization about going and talking to an inner advisor. I led up to it by having her talk to different animals, plants, inanimate objects, getting messages from what they "said" to her. She saw herself as a weeping willow in one case, and that really had significance for her. She was absolutely blown away. It gave her clues that she wouldn't have gotten from logical analysis.

—DIANE, CAREER COUNSELOR AT A RESEARCH FACILITY

TUNING IN

The Visioning and Exploring styles start with an intuitive insight, hunch, or hypothesis; then they gather information to confirm and "fill out" their intuition. The difference between these two styles is that Visioning searches for a clear mental "picture" of the future. Exploring often employs symbols to sense what is metaphorically possible.

Modifying and Experimenting techniques structure information and point out where to look for new ideas. Visioning and Exploring techniques take advantage of our right-brain capability to perceive whole solutions in sudden leaps of logic. Our intuition is more fluent in images, sounds, and symbols than in words—as in our day and night dreams. Intuitive techniques take advantage of the insights prompted by these images, sounds, and symbols.

While the road to your intuitive insight is often paved with logical, linear thinking, the logical, *without* intuition and emotion, is actually irrational, because it is not based on our full capacity for problem solving. Logic alone is not whole, and thus cannot produce whole, reality-based solutions or promote the integral, long-term health of any person or organization.

The realm of intuition is *not* unreal or untrustworthy. Our intuition remembers data that our conscious mind has stored away. It is our inner, intuitive world that is constantly giving us the guidance and answers to our questions about living and problem solving, *especially* when our logical, linear thinking reaches its limit.

When using intuitive techniques, an important assumption—or truth—is that at some level *you already know the answer.* You already have that which you are seeking. It is as if you had misplaced your favorite jewelry somewhere in your top drawer; if you keep looking, you will eventually find it. This is a different perspective from, "Is there an answer?" or "Will I ever solve this?" The assumption that you *already know* can open the main door to the solution.

> When using intuitive techniques, an important assumption—or truth— is that at some level *you already know the answer.*

To tune in properly to your intuition, it is important to realize that your intuitive self is *not* the same as your subconscious. Your subconscious includes memories and related thoughts and emotions, which may actively affect your day-to-day life. Your intuitive self comes through when such subconscious rumblings have been quieted.

In this chapter we'll look at eight Visioning and Exploring tools I've found to be most useful in solving work-related challenges. For Visioning, the tools are the wish list, future annual report, and visualization. For Exploring, they are guided imagery, analogy, forced association, dreaming, and drawing. These are all effective means of using your intuition to evoke new insights and new ideas.

USING VISIONING TECHNIQUES

Visioning techniques all reflect the Compass question (see pages 73–73): "What ideas would give us an ideal future?"

Wish List

This is the easiest technique to describe but sometimes the hardest for people to use because they must "let go" and let themselves be "unrealistic." Simply put, use of the wish list technique is a matter of temporarily assuming you have *all* the resources you'd ever need and can have *anything* you'd ever want—as if you have a fairy godmother or genie who is ready to grant you any wish. All you have to do is wish for the boldest, most unlimited, most outrageous thing you want. What *do* you wish for?

For example, if you had $20 million and gave yourself the next ten years to do absolutely anything you want, even if you'd never even started learning or training for it before now, what different things do you wish you could do? Let yourself dream.

- Travel throughout Asia for a year?
- Race sports cars?
- Research dolphin behavior and communication?
- Be a sportscaster or a golf pro?
- Help inner city children get a better education?
- Start your own business?
- Visit and study in monasteries throughout the world?

Take a few minutes to make *your* wish list.

Whatever your answers, what do you discover about yourself? Pick one thing you brainstormed and answer, "What would it actually take for me to do this, assuming I had all the money, family permission, and whatever else I'd need?" Finally, "What would it take for me to do this in the coming years, even in my present circumstances?"

The difficulty for some people is that the wish list technique starts with an "unrealistic" premise of unlimited resources; we're so conditioned to "be practical" within our present circumstances. However, this technique often uncovers the seed of an idea that you *can* make real! Its power comes from your willingness and courage to think beyond your normal limits. The next time you're in a brainstorming session and thinking, "When is this blue sky session going to get real?", remember to open up to the possibility of a stretch idea that could catapult you to the next level—to what would then seem realistic.

Future Annual Report

At SRI International, we once worked with the top executives of Nokia Electronics in Finland to envision where they wanted to lead their company. The first exercise was to write, in some detail, their potential annual report for seven years in the future: What did they see as their products, services, organization, revenues, profits, and so forth, as well as what would their global industry be like? This tangible, detailed exercise captured their dreams of what they wanted to become. After that, we had them take specific parts of the report and strategize what it would take to get there.

Another version of this exercise is to jump three to five years into the future and write a news article, "Looking Back Three to Five Years," describing your most outstanding team/company accomplishments for those years. All the key achievements you would ideally like to see, assuming everything goes perfectly as you envision, should be included. For example, your article might read:

Since 1993, sales of our division have grown at a rate of 15 percent annually, and we've doubled in size over five years from $250 million to $500 million. Even more astounding, our profits have quadrupled, due in part to the breakthrough work of our quality teams. We established a new Quantum Quality program, educated everyone in breakthrough creativity techniques, and even got our customers' customers involved in defining what we could do better. We cut product development time by 10x and received the industry award for most outstanding customer satisfaction.

Key achievements, therefore, were:

- Establishing a new Quantum Quality program
- Educating everyone in breakthrough creativity techniques
- Getting customers' customers involved
- Cutting product development time tenfold
- Receiving the industry award for most outstanding customer satisfaction

The final step in this exercise is to take each of these idealized future achievements and brainstorm first steps you can take, in present time, to move toward each of them. Like the exercise the Nokia executives did, this technique produces a list of ideal goals, but one tempered by more tangibly "living in the present," without sacrificing the level of imagination and attention to detail that allows people to let go of limited thinking.

Visualization

In visualization, you use your imagination to come up with realistic, vivid scenes of the future. It's different from fantasy because the images are like "actual movies about the future." (*Fantasy*, as I use the word, is more like flying on a magic carpet, talking to a bird in flight— some of the metaphorical images that are so useful in the Exploring style, as we shall see.)

For example, I consulted with a company that wanted to expand their bowling business. Instead of defining the project as "What can we do to replace our automatic pinsetter technology?", we chose a Visioning approach and asked "If we were customers, what would be our ideal experience of being in a bowling center?" This broader definition opened up all sorts of room for people to wish for anything they'd like to have happen. One person said, "Well, I'd like to have my personal bowling coach go with me wherever I go bowling to help me improve my game." That wish, among others, is now being turned into a reality through computer and video technology. Visualization can help you to pay attention to your dreams and wishes so that you're more likely to be satisfied with the outcome.

Apply this exercise to your career to find ideas that reflect your best wishes for the future. As you think about your career, keep the question in mind, "Where would I like to be in my job and career in the long term—in say, the next five years?"

Visualization starts with a period of relaxation. Have you ever seen a sports team or a player lose a game by being either too tense or too lackadaisical? It's the winning players who find a balance between being loose and fluid and still maintaining a great deal of concentration. Creativity is greatly enhanced when you are in this state of relaxed attention for two reasons: When your mind is empty of mental chatter, you're more open to ideas and new solutions. And when you're relaxed, you can more easily let go of the emotions that can block creativity such as anger, overconfidence, embarrassment, and fear.

To begin, sit comfortably with your back fairly straight and your feet on the floor. This will help to keep you attentive while you're relaxing. You may wish to close your eyes if that feels more comfortable. Begin by focusing on your breath, noticing whether it is deep or shallow, fast or slow. You don't have to change it, but if you want, you can take a deep breath or two and then breathe at a pace that makes you feel the most comfortable. Be sure to let go of any of your day-to-day concerns. Let them just slip away as you relax and concentrate on your breathing.

Each time that you inhale, imagine a light, warm breeze swirling through your lungs, through your abdomen, and throughout your body. Everywhere it goes—into your arms and legs and head—it massages away, it blows away any tension that you're feeling. As you exhale, the air gently carries all tension away and you begin to feel more and more relaxed with each breath. Feel yourself becoming more relaxed yet staying very alert and very aware of your breath.

Remember that the purpose of this exercise is to find ideas that reflect your ideal work in the future. The first time through this exercise, you might not get a totally clear picture. If that happens, try it again.

Eventually, this exercise will help you to discover your ideal situation. As you think about your career, you might ask, "Where would I like to be in my job and career in the long term?

Now, imagine that in front of you there are five calendars for the next five years. A strong gust of wind begins to blow the pages away. As they peel off, one after the other, you realize that you've been transported five years into the future. Imagine that it is actually the year that is marked on the last calendar page.

Describe your ideal work day or week or week in that year. Be sure to take the time to write down the first things that pop into your mind, no matter how wild, crazy, or impossible they seem.

1. First, imagine waking up on a Monday morning and getting ready for work. In as much detail as possible, what are you doing? Are you getting dressed? Exercising? Eating breakfast? Reading the newspaper or a magazine? Imagine feeling very refreshed and eager to go to your job because you'll be doing exactly what you love to do.

2. Now you're heading off to work. What kind of transportation are you taking? If you're in a vehicle, feel it sway on the curves of the road, or the track, or gliding effortlessly on the water. If you're walking, feel your feet as they move along the ground. Imagine all of the sounds around you. Remember, this is your ideal future and your ideal way of getting to work.

3. Go into your workplace and notice your surroundings. If there are people there, greet them and then go to your desk or work space. Now, take a look at the "to do" list you have written down for Monday or the entire week, imagining that everything on the list is something that you're looking forward to doing. What's on your list? Take time now to actually compose this "to do" list. Write down everything you'd ideally like to see on it. Imagine yourself going through the day doing the first thing on your list, then the second, and so on. Be as vivid as possible in your imagination—actually have the conversations you'd like to have . . . make the things you'd like to make . . . hear the things you'd like to hear.

4. Now check up on a situation that had troubled you five years ago and notice that it's turned out perfectly. Envision the solutions to that situation. How do you feel about achieving all this? What does that say about you?

5. Now see yourself firmly in this picture of the future and look back. Imagine the steps you might have taken to get there with

as much detail as you can. Imagine the journey year by year until you've covered all five years.

Now, in case the steps seem a little fuzzy, try it again. Relive the steps you took to get there once again, even more vividly. How does it feel, knowing that you're going to succeed? Finally, check your "to do" list and see if there's anything you'd like to add to your ideal picture of your future workday.

When you have finished with this visualization, write down all the key elements. As the final step, brainstorm ways you can begin to actualize what you have visualized. This is where the present-time practicality part of idealizing enters the picture!

USING EXPLORING TECHNIQUES

Exploring techniques all ask: "What ideas could start with totally new assumptions?"

Guided Imagery

Guided imagery implies the use of symbols, scenes, or images as windows to intuitive creative thought. A circle, a gurgling stream in a fragrant meadow, or a snake eating its tail may somehow hold the key to the solution you're looking for. Imagery is a vehicle for communicating qualities, bringing paradoxes together, and expressing the meaning we ascribe to information and experiences.

The right brain communicates in images rather than words. You can dialogue directly with your intuition through images and then convert the qualities of the images into words. This dialogue can be in the form of asking questions and looking inside for whatever image comes up.

For example, I once worked with executives from a department store chain and a savings and loan association. They wanted to identify the corporate values for operating a new joint venture. After discussing demographics and other logical data, I had them close their eyes, relax, and ask their intuition for images that symbolized the key "corporate culture" values for making their joint venture a success. One person imagined a big family dinner; another saw herself talking with a close friend; another saw himself driving a sports car on the California coast. We then discussed the qualities found in these images, such as respect and service. They formulated their own meanings for these values, which became the key principles to communicate with the public and to practice with their employees. This shows the combined power of physical relaxation and intuitive imagery. It also shows how the imagery can be nourished by logical analysis but can give deeper answers than logical analysis alone can provide. Imagery is not independent.

There are a number of guidelines for using imagery:

1. Relax. Soothe both your body and mind using breathing or another technique.
2. Clearly ask your intuition for an appropriate image (e.g., "Give me a symbol, scene, or image that represents a new advertising theme.").
3. Accept whatever images emerge . . . surrender. (Don't judge or sort through; take what's there.)
4. Make the image vivid. Let emotions surface and tune in all sensory modes (feelings, sights, sounds, smells, tastes).
5. If the image is not easy to understand, ask your intuition for another one.
6. Honor all intuitive messages. Enjoy them.
7. Look for the *qualities* in the image (rather than getting caught up in the literal meaning).

The more fully you create an experience in your mind—with clear, multisensory images—the more powerfully your intuition can communicate to you. Sometimes you may wish to augment the imagery process with musical selections.

When you get an image, talk to it and see what it says back. If you receive an image, for example, of a red sports car speeding past a luxurious old ranch home on a road to Las Vegas, you can ask each of these symbols to tell you what they are doing in your image.

At first, images in your mind may be hard to understand, or you may not like them. If you get only partial information, you can dialogue to fill in the gaps. If an image is confusing, ask for another image that is easier for you to understand. Your intuition will gladly oblige, especially if you say, "Thank you," for all images it offers you. Your intuition is a friend of yours. It's a part of you. If an image seems frightening or disturbing, keep asking for the next "deeper" image. Finally, one will emerge that you can work with fruitfully.

As we learn to trust our intuition more and more, we are able to find and accept the truth inherent in the images as soon as they come up. Thus, our vision and insight become more powerful and creative, leading to more effective innovation and personal expression.

A team of specialists from a Japanese software company was working with consultants to identify new business opportunities in software. As part of a three-day workshop, I led them on an imaginary ocean dive, seeing fish, picking up artifacts, and finding a treasure chest. When we discussed what they had imagined, the qualities inherent in their images spawned many new ideas. Wet suits gave us ways to "warm up" the user interface with a cold technology. An octopus gave new ideas for developing the "architecture" for elaborate computer systems in artificial intelligence.

You can try the same exercise, applying it to one of your own work challenges. After reading the exercise below, close your eyes and actually take a few minutes to experience it. If you prefer, have someone read it to you, or tape record it to play back to yourself, so you can more easily follow the guided imagery. (Note: this exercise may seem similar to the visualization previously described in this chapter. The difference is that visualization uses your imagination to create vivid "photographs of the future," as if you were living in them today. Imagery allows you to use fantasy to create allegorical worlds that don't have to be so "realistic.")

Think of a situation at work that needs improvement or special creative insight. Write this down in a sentence or two on a piece of paper as if you were a newspaper reporter giving a completely objective overview of the situation. Now close your eyes and lead yourself into a state of deep relaxation.

Imagine that you are on your favorite warm, sunny beach, perhaps in the Bahamas or the Hawaiian Islands. Take in the whole scene with all of your senses. Feel the warm breeze blowing across your face and the smooth grains of sand massaging your feet. Hear the waves rolling gently onto the shore, and the leaves from the palm trees and grasses brushing softly against each other as they sway in the breeze. Smell the salt water and the sweet smoke of a campfire burning nearby. Look around and see the curve of the shore and the people with you on the beach. Several ships may be passing by on the horizon.

You put on your scuba-diving gear. You feel confident. Your scuba-diving lessons prepared you perfectly for a dive in this warm, clear water. You carry the single tank easily on your back as you walk to the water's edge, put on your flippers and mask, and insert the regulator into your mouth. The air draws easily and you breathe naturally.

Excitedly, you wade into the waves until the water reaches your chest, then you dive under and begin to swim about ten feet below the surface. As you look around, hundreds of beautiful tropical fish—glowing oranges, blues, and pinks—swim around your arms and legs and dart in front of you. You continue to breathe easily, swim further out from the shore, and dive a little deeper. You are still in very safe water. There are no dangers anywhere.

Then as you gaze down to the ocean floor, about fifteen feet below you, something captures your attention. You swim toward it. If it is alive, you trust it and it trusts you. No danger exists for you . . . or it.

Ask it to speak to you, to say how it represents a solution to your situation. Have a dialogue with it. Ask it to clarify anything you want to know. Test its insights against your own feelings and thoughts. Acknowledge its contribution to your thinking. Then thank it and swim on, knowing that you will remember everything it told you.

As you swim further, you notice below you a small, sealed chest nestled in the sand and surrounded by dark-green seaweed. You swim down to it and open it. Inside you find a piece of paper folded in half.

As you unfold the paper, you see that on it is written the message in response to the work situation that needs improvement or a special creative insight. You read the message. As you swim on, you begin to contemplate how the message might be a solution to your situation. You test it against logical considerations.

You return to the beach, take off your scuba gear, and lie on the warm sand. The warm sun and warm breeze caress your skin.

You reflect on the solutions you have found, noting to what degree they solve your situation.

This is just one type of exercise that shows how you can involve all your senses in tuning in to your creative intuition. After all, no one but you wrote anything on that piece of paper, even though you may have been surprised by the message you received. This exercise also shows how intuitive images can be enhanced with linear, verbal messages, thus giving you fluency in both.

Analogy

An analogy is a similarity between two conditions or things otherwise dissimilar. The use of analogies assumes that if two things are alike in some respects, they must be alike in other respects as well. Analogies serve to help "make the familiar strange and the strange familiar." From either of these perspectives, you can often find new approaches and new insights into the nature and possible resolution of the problems and questions you are working on.

To use *personal analogy*, identify yourself with an object or process in order to get a new perspective on the problem. For example, if you were trying to invent a new typewriter, you might ask yourself, "If I were the carriage return, how would I feel? What would I want?" Or if you were trying to invent a new electronic printer, you might imagine, "If I were a piece of paper, how would I like to have characters printed on me?"

To use *direct analogy,* make a comparison between parallel facts in two different fields to shed new light on the problem. For example, if you had been Alexander Graham Bell trying to invent the telephone, you might have compared the eardrum and bones of the human ear and how they work with the way some other membranous material might behave with "bones" of metal. As another example (previously mentioned), the inspiration for Velcro came from observing how burdock burrs cling to clothing.

To use *symbolic analogy,* use an image that might be technically incorrect but that colorfully describes the implications of a key concept of the problem. For example, to cover buildings where the outside surfaces take a beating from the elements, your analogy might be "a paint that grows thicker with age."

Similarly, you can take the *purpose* of a solution and imagine ways to fill it: "_____ (Something) that _____(performs a function) like a(n) _____ (analogy)." For example, you might want to invent "*new clothing fibers* that *change color* like a *chameleon.*"

To use *fantasy analogy,* imagine anything without regard to real-world plausibility and see what real-world ideas can spring from the exercise. For example, if you were trying to invent new arthroscopic surgery devices (which are inserted into the body on thin wires to perform microsurgery without major cutting of body tissue), you might imagine being able to shrink people to go on a "fantastic voyage" through the body to make repairs.

Analogy and imagery go hand in hand. Analogy tends to be more directive in generating new ideas, because you start with a comparison point (e.g., the starting point for Velcro was the burdock burr). Imagery, on the other hand, is usually more open-ended, having no beginning point for comparison. Both are extremely useful on their own and in conjunction with the other intuitive methods and the structures of the Modifying and Experimenting techniques.

Forced Association

When you put two concepts together that seemingly have nothing in common, you might be very surprised to see what ideas emerge. In a workshop to identify new ideas for constructing walls, participants were asked to make a connection between wall construction and spiders. One idea generated was to manufacture an adhesive webbing that would make it easier and faster to put up inside wallboard. Another idea was a new design for a caulking gun.

Or suppose you are wondering, "How can I improve my relationship with my boss?" You can ask, "How is this relationship like a pencil?" If you imagine a yellow pencil with an eraser, you might think . . .

- Eraser . . . We both keep bringing up past mistakes.
- Lead . . . I procrastinate. I need to get the lead out and confront this.
- Yellow . . . I feel timid.
- Gold ring . . . He's doubting my commitment to work.
- Wood shaft . . . I'm getting shafted by taking on too much.

From this thought process, you can identify many ways to respond to the situation.

Dreaming

Solutions can come to us when we don't expect them, after some "gestation period" in our minds. This method takes advantage of our wonderful ability for both daydreams and night dreams. Ray Bradbury, the science fiction writer, once said that he often discovered preciously good material in the half-awake, half-slumbery time before real sleep. Often he forced himself completely awake to make notes on these ideas. You can coach yourself to receive dream images by asking your intuition, "Give me a dream about _____ (the problem you're working on). Awaken me as soon as the dream is over." (With practice, you will be able to dream and wake like this.) As soon as you're awake, *don't* open your eyes but *do* review your dream. Then open your eyes and get the pad and pencil you have left by your bedside and quickly write down the main elements of the dream.

The key is to be willing to write down the key images or words that come to mind as soon as you realize they are there. The insights can be hard to recapture, so take advantage of their first visit. Later (in the morning, for example), you can fill in gaps and other details you can remember, settings, feelings, sensory images, and qualities you can distill from it all. As in other interpretations of imagery, look for the qualities represented by the images, treating them as metaphors rather than taking them too literally.

This process also works well after relaxation, meditation, and just plain daydreaming. (Keep a pad with you in the car for insights while driving and in the bathroom for insights while bathing or shaving!) Daydreams can be invoked simply by creating a fantasy about some ideal world or situation you would like to be in. You can also develop a wish list of items in your daydream that would combine to solve the problem you're working on. You will then evoke either images or words that you can write down—perhaps even "write" them in your daydream—to help bring the insights into your waking consciousness. You may even find that you can play "movie director" for your daydream to guide the course of events partially.

Drawing

Because your intuitive consciousness communicates more easily in impressions and symbols than in words, drawing is a marvelous way to bring out creativity. Drawings can both *evoke* and *record* creative insight, and different techniques have been developed emphasizing one of these two purposes over the other.

Evoke

To elicit deeper insight, drawing relies on producing intuitive symbols, sometimes archetypal. One exercise to help diagnose a problem situation is to become deeply relaxed and ask your intuition for symbols, scenes, or images that represent your situation. (This can also be done as a guided fantasy, similar to the one given earlier.) After receiving the symbols, use as many colors as possible and draw the symbols on a large piece of paper as your *hand* wants to draw them. (You may wish to use your "opposite" hand to give you less conscious control over the drawing.) Then fill in the first word that comes to mind for each of the symbols. Write a paragraph combining all the words, and expand on those thoughts in a free flow of thoughts and feelings.

Another example of using drawing to evoke insight is to establish a *theme* for a meeting (for problem solving, strategy development, etc.). Over the course of a few days before the meeting, one person generates images that represent that theme. The meeting then begins with the image placed next to the agenda and objectives to elicit comments about the purpose of the meeting. This almost always stimulates the expression of very inspiring principles and values. In turn, these values can energize and empower the group to embrace the theme and engage in the meeting wholeheartedly.

For example, a successful social service agency held a meeting with the theme, "After Success, What? 2000 and Beyond."[1] The image the the facilitator developed before the meeting is at the top of page 178.

As the participants discussed the image, the star came to mean their success, and the heart inside it was the source of their success. The road symbolized going on another journey toward mountains that represented new challenges. They emphasized that they didn't want to become complacent; rather, they wanted to take on new risks. The sun nearby was their very dynamic past, and the more distant sun was their dynamic future.

As another example of how drawings can help conceptualize the nature of the problem you are working on, the following drawing was developed in the course of a strategy conference.[2]

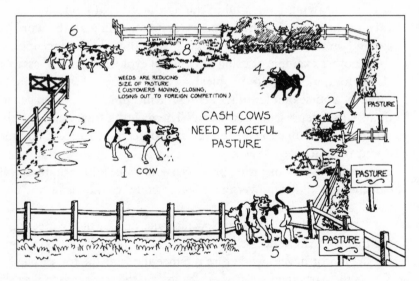

The central cow (1) symbolized the company itself, and the other animals were competitors:

- Competitors with more energy-efficient products (2)
- Competitors with different high-quality features (3)
- A competitor who produced very large-scale products (not direct competition) but who also was licensing its technology for smaller applications (4)

- Future competitors who could enter the market using emerging computer capabilities (5)
- Competitors with narrowly focused but high-volume applications (single customers) (6)

The water (7) was the invasion of new technologies, while the weeds (8) symbolized the natural turnover of customers.

After this drawing was shown, the president of the company studied it for the remainder of the day. The next day he came into the meeting room excitedly saying, "I know what we're going to do!" He described a strategy of acquiring one cow to avoid competition, changing pricing strategies to fend off other cows, and so on. The image gave him a total sense of how to rejuvenate his business.

Drawings are also essential for conceiving many engineering and scientific innovations—witness the extraordinary power of computer-aided design and engineering programs to make drawing processes more elegant and time efficient.

Drawing can be used in less elaborate ways, too, to deliver insight. After a period of deep relaxation or contemplation, if you have had your intuitive self working on a problem for you, draw an image of the current state of your problem/answer. Ask yourself, "What is the current state *today*?" knowing that you don't need a final answer right away. Suspend judgment—especially those voices from age eight that said you weren't good at art in school—and use colors or pens or even magazine cutouts. Try letting the images flow without conscious direction, as if the items on paper were telling you how they wanted to be. Then put words to the images—whatever words come through your hand. Again, use the results as a "status check" to see what is in your subconscious, impressions that you can always modify if you want to.

Record
There are two general methods of recording ideas as an individual or group generates them. The first is more linear, in traditional outline fashion:

I. _____
  A._____
    1. _____
    2. _____
  B._____
    1. _____
    2. _____
II. _____
  A._____

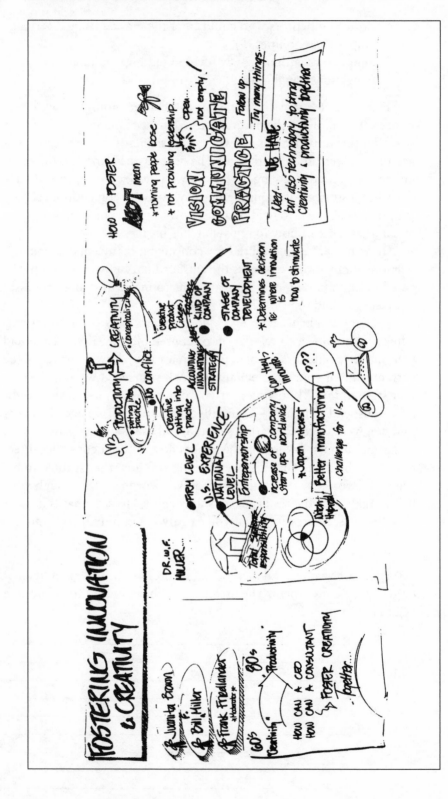

The same thoughts can be "grown" organically through pictorial means. An example of this is shown on page 180. For many of us, this method of making pictures of, sketching, our ideas is closer to how our thoughts naturally grow from one to another. Later, this pictorial outline can be translated into the linear type. This translation could be important if the thoughts have to be written into a report, which by nature is linear (i.e., having one thought after another, one paragraph after another, one chapter after another).

BECOMING EVEN MORE FLUENT

Without changing your basic profile of preferred styles, you can gain greater fluency in all four styles by using them in combinations. For example, a group of scientists at Eli Lilly & Company defined a challenge: "How can we foster more creativity in our laboratories?" Given the profile of the group, I led them through pairs of opposite approaches: a Visioning technique followed by Experimenting, then a Modifying exercise followed by Exploring.

In the Visioning technique used first, I asked the members of the group to visualize their ideal *wish list* for having anything they wanted to meet the challenge, with no restrictions or limitations on resources. With those results, I had them try an Experimenting technique, *matrix analysis:* "List the two main variables in your issue, and elaborate on the sub-variables within those two. Generate ideas for implementing the different cross-relationships between the sub-variables' attributes." That exercise produced a more refined set of ideas to meet the challenge they had defined.

For the Modifying technique, *force-field analysis,* I told them: "Select one item from your wish list. Complete a force-field analysis by:

- Expressing your wish as a goal.
- Describing your best and worst possible outcomes.
- Describing the positive and negative forces that are tugging for and against you.
- Generating ideas for making the positive forces even stronger or the negative forces weaker.

This technique gave people a sense of practical steps to take with their "blue sky" wishes. The Exploring method, *guided imagery,* was last because the group was, for the most part, skeptical of this approach to new ideas, and I was still building credibility with them. The purpose of this tool was to find the key criteria for developing an action plan and implementing their favorite ideas. I led them through a deep relaxation exercise and an imaginary dive to the ocean floor to find a special object. Later, in their imagination, they walked on a beach and met a wise person who helped them understand the significance of the object they'd found.

In this last exercise, many of the workshop participants had very moving and insightful experiences. However, one woman came up to me at the break and complained that the symbol approach to intuition was limiting to her. She explained that she didn't use an intermediary, such as a symbol, to get intuitive insights; "she just got it" in a flash. I realized that she employed her intuition in a Visioning way, to *converge on* an answer; the Exploring technique used intuition to *diverge into* broader considerations—thus her difficulty with the method.

Idea-Generation Matrix

To become a true master of the art of idea-generation, you can distinguish between *idea-stimulation* techniques and *idea-collection* methods as you strategize how to facilitate a group. Wish-listing is an idea-stimulation technique—a way of stretching to an ideal future (versus modifying the present). Use of Post-it notes is an idea-collection method—a way of writing down ideas and their relationships to each other.

> **To become a true master of the art of idea-generation, you can distinguish between *idea-stimulation* techniques and *idea-collection* methods**

To generate ideas, you always need both: idea-stimulation and idea-collection. When you vary the idea-stimulation techniques, through use of the different Innovation Styles, you gain more participation, by people of different style preferences, and you get a more well-rounded "buffet table" of ideas to choose from, both breakthrough and incremental. When you vary the idea-collection methods, you change how a group is interacting and recording their ideas, and thus maintain a higher level of energy.

There are two key variables in learning how to generate a more creative and comprehensive set of ideas. The first is the *Idea Generation Strategy*, based on the four Innovation Styles. The second is the *Idea-Collection Method*.

You can use the *Idea-Generation Matrix* (opposite) to strategize an idea-generation session. On the left, list various idea-collection methods; across the top, list idea-stimulation tools organized by the four Innovation Styles. As you switch from one idea-stimulation technique to another, also change the way the group interacts to collect their ideas. For example, use a large sheet of paper on a "group wall" to construct a matrix for Experimenting ideas, use Post-it notes to get ideas from wish-listing (Visioning), use a flip chart to write ideas from a force-field analysis (Modifying), and have each person draw on their own pads of paper a symbol and its related ideas (Exploring).

IDEA-GENERATION STRATEGIES

	Visioning	Modifying	Experi-menting	Exploring	All
IDEA-COLLECTION METHODS	Wish List Future Annual Report Visualization	Force-Field Attribute List-ing SCAMPER	Matrix Analysis Morphological Analysis Nature of Business Alternative Scenarios	Guided Imagery Analogy Forced Association Dreaming Drawing	Compass
Flip Chart					
Post-its					
Methods					
Group Wall					
Electronic					
Other					

The key to dynamic facilitation is to select one collection method for each idea-generation tool. Vary the tools and methods to maintain the most energized creative thinking. I once worked with a container company on a business strategy that involved the subject of recycling. We used a combination of Innovation Style techniques to develop the alternative strategies for introducing a new container.

We initially stated the objective as developing an economically feasible, practical strategy that would meet environmental concerns for the new container. The container had many potential environmental advantages of which the public was generally unaware.

One of the linear techniques was to portray the arenas for strategy alternatives as a 3-D matrix in which we pictured various mixes and matches of issues, strategy components, and stakeholders.

ISSUES	STRATEGY COMPONENTS	STAKEHOLDERS (those with an interest in the final solution)
Recycling	Economic/technological incentives	Consumers • Traditional middle class
Litter		• Achievers
	Education/PR	• Societally conscious
		• Others
		Industry corporations
		Legislators
		Others

First taking recycling as a key issue, we explored many of the demographic and attitudinal descriptions of the society and then brainstormed strategy alternatives in each of the "strategy component" areas. In some cases we said, "Pretend you are a member of this particular consumer group; what would you want to see as the final strategy of this corporation?" Once we had developed strategy ideas with recycling as the prime issue, we did the same with litter.

A primary component of creative strategizing is to alternate among the four types of techniques. This keeps participants refreshed and allows us to get maximum practical insight. After the 3-D matrix exercise, the participants formed groups of threes—taking the roles of consumer, corporation, or legislator. They were instructed to maintain silence and to use crayons to "negotiate" (by making lines, symbols, figures, etc., on paper) a solution where everyone wins: in essence, to produce a portrait of a win-win solution. Although at first unsure of what to draw, they eventually produced a visual statement that we could discuss and determine the qualities the images represented. This became important information to store away, to revisit at a later time with more linear techniques, such as a brief version of alternative scenarios.

Near the end of the day I had the participants close their eyes and, with music, led them into a deep relaxation state. Using very general instructions to guide their imaginations, I took them on a tour of a vacation spot of their choosing. After walking on a path awhile (one person, I found out later, was canoeing on a stream), they saw something that caught their attention and examined it closely. Then they attended a party in their honor where different stakeholders came up to congratulate them on the final strategy.

When the exercise was over, we discussed the qualities they discovered in whatever had caught their attention, plus the comments made to them at the party. One person saw a snowflake and fresh snow at a ski resort, and for him this symbolized the new and somewhat fragile territory his company was embarking on. Another person saw a fish he had never seen before, swimming slowly and unafraid in the currents. He saw that the situation was new yet familiar; and when he asked the fish to speak, it advised "move slowly and test the currents, but be unafraid." Other images reflected very similar themes (a good test of the intuitive "rightness" of the group's perception of the optimum solution).

As a result of using the four styles of idea-generation, four possible company strategies emerged from the various image-derived themes, some more aggressive in promoting recycling and some more conservative. A summarization of costs/benefits/risks was drawn up and presented to executive management. The summary showed what research would be needed to verify how each strategy alternative might (a) differentiate the company from its competitors; (b) gather higher market share; (c) improve legislator relations; (d) potentially raise stock values; (e) implement corporate concerns for the environment; and (f) provide the highest win-win for all stakeholders.

Your use of multiple techniques can elicit a much greater variety and depth of alternatives. Your final solution has both incremental and breakthrough components, leading to quick results as well as long-term success.

IN CLOSING . . .

Intuitive approaches to creativity can open our minds to our internal wealth of insight and wisdom. Training in methods of intuitive thinking becomes an important new dimension to using the more linear, or logical, idea-generation techniques.

When we've developed fluency in the use of all the tools associated with the four Innovation Styles, we can often instantly translate our intuitive "leaps of logic" into language, and our ideas come out in verbal form. It may happen so automatically, so quickly, that we don't even realize how truly fluent we have become in thinking and expressing ourselves creatively.

Thus, you can realize a stronger connection between your intuitive answers and your deeper sense of purpose and meaning in life. Your answers—to whatever problems—will begin to feel richer, with more personal intention to make them real in the world.

PART III

Revitalize the *Soul* of Corporate Creativity

You know what I'd like to do, Caslow? I'd like to create a far-reaching, innovative program that will open a lot of channels, offer great opportunities, link up with all kinds of things, and enable something or other to happen. Any ideas?"

Once there were two knights, Sir Vival and Sir Thrival.[1] Sir Vival loved to fight. He saw all of life in terms of competition. He fought every situation, every person, and every event that didn't fit into his ideal picture of life. Anything that dared ask him to adjust to it was seen as a Change Dragon to be slain. Because Change was always upsetting his ideal life, he was always doing battle; and when his Change Dragons were asleep, he was too tired to do anything but sleep also. His life became a matter of constant battle, and he grew weary. Mere survival became his ultimate victory.

Sir Thrival also loved competition, but he could distinguish between fantasy opponents and true challenges. His Change Dragons were fewer, and he could devote more time to anticipating their next moves. He enjoyed the sport itself, but he recognized that slaying the dragons would bring an end to his sport. His competitiveness was a type of collaboration, for without each other, there would be no stimulation or sense of gain. Ironically, although it appeared that he took his battles less seriously, he actually thrived, living strong and healthy for all his years.

These mythical characters embody two different ways we typically handle change and competition. Sometimes we may respond to seemingly unending demands for change by adopting a "survival" mode—a defensive posture that ultimately exhausts us and those around us. We hang on for dear life trying to keep things the same, avoid change, and get a chance to rest.

As an alternative, even during times of onslaught, we can promote strategically appropriate creativity in a way that *rejuvenates* us, that gives *vibrancy* and *health* to our organizations. This requires that we replace the sometimes unconscious motto of "Protect what we have" with the inspiration to "Create what we want."

In this context, this section provides you with new notions for inspiring an organizational vision, managing knowledge, and developing an innovative culture.

CHAPTER 11

Inspire Growth with *Purpose, Vision*, and *Values*

I had a boss who was a real visionary. She used to get up in meetings and talk about her vision for the nurse practitioner program and health care.

We replaced the medical model with the self-care model. We replaced it by going inside ourselves and understanding our own self-care process. We would work weekends and nights and drive to different cities, but we were all really alive.

We went through a staffing process that was transformational for our medical school, producing a values statement about who we were and what we were doing. It gave us an intense sense of belonging and commitment. People who didn't like those kinds of values and vision left, which was fine. It wasn't a wrenching leaving; they just got very clear that this was the wrong place for them.

We were invincible. I think part of learning about your own creativity is pushing through what you think are your limits.

—CYNTHIA, CONSULTANT AND FORMER HEALTH-CARE PROFESSIONAL

DISCOVERING A SENSE OF PURPOSE

Where is your life going? What do you stand for? Without a sense of *purpose* and *vision* about our lives—a sense of self—we may feel adrift, constantly reacting to changes in life without much sense of power. The same is true of our work groups and our organizations.

Your organization's *purpose* answers the questions: What do we stand for? What are our values? In the long term, what do we want to be? What are we *called* to be? What is our business and our ultimate contribution to the society and economy we work in?

Your organization's *vision* is a description of the medium-term (five years, typically) implementation of its purpose. Ask yourself and your organization, "What will we be producing in five years? How will we be organized? What values will we be emphasizing? What is the role of innovation for us (in products, marketing, manufacturing, etc.)?"

The vision may remain the same while particular financial, product, and human resources goals may change. Or the vision itself may change every few years. Throughout such changes, the purpose provides a fundamental continuity and stability for your organization.

Thomas Watson, Jr., son of IBM's founder, described the importance he placed on shared purpose and vision this way:

> *I believe the real difference between success and failure in a corporation (is) how well the organization brings out the great energies and talents of its people. What does it do to help these people find* common cause *and* sense of direction *through the many changes which take place from one generation to another? . . . If an organization is to meet the challenge of a changing world, it must be prepared to change everything about itself except (its core) beliefs.*[1]

In their book *In Search of Excellence,* Peters and Waterman spoke of the principle of "Hands-On, Value-Driven . . . in touch with the firm's essential business."

> *Let us suppose that we were asked for one all-purpose bit of advice for management, one truth that we were able to distill from the excellent companies research. We might be tempted to reply, "Figure out your value system. Decide what your company stands for. What does your enterprise do that gives everyone the most pride? Put yourself out ten or twenty years in the future: what would you look back on with greatest satisfaction?"*[2]

For corporate purpose and vision to have inspirational value, it *must* be based on how the organization can serve—not just its customers, but society and the environment. Missions based only on "increasing shareholder wealth, making a profit, growing the business, beating the competition" all fall short because the human urge to serve is deeper than the urge to acquire. Recently, Hewlett Packard Labs noticed that their organization's mission, "To be the best R&D facility in the world," had lost its inspirational power. Over several months they got everyone involved in discovering a new mission that would be fresh and intrinsically motivating. In the end, their new mission had changed only *one word*: "To be the best R&D facility *for* the world."

> **For corporate purpose and vision to have inspirational value, it must be based on how the organization can serve**

We are always more inspired by giving ourselves to a cause that's bigger than ourselves. When we've understood our own personal purpose and values, that cause becomes an extension of ourselves. It's the work-equivalent of feeling a spiritual oneness. For example, in the 1970s Charles Schwab had a keen ethical insight that inspired a business breakthrough. He saw that Wall Street brokers were in an untenable conflict of interest: They were supposed to look out for their customers' investment interests, yet they made more commissions by convincing those customers to make more trades. He also realized that hordes of well-educated investors didn't really need advice; they needed reliable transactions. Doubly armed, he founded the first discount brokerage firm to handle trades, and dumbfounded Wall Street by breaking the rules of conventional wisdom, paying no commissions to traders.

Over the years, Charles has broadened his sense of purpose: To stimulate every household in America to become investors in their future, whether or not his firm handles their investments. As the market expands, surely Schwab and Company will get their share. Their vision is to be different, not just better, and to be considered the premier provider of financial services in the world.

To get there, Schwab pioneered services such as One Source, the first "one-stop shopping" for no-load mutual funds from many companies (with no transaction fees charged to Schwab customers). Charles' dedication to ethical principles endured through tough negotiations with the supplying mutual fund companies. Many of them wanted to issue a special class of mutual fund share, in which customers would pay higher management fees than the company would charge to their own direct consumers; they planned to make up for the no-load basis that way. Schwab refused to have their customers pay more and didn't offer mutual funds from those companies.

Today, the company attracts employees who are themselves dedicated to this "high road" strength of character. Indeed, when customers wanted Schwab to offer guidance, employees vocally worried that the company's "no conflict of interest" stance might get compromised. Charles and his staff worked hard to find the "Schwab Way" to respond to customers' needs without sacrificing their values.

DEVELOPING CREATIVE STRATEGIES

Your organization's purpose, vision, and environmental factors most clearly come together in the development of the organization's strategy. A strategy provides the first major link between your current reality and your shared vision. Purpose provides the fundamental direction, vision provides the destination, and strategy development provides the compass.

In its most basic terms, a strategy really *is* a statement of creativity: What future does your organization wish to create for itself? Strategy development must encompass what the people in your organization want to *be* as a group (your overall mission, purpose, business definition and short-term vision), what they want to *do* (your strategy and tactics), and what they want to *have* (your goals and achievements).

The strategy development process is potentially the most vital way of establishing a culture of creative strategic management as both an operations ("line") and support staff function. As Jim Bandrowski notes:

> *Strategy development is a creative exercise . . . developing insights into your business and your markets, generating a wide variety of strategic options from which to choose, flushing out the best alternatives, and ensuring that plans are not only formulated but carried out.*[3]

Most strategic planning processes are dominated by analysis—financial, market, competitor, technology, and so on—with relatively little attention paid to creativity. It is rare to even hear the words *creative* and *planning* in the same breath. How sad! Many elaborate plans become an end in themselves. They then sit on some manager's bookshelf until the next round of strategy development.

Consider, by contrast, musicians. They sometimes play with such connection—a communion, or attunement, if you will—that the performance rises above the composition itself. This is their "peak performance." A mediocre score cannot elicit an inspired performance. Yet, the strategies most organizations develop are composed as mediocre pieces, using an uninspired process and leading to uninspired implementation.

There are two popular perspectives on strategy development: *strategic road-mapping* and *strategic positioning*.

Strategic road-mapping typically:

- Defines a goal or destination for the business and a map for getting there.
- Assumes a future dominated by "certainties" (due to short time periods and/or stable environmental trends).
- Employs single forecasts with +/- variations.
- Emphasizes organizational structuring to implement the strategy with strong controls.

This perspective assumes there's a HERE (point A) and a visionary *destination*—THERE (point B)—and the strategy is the straight line between the two (see p. 193, top). Strategic road-mapping assumes a controllable pathway from A to B, in which any deviation "off course" needs to be fixed. It makes no easy allowance for learning and adjustment along the way.

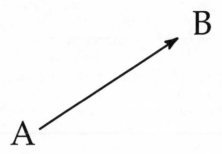

Strategic positioning typically:

- Defines a direction for the future business and a compass for midcourse changes.
- Assumes a future dominated more by "uncertainties" (due to longer time periods and/or more turbulent environmental developments).
- Employs qualitatively different future scenarios.
- Emphasizes organizational capabilities and flexibility to implement the strategy opportunistically.

This perspective assumes there's a "here-and-now" point surrounded by a "field of all possibilities." Strategic criteria define the range of a visionary *direction*.[4]

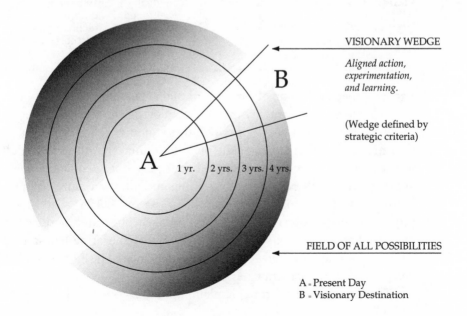

Within the visionary wedge lies uncertainty—*and* the opportunity for experimentation and learning along the way. This wedge eliminates most of the field of possibility, so people can responsibly choose which experiments and learning align with the general sense of direction. For example, one electronics engineering company bought a software company primarily to *learn how* to manage one, since software would play an unknown but important role in its future success. Anything within the three to five- year wedge is fair game for creative experimentation and midcourse corrections in visions, strategies, and tactics. Anything outside the wedge is not pursued.

Peter Georgescu, Chairman and CEO of Young & Rubicam notes: "Opportunities and ideas to drive incremental growth are drying up. As the '90s draw to a close, so will the viability of this strategy; companies will be forced to focus on the top line."[5] Concentrating only on short-term goals and quickly testing to see if they will bear fruit is a recipe for disaster; Jerome Weisner, former president of MIT was fond of saying, "That's like planting a seedling and a short while later yanking it out to see if the roots are healthy."[6]

A healthy mixture of short- and long-term goals can emerge by using the Innovation Styles model covered in chapter 4. It offers four distinct questions for strategic planning:

	Modifying	Exploring	Visioning	Experimenting
Strategic Planning	How can we build on our core strengths and capabilities?	How can we rewrite the rules of competition?	How can we be ideally positioned within the industry?	How can we synergize different technologies, partnerships, etc.?

Each approach offers one-fourth of the viable possibilities for a robust, creative vision and strategy. Many strategy development processes dwell too much on only one or two of these questions—usually because they are the favorite styles of the people running the show. Using all four to set a "buffet table of possibilities" gets more people involved, engages everyone's best way of thinking, and allows a more comprehensive set of options. As seen in the graph on p. 195, sustainable growth occurs in alternating cycles of breakthrough and incremental change. The Exploring style leads the way in generating leap-ahead strategies, while Modifying optimizes, in incremental fashion, what has been initiated by past strategies.

The New World of strategic planning will be one in which transi-

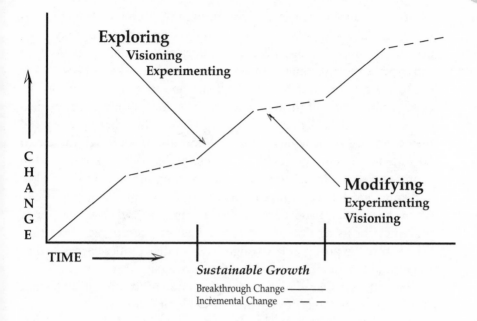

tions happen with greater and greater frequency, and the create-sustain-end cycles will happen faster and faster. Rather than going "straight line" from Point A to Point B, strategic direction will be established by identifying the "wedge" in the circle-of-all-possibilities where experimentation from Point A within the wedge will lead to the best Point B on the circle's outer rim. Using the four approaches to idea-generation found in the Innovation Styles model will give you the most robust strategy possible.

CREATING A SHARED VISION

Many managers find that developing a strategy is much easier than implementing it. They make the crucial mistake of considering implementation as the last step. In a very real way, it's the first consideration.

Operating by a shared vision requires attunement as well as alignment. We often overemphasize the role of communicating the company vision without tapping into employees' intrinsically motivating life purposes. Recall the discussion in chapter 1 of Barry Posner's research, which showed that clarity about personal values was much more important to job commitment than clarity about company values. The corporate vision must be created through the inner, intuitive guidance of leaders at all levels of the organization.

It is when you can align personal and corporate values and vision that you produce true magic. If you are like most people, you really want to produce quality work for an organization whose purpose is meaningful for you. When we feel a connection between our own values and purpose, the organization's values and purpose, and how we can express them through our jobs, our motivation skyrockets.

In one case I consulted with the board and staff of a shelter for battered women. Half of them believed their organization was established solely to provide a shelter for women in need. The other half believed they were also to provide community education. Although these two notions may seem very close, conflicts arose when resources were short—for example, when there was a staffing shortage at the shelter and someone was committed to speak to a community group. Only when the second purpose was agreed to, and only when a clear set of priorities for using time, people, and financial resources was established, was the group able to align itself to deliver its services and to feel attuned as an internal community once again.

How does a *shared* sense of purpose and vision emerge? In part, it takes a dedicated executive who is capable of *visionary leadership*, a "corporate hero." As stated by Deal and Kennedy in their classic, landmark book, *Corporate Cultures*,

> *We are not talking about good "scientific" managers here. Managers run institutions; heroes create them.*
>
> *Heroes . . . are driven by an ethic of creation. They inspire employees by distributing a sense of responsibility throughout the organization.*
>
> *There is more tolerance for risk taking, thus greater innovation; more acceptance of the value of the long-term process, thus greater persistence; more personal responsibility for how the company performs—thus a work force that identifies personal achievement with the success of its firm.*
>
> *The success of these visionaries (like Henry Ford, John D. Rockefeller, William Kellog, Harley Proctor and others) lies not only in having built an organization but also in having established an institution that survived them and added their personal sense of values to the world.[7]*

A strong, visionary leader is vital to having your organization's members work together to fulfill a purpose and vision. Yet the presence of such a leader is insufficient: the purpose and vision must be *shared*. Your top managers must extend themselves and communicate with employees to find out what *employees* believe and want the organization to stand for. To ask that question virtually always elicits a statement of high values, for which employees would give 100 percent if the organization's purpose were truly defined and practiced that way.

What does the leader listen for? It's more than just "new product ideas." As Peter Russell and Roger Evans have so eloquently stated,

We are being forced to challenge many of our assumptions. We are all undergoing a crisis of values. Every one of us is being asked to listen to the voice within and let it speak through our decisions and actions. The voice within is that part of us that feels that something is not quite right, the feeling that there is more to life, the urge to follow a higher purpose. It is not always easy to hear. It is the willingness to listen to our own inner worlds that is the mark of the creative manager. [8]

Collectively, an organization also has an inner voice that prompts everyone to match corporate values to the needs of the larger whole of life. This inner voice may be at odds with an existing corporate culture and those in authority who wish to preserve power and silence the voice of what nearly everyone knows is true. However, the organization's inner voice bears the most potent source of power. As Robert Quinn tells us:

> **The organization's inner voice bears the most potent source of power.**

The organizational voice always wants the organization to succeed. In seeking the collective good, the inner voice does not distort the needs for sacrifice and change by deferring to the preferences of a particular individual. The inner voice leads to realignment and an increased flow of resources. The inner voice finds roots in the moral core of the organization. When individual effort disconnects from the inner voice, people begin to lose vitality. Human commitment begins to decay.[9]

Here lies the greatest opportunity for revitalizing the soul of your corporation's creativity. First discover and tap into the "soul purpose" of people throughout your organization. In the end, you will all firmly embody the purpose, vision, and strategy of your company—generating ideas, making decisions, and taking action with the enormous power of your collective spirit.

Intuition can play a key role in finding this inner voice and creating a personally compelling business vision that meets future business conditions. In 1971, the Rolm Corporation was still a fast-growing maker of heavy duty computers, but mainstay orders from the Department of Defense looked like they might dry up. Kenneth Oshman, co-founder of the company, decided to explore the new market for computerized telephone equipment, even though at first that opportunity didn't appear very fruitful. "We didn't have a strong enough gut feeling that anything else was right for us, so we decided to see how we could turn this into a business." This intuition led Rolm to develop computer-controlled switching equipment that was far more sophisticated that anything AT&T or other competitors had. Rolm's business thrived, growing to $660 million in revenues before IBM acquired it.[10]

Intuition gives us foresight into the future, anticipating "What is most likely to happen (given, at least, the current forces of change) and what will the needs be?" Personal purpose gives us our internal navigation system for engaging in what we have the most energy for contributing. Strategic vision happens at the intersection of intuitive foresight ("What is needed?") and personal purpose ("What do I stand for?"), answering the question, "What future do I want to create, in the field of all possibilities?"

INTUITIVE FORESIGHT
- What is needed?"
- What do I anticipate the future to be like in the year _____ ?
- What are some primary issues and needs that catch my attention and interest?

PERSONAL PURPOSE
- What do I stand for?
- What is my purpose in life and work?
- What do I most want to engage in and contribute?

STRATEGIC VISION
What future do I want to create, in the field of all possibilities?

As an exercise to create your vision for the future, try these four steps . . .

1. Anchor your company in future time, asking questions such as:
   - *Where are we?*
   - *What are we doing?*
   - *Who is around us?*
   - *What are people saying?*
2. Tune in intuitively to foresee what the world might be like in the future, asking questions such as:
   - *What is happening in the world?*
   - *What are the hot issues?*
3. Imagine what your company has contributed to the world, asking questions such as:
   - *What are some new technological advances or changes that we would not have dreamed would have occurred?*
   - *What is the latest innovation that is revolutionizing the way challenges are being solved?*
4. Focus on your own role in creating this future, asking questions such as:
   - *What have we done along the way to help the company attain this success?*

- *How have we worked with others, or supported them in some way, to respond to these challenges?*
- *What did we do to help us work better together and capture or take advantage of the technologies, innovations, rapid change that was emerging—early on—ahead of other companies?*
- *Where was our time most wisely spent?*
- *Where did our time really make a difference, and what was the difference it made?*
- *What did we stop doing to allow this to blossom or develop more fully?*

Sometimes, your vision will emerge without such deliberate considerations. Mary Kay Ash first started out by retiring from a mediocre career in sales at a catalogue sales company. "I felt there were many women like me who were qualified to do a lot more than they were doing. My idea was to write a book that would help them over the obstacles I had encountered." She spent three weeks jotting on a legal pad all the business practices that she felt stymied women's advancement. On a second pad she enumerated all the practices she felt were helpful and worth emulating. "Inadvertently, I had put on paper the marketing plan for a company that would give women open-ended opportunity."[11] Those pads turned not into a book but the business prospectus for Mary Kay Cosmetics.

Innovation remains important in *all* areas of your organization's life. However, the emphasis for innovation may shift depending on the growth cycle of your industry and products. For a while, when costs are the driving force behind competitive advantage, innovation may be aimed inward at production and support efficiencies. Another time, innovation in new products carries the torch and gets the resources. At other times marketing innovations are the keys to success. Only with a purpose and vision in hand (and heart) can goals and objectives begin to make sense to people throughout your organization and the role of innovation remain clear.

CONDUCTING INNOVATION SEARCHES

Innovation Search workshops, by bringing together a diverse group of specialists, can spark the heart of creative strategy development. These workshops require workshop management as complex as the topics themselves. For example, one health products company wanted to see how some of the more sophisticated technologies, such as ultrasonography, might be used in producing their products. In other cases, we conducted workshops aimed at:

- Helping one division of a chemical firm establish a broader vision of the nature of the business (including specific business opportunities).
- Developing a financial institution's business strategy for the entire Asia-Pacific region.
- Identifying business opportunities for 1990–95 with a Japanese company in the software industry.
- Formulating new business opportunities for using excess engineering personnel in a nuclear engineering firm.
- Inventing a new portable printer.

For projects such as these, pure "number crunching" and other analytical thinking would have missed ways to take advantage of many of the key opportunities identified. Intuition was needed to link together so many facts and diverse interests. Without it, there would have been no way to formulate and coordinate the investments in systems, promotions, and human resources needed to make the strategy operable.

The search for innovative solutions in these workshops unfolds along the same lines as the Creative Journey process. There are six steps to producing an Innovation Search (or Business Opportunity Search); these steps coincide with the first three steps of the Creative Journey.

STAGE I (The Challenge)
1. Identify goals, criteria, capabilities
2. Gather technology and market information
STAGE II (The Focus)
3. Select focus areas and related creativity exercises
4. Select and prepare participants
STAGE III (The Creative Solutions)
5. Generate alternatives in a variety of settings
6. Screen alternatives for top concepts

The only decision made in the workshop is "what concepts offer the most potential, given this assembly of talent and expertise?" After screening alternatives to select top concepts, these concepts must undergo more rigorous feasibility assessments. After the feasibility studies and a final decision, the Completion stage of the Creative Journey can commence: implementing the solution and celebrating the results.

Stage I—Conduct Preliminary Assessment

First, you develop the groundwork for the *content* of the workshop by meeting with the principal stakeholders of the project. Develop a consensus regarding the following issues:

Identify Goals, Criteria, and Capabilities
- Goals. What are the objectives of the overall project? What are the objectives of the Innovation Search workshop in relation to the project objectives? How does the Search fit into meeting the project milestones?
- Criteria. What are the general parameters by which to focus the Search?
- Capabilities. What are the organizational capabilities and resources—financial, technological, human, and so forth—upon which to build the ultimate solution?

Gather Background Information
What information is needed to provide a substantive groundwork for idea-generation—market and technology trends, for example?

Stage II—Prepare for the Workshop
Next, you prepare the groundwork for the *process* of the workshop:

Select Focus Areas
What are the topics by which to organize and guide the idea-generation discussions? For example, a chemical company wanted to identify new applications for a resin product they had invented. As criteria to guide their search, they wanted business opportunities that:

- Could be commercially developed for either the short term (three to five years) or long term (five to ten years)
- Offered a competitive advantage by quality, cost, price, or distribution (either a "large market share" or "specialized niche markets" were acceptable business approaches)
- Were in healthy, technology-oriented, growing industries
- Did not require direct sales to consumer markets
- Had a broad base of customers
- Used currently developed properties of the resin product
- Might or might not depend on the company's engineering manufacturing, or marketing capabilities (they would make an acquisition if necessary).

The first two focus areas were technology-oriented to look for opportunities across all possible markets, based on both the resin products' physical and chemical properties. These focus areas were planned to occupy two-thirds of our total idea-generation time. Four market-oriented focus areas were chosen for the remaining one-third of our time. This ensured that we would consider the needs of four key industries that might use the product.

As another example, the project with the Japanese electronics company began by constructing four alternate scenarios for the year 2010. We first examined each for the range of market needs that might be expected. Those market needs were combined in a matrix with technology trends, including: biotechnology, advanced materials and processing methods, fuel cells, optics, electronics, electro-active and "smart" polymers, specialty chemicals, membranes, robotics, artificial intelligence, digital communications, optical electronics, chemical synthesis, energy conversion, and software.

From this analysis of market possibilities and emerging technologies, plus a knowledge of their corporate capabilities, focus areas were selected to organize the Search workshop.

Select and Prepare Participants

Who are the best people to attend based on (a) specialist expertise, (b) importance for eventual implementation, and (c) comfort/skills in group settings? (These may be people from outside your group and even outside your organization.)

In the resin product Search, the participants included the company's project manager, new venture manager, director of research, research and development manager, market development manager, the product inventor, and another senior scientist. We supplemented this talent with specialists in particle technology, catalysts, membranes, and the four target industries.

In addition, what articles, technology briefs, market analyses, or other materials would help the participants to arrive at the workshop on a common ground, ready to work closely in multidisciplinary problem solving with people of different specialties? If presentations will be given (on market trends, etc.), what preparation and coaching do the presenters need?

For the resin product Search, a workbook with over 400 pages of articles on various industry trends and technology developments was prepared for all participants. Although each person didn't read every page, it helped give everyone a common vocabulary for the workshop. Video and other media are also excellent tools for such preparation.

The presenters were coached to give a twenty-minute talk on pertinent subjects designed to *stimulate* the group, not to solve the problem. Roughly five minutes were devoted to an orientation to a subject, ten minutes to details important to our idea generation, and five minutes of specific initial ideas.

For each focus area, what techniques might best stimulate ideas? What combinations would keep the flow going? Which ones would work best with the whole group, with subgroups, and/or individually? (The resin products search included exercises such as matrix analysis, analogy, reframing questions, force field, and brainstorming.) How can the Search workshop environment be dressed up to help focus the imagining and enliven the climate for creativity?

Stages I and II can span a period of four to eight weeks to give time for each person to prepare adequately.

Stage III—Conduct the Workshop

Managing the Search workshop usually requires a skilled facilitator (or facilitators) and a second (or third) person as recorder and subgroup leader. This allows the key stakeholders to participate freely in the discussions while the group process is being properly guided.

Generate Alternatives

By following the guidelines covered on pages 136–137, the facilitator and recorder may become rather invisible to the workshop. The attention should remain on the quality and quantity of ideas being generated. This is as it should be, though an observer might misconstrue the facilitator's limited participation.

After introductions, start the Search with a discussion of objectives and criteria to make sure that participants have a common understanding. This also gives the key stakeholders a chance to answer questions and modify or amplify their needs. Then, be sure to set the climate for creative interaction by introducing ground rules such as the following:

- Give all your ideas—even wild ones.
- Give your ideas freely and spontaneously (the facilitator can guide this).
- Don't wait for the "right time."
- Share your ideas with everyone—avoid side conversations.
- Draw or sketch your ideas if you desire.
- Make sure your ideas and others' are recorded properly.
- Build on others' ideas—avoid idea killers.
- Enjoy, have fun, and use humor!

Then proceed with your agenda, including the creativity exercises, and employ other techniques as the need arises. As ideas are recorded, periodically have them put into a word processor or computer so that a printout will be available for reviewing the ideas. Make sure each idea is assigned its own number, no matter what focus area it was recorded in.

Screen Alternatives

In a two- or three-day Innovation Search workshop, you might record 300 to 600 separate and overlapping ideas for all the focus areas. There are many ways to group the ideas into concepts (a "concept" might represent anywhere from one to twenty-five or more "ideas") and do a preliminary screening of the criteria. One process involves the following five steps:

- *Review the criteria for the Search.*
- *Have each participant skim all the ideas,* briefly marking the ones that strike his or her fancy.
- *Have each participant go through his marked ideas and begin assembling them into concepts* that represent possible answers to the workshop problem/objective. Document each concept with (a) a title, (b) a description, and (c) reference numbers to individual ideas included in the concept.
- *As a full group, have each person present a concept.* Ask others if they have a similar concept they would like to add/merge with the presenter's. Give the presenter veto power over whether she wants the others' concepts added (this stops any tendency to argue rather than build on concepts). Any concepts that were offered by others and vetoed by the presenter may be introduced at another time. Move on to the next person and continue this process until all concepts have been presented. My experience has shown that, on the average, if 10 people each begin with 10 concepts (a total of 100 concepts), approximately 40 concepts will emerge from the synthesizing process.
- *Apply some ranking method to specify which concepts, in the wisdom of the group, most deserve a more detailed evaluation to determine their attractiveness in meeting the objectives.* In some circumstances, this ranking can provide a final decision, but usually a much deeper level of investigation is needed. One quick method for ranking is to have each participant assign two points to each of his "top third" of all concepts, zero points to each of his "bottom third," and one point to each of his "middle third"— based on the criteria. Then add everyone's point assignments to produce a prioritization.

EVALUATING TOP CONCEPTS

Before you make final decisions, certainly you must assess market, technical, and organizational feasibility. One chemical company estimates that for every 300 products from their R&D labs, three make it to the marketplace and one makes it big. It is more typical across industries that for every 100 products, twenty-five get analyzed seriously, ten go into product development, four get market tested, two get marketed, and one gets added to the product line.

Too many criteria or excessive quantification too early can kill promising ideas or discourage new ones from even being posed. Too much quantification can also lead to the "creation" of data merely to satisfy the system. Conversely, waiting until later in a project's life to apply key criteria can waste valuable resources.

In the consumer products company discussed earlier, management discovered that the presence of a four-page form with twenty to twenty-five criteria discouraged the submission of new product ideas and encouraged "hollow" market projection data. They instituted a new procedure saying,

We as managers need to ask four questions early in a project:

* *Does this fit with corporate strategy?*
* *Does someone (consumers) want this?*
* *Is the technology likely to be available?*
* *Do we have the people to champion it and do it?*

When submitting your idea, simply address each of these issues. For example, if your idea doesn't fit with corporate strategy, tell us why the strategy should be different.

When you have a great idea and can't wait to work on it, you may find it hard to answer such questions patiently. But if the evaluation process is conducted well, it can hone and sharpen the idea in your mind and enable you to make a contribution with significant impact.

There are any number of evaluation methods available, depending on the idea, the purpose of the evaluation, the criteria, and the style of analysis preferred by management.

In one case, the industrial products group of a Fortune 500 company wanted to determine a new match between "What do *we* want to be?" and "What does the *market* want us to be?" We conducted an Innovation Search to identify possible new business concepts for the next five to ten years. The top concepts were then evaluated through a value-indexing process.

A value-indexing process is an alternative to a strict, quantitative approach to decision making. It gets people involved in choosing the opportunities that best fit the purpose and vision of the organization. The entire evaluation process, not just the criteria themselves, can complete the learning cycle that forges group cohesion and the commitment to make a difference *together*.

A set of sixteen criteria were defined and divided into two categories:

- Eight "external attractiveness" factors (those related to markets, competition, technology, etc.)
- Eight "internal fit" factors (those related to corporate capabilities, business purpose, etc.).

External factors are usually less under the organization's control than internal factors.

Statements were developed describing relative levels of meeting each criterion factor. For example, "potential growth rate" had levels similar to: 0-5 percent, 5-9 percent, 10-12 percent, 13-15 percent, 16 percent or more. Each statement was then assigned an index value on a 1-10 scale, such as:

POTENTIAL GROWTH RATE	INDEX VALUE
16+%	10
13–15%	8
10–12%	5
5–9%	2
0–5%	0

Data were gathered on the top twelve business concepts from the Innovation Search to rate each concept on the 1-10 scales. For example, if the estimated growth potential was 14 percent, a score of 8 was given for that criterion. These determinations required extensive discussion among the members, a key part of the process.

At the end, weighted scores were averaged for all "external attractiveness" and for "internal fit" criteria. For example, a concept might have averaged 50 for external attractiveness and 60 for internal fit. The scores for each concept were plotted on a matrix (page 207); the numbers within the boxes show the priority for investment (1 being the best).

The example with scores of (50, 60) would have fallen in section 4. A concept may be very attractive but a poor fit (quadrant 5), or perhaps a very good fit but very unattractive (quadrant 6). It is usually easier to modify the internal fit (move from a 5 to a 2 or 1) because

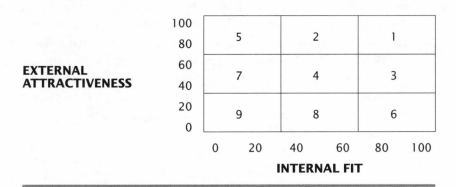

internal factors are more under management's control. Therefore, the business opportunities would receive a 1 to 9 priority for development.

The discussions surrounding the interpretation of this matrix and the decisions about which specific business opportunities to pursue were important to the group's alignment and attunement. Even more important, a purpose and vision emerged that redefined the overriding nature of their business.

IN CLOSING . . .

We are seeing evidence of a growing evolution of consciousness, under the name of sustainability—not just for the conservation of Spaceship Earth's limited resources, but for the just distribution of wealth among the planet's population. Many companies' full-time staffs are looking at how to make healthy business decisions that put the planet first, knowing that business health cannot be sustained at the expense of exploitation.

Business is perhaps the most powerful force on the planet today—more than governments, more than education, more than the churches. Business decisions affect not just economies but entire societies—not just immediate concerns, but the long-term macro problems of poverty and environmental well-being as well as personal security and prosperity. Business crosses national boundaries as no political institution can, and the corporation is far more flexible and adaptable than the bureaucratic structure of government.

Proceeding from that truism, we have the opportunity to put our deepest values to work. Business leaders (at all levels) have the opportunity—and the responsibility—to become the first true *planetary leaders!* Living and working with well-being, truth, peace, right action, and love as the ultimate goals can become quite natural. These deepest human values may be labeled differently or called by different names among the diverse peoples of the world, yet they have a common heritage in our humanity that is beyond cultural and personal differences.

Will people in business step up to this responsibility, individually or together? Can we inspire our organizations and societies to achieve economic and social transformation? Will *you* dedicate your company's business strategies and organizational culture to this cause?

CHAPTER 12

Create and Manage
Knowledge

After many years of using my creativity to format computer printouts, manipulate data, and make worksheets, I was given the opportunity to break out of the numbers world into the world of people. I volunteered as leader of a yet untried project—to organize a career fair. I was asked to develop the idea, sell it to management, and then make it happen. This task proved to be the high point of my twelve years of working experience. The project took four months (I was holding down my regular job at the same time) and involved leading over 100 people. The experience charged my batteries and I was high for about three weeks after. I found I really enjoyed and was good at visualizing what an idea could become and then backing up to start creating it.

—ALLISON, FORMER ACCOUNTANT IN A COMPUTER COMPANY

CREATING NEW KNOWLEDGE

A blip on the radar screen of history—one that we may have all taken for granted, as we did with cheap petroleum and Iron Curtain countries—has passed. The people with financial capital no longer own the means of production, as they had since the Industrial Age began a hundred years ago.

Today, issues of knowledge and intelligence dominate the business scene. Knowledge has become the "raw material" of what we make and sell. A beer can, a pharmaceutical drug, an athletic shoe, a biotech seed, a report on new methods of mining . . . all these are "bundles" of the intelligence that goes into inventing, packaging, and delivering them.

Knowledge is the compilation of a group's "know-how" and "know-what." However, knowledge is not the same as intelligence. While knowledge is a synthesis of information, intelligence is what it takes to create knowledge.

Intelligence is the ability to:

• Imagine	• Add to a body of knowledge	• Intuit patterns in data
• Learn	• Transfer knowledge and skills	• Intuit future trends and events
• Reason	• Envision what's possible	• Relate to different types of people
• Create new insights	• Make wise, value-based decisions	• Generate alternatives

Intelligence is the #1 asset of any company, the precursor to financial wealth. Where does this intelligence asset reside? First and foremost, in you and your colleagues. People take some of the company's asset base with them when they go home at night, and the company has only a probability, but no guarantee, that it will be back. The company, to some degree, "rents" your intellectual capital and takes ownership of it only when you convert your ideas into products, services, or work processes. (In a similar fashion, another portion of intelligence assets resides in customer relationships—and they aren't owned by the company either.)

To appreciate the critical role of knowledge management, we must clearly understand how every product, service, and work process is a "bundle of knowledge." For example, a Nike pump shoe is, in essence the intelligence that has been bundled into the ability to conform to a foot (a "more intelligent shoe"), aided by special knowledge about manufacturing and distributing it at a value to customers.

A product or service finds a successful niche in the marketplace to the extent that the knowledge bundled in it is considered fresh. All of life—from a flower to a dolphin to a human—depends on the movement of energy and information. Stopping that flow means death. When the knowledge contained in an offering (product + service) is new, the offering thrives. When the bundled knowledge becomes outdated, the offering dies.

> A product or service finds a successful niche in the marketplace to the extent that the knowledge bundled in it is considered fresh.

Similarly, the speed with which new knowledge is bundled and brought to the market can make or break a business. For example, in the 1980s, typical Japanese cars were produced in about three years, from design to showroom, while American cars took four to five years. For cars in the showroom with the same model year—that is, competing directly—the technology (knowledge) built into the Japanese cars was only three years old, while in the American cars the knowledge was up to five years old. No wonder Japanese cars were judged more innovative!

Ultimately, knowledge management starts with the creation of new knowledge—the "stuff" with which people innovate new products, services, processes, and management methods. Can you tell someone, without showing them, exactly how to tie a shoe? This is *implicit* knowledge—personal and often hard to put into words. Implicit business knowledge is the asset that goes home each night. A key challenge of knowledge management is to *articulate and document* all important knowledge, making it explicit and openly available within the organization . . . that is, to make implicit knowledge *explicit*.

Ikujiro Nonaka and Hirotaka Takeuchi have created the classic model for knowledge-creation[1]. This cyclical process starts with (1) personal experience, which is (2) articulated into personal theory/concepts, then (3) combined with others' concepts into a model, which then becomes (4) integrated as the "way things are" in the culture . . . until some new knowledge expands beyond or replaces this "old knowledge:"

	IMPLICIT KNOWLEDGE	**EXPLICIT KNOWLEDGE**
PERSONAL KNOWLEDGE	(1) Personal experience	(2) Personal concepts
GROUP KNOWLEDGE	(4) Integrated experience (socialization)	(3) Combined models

Despite our pictures of studious people staring intently at computers, most new knowledge is created in dialogues, in community! Knowledge-creation takes much more than just "communication," which comes from the Latin *communare*, meaning "a shared space." Communication occurs when we share the same context and meaning but it can be only one-way. Knowledge-creation requires two-way "conversation," from the Latin *conversare*, meaning to "turn around." We have to "turn around" our old beliefs and paradigms to invent new knowledge, and that is hard to do alone, without conversation.[2]

In fact, the best way to guarantee a steady stream of new knowledge is to bring together people who are as different as possible from each other to generate multiple perspectives. Productive conversation depends on transforming *debates*, which focus on "who's right and who's wrong," into *dialogues,* based on open-minded wondering and sharing of ideas:

DEBATE	DIALOGUE
Knowing	Finding out
Answers	Questions
Winning or losing	Sharing (not always consensus . . .)
Unequal	Equal
Power	Respect or reverence
Proving a point, defending a position	Listening, exploring possibilities

Marvin Minsky, father of artificial intelligence, says that you don't know something until you know it in more than three ways.[3] What may seem like misunderstanding could actually be the root of a new idea.

MANAGING KNOWLEDGE

Fundamentally, knowledge management manages all knowledge as a central resource for the benefit of the organization as a whole—identifying, creating, capturing, conserving, organizing, transforming, transferring, delivering, and applying a group's collective "know-what" and "know-how." (Knowledge-creation, therefore, is a subset of knowledge management.)

Knowledge management requires people networking, computer networks, and (ultimately) global, multimedia linkages to facilitate group dialogues. Only then will the right people engage with the right information at the right time in a user-friendly manner. We're all knowledge managers, charged with helping each other capture and disseminate knowledge beyond the small group that may originally have created it. (Again we see how our relationships are the underpinning of successful knowledge-creation and innovation!)

The term *knowledge management* is the new "hot date" at the corporate prom. Its popularity derives in part from its easy fit into traditional management thinking. ("We can manage knowledge like we manage other inventory"), which makes sense when you primarily convert *material* resources into products to produce wealth. When a resource was used to make something, it couldn't simultaneously be used to make something else. For example, a piece of copper could be used for wire, pots, or art, but once some copper was used for one thing, there was less of it to use for another. In this paradigm of inventory (material) management, control is the key issue.

However knowledge follows a different course than material, which has a physical form. When knowledge contributes to making one thing, the same amount of, or more, knowledge still remains for another use. Knowledge has an additive or multiplicative nature when used, whereas material resources have a subtractive nature. When we try to apply the old "control" notions to managing knowledge, we actually stifle its creation and artificially limit its potential abundance as an internal resource.

To reinvent the rules of group knowledge-creation and sharing, we must explore five domains:

1. Expanding personal intelligence
2. Promoting informal communities of practice
3. Formalizing knowledge management
4. Accessing "outside" information
5. Using information technology

EXPANDING PERSONAL INTELLIGENCE

The old notion that personal intelligence is fixed doesn't hold true. To actually increase your intelligence, and thus the knowledge you create, you can actually get smarter by following four practices:

1. *Reprogram the "default settings" in personal thinking habits.* We all have certain negative mental and emotional habits, such as paying special attention to fear and crises or needing to "be right." Our brains have evolved to *automatically* think in "survival" terms, which can actually hinder intelligence. Through personal insight and taking advantage of diverse viewpoints in groups, you can adjust the following "survival/default settings":
   • Narrow thinking (looking at only a few things)
   • Fuzzy thinking (not differentiating between things)
   • Sprawling thinking (being overwhelmed by information's complexity)
   • Overly dramatic thinking (sensing most immediate fear issue)
   • Recent thinking (only "first, last, recent events" recalled)
   • Denial thinking ("this isn't happening"; shock)
2. *Build stronger relationships for sharing insights and ideas.* Scientists have long recognized that peer interaction stimulates new thinking better than anything else. Communities of practice clearly provide stimulation for generation of new knowledge by springing up around common interests or issues, though not necessarily project-oriented, management-sponsored ones.
3. *Promote "brain-healthy" habits.* How well we eat, drink, exercise, and sleep all have a huge impact on optimizing our intelligence.

4. *Develop more powerful intuition.* Intuition is perhaps the most neglected means of expanding intelligence. As Jonas Salk once said, "Intuition tells the thinking mind where to look next," often through the language of images and metaphors. Intuition allows us to see patterns and trends not evident in normal information but essential for interpreting data, seeing into an ambiguous future, and making decisions that are more likely to pay off.

Developing intuition is perhaps the most critical practice of the four, because it's essential for creative ideas and for wise, responsive decisions. Despite its increasing quantity and complexity, information doesn't keep up with the speed and complexity of the world; thus, there is *never* enough information from which to make a fully informed decision. With high-quality, global competition, speed is essential for getting new ideas developed, out the door, and into customers' hands. To be a leader, a company must constantly do things faster.

As decisions become more complex, the time to collect enough information is getting longer while the time needed for making a timely decision is getting shorter. Even if complete information were possible, it couldn't be kept up to date fast enough to keep pace with the shrinking windows of time for decisions. Intuition is the only survival skill we have that allows us to deal with this quandary. We've already seen how intuition plays a role in generating options, now let's examine its optimal role in making decisions.

Develop More Powerful Intuition

With intuition, you don't foresee a predestined future; you sense the possibility of events unfolding. You can then act, within limits, to co-create or to alter what you intuitively sensed. At the New Jersey Institute of Technology, research funded by Chester Carlson, inventor of xerography (Xerox), showed that 80 percent of CEOs who had doubled their company's profits in a five-year period proved above average in precognitive powers: "Things don't come to mind readily but all of a sudden, like pulling thoughts out of the air. You have to get your inspirations somewhere, and usually you get it from reading something else."[4] Westin Agor, famous for his decades of study on intuition in executives, found that more and more executives are defining their jobs as being the intuitive force in the company—seeing patterns and possibilities that no one else is in the position to see.

Intuition has a bad rap, sometimes deservedly so. We all know the stories of people who made foolish decisions in the name of "intuition" or were "shooting from the hip" and somehow found the right target.

Yet intuition is such a profoundly critical skill—perhaps the most essential one for making strategic choices—that it would be a grave error not to address it. Take, for example, multimillion dollar acquisitions: What would be the benefit if somehow you could double your success rate in strategizing, choosing, and managing them? What about even a 50 percent increase in "wins"?

In 1952 Ray Kroc bought the ability to franchise Richard and Maurice McDonald's restaurants, creating a chain of 228 between 1952 and 1957. He received only 2 percent of the gross and had to turn over more than 25 percent of that to the McDonald brothers. In 1960 he asked them to give him a price to buy everything, including the name. They said $2.7 million, which Kroc's attorney thought was exorbitant. Kroc recalled, "I'm not a gambler and I didn't have that kind of money, but my funny-bone instinct kept urging me on. So I closed my office door, cussed up and down, and threw things out the window. Then I called my lawyer back and said, 'Take it!'"[5]

In any major decision, there is information to be gathered using both logic and intuition. Intuition is a highly disciplined, *information-gathering* process with five steps:

1. *Ask*: Gain focus with clear questions. Your questions can have either a broad or a narrow focus. This is the difference between, "What's my purpose in life" and "What should I order for lunch today?"
2. *Access*: Let go of expectations, wishes, hopes, and fears. Record all impressions—symbols, sights, sounds, sensations.
3. *Interpret*: Be your own final judge; only *you* can interpret what a particular impression means.
4. *Integrate*: Combine your intuitive information with other sources of knowledge and experience.
5. *Act*: Practice and learn from your results. Begin practicing on small things. Come from an attitude of curiosity and confidence.

Therefore, decisions are not be be made solely from intuition, but using intuitive information combined with other sources of knowledge and experience. Let's look in more detail at what you can do to free up your intuition at each step of the process.

Ask

Like a lens on a camera, questions focus your intuition, to allow you to get a clear picture—wide-angle or very close up. Dr. Benjamin Libet, physiologist at the University of California at San Francisco, claims the brain begins to ask for something and actually initiates the action about 0.4 seconds before the brain's owner is aware of wanting it. However, the quality of the questions you ask drives the potential quality of intuitive insight. Two important questions to ask yourself here are:

- How do I limit my focus by my habitual ways of looking for specific types of information?
- In the past, what questions *didn't* I ask when I made decisions that didn't turn out well?

Most of us prefer certain types of information, but if you are overly focused on one particular way of receiving information, you will limit access to your intuition. For example, looking at past business decisions that didn't work out for you, what questions did you *not* ask? Did you overlook questions like:

- What am I missing in this situation? What are the obstacles to success?
- What are the opportunities here? What do I need to do differently?
- What will happen in the near future? Long term? How will things change as a result of ____?
- What information do I need for a wise decision?
- Is this a wise course of action (yes/no)? If yes, how can I optimize it?" If no, what can I do to turn it into one?

Access

Next, you access your intuitive source. Notice all of the images and impressions you receive after you ask your question. You will most likely receive your intuitive information in symbolic form: seeing an image or scene or word, hearing a piece of music, getting a physical sensation, feeling an unexplained emotion (an inner fear, contentment, or "yes"). Jonas Salk commented,

> *Our subjective responses (intuitional) are more sensitive and more rapid than our objective responses (reasoned). This is the nature of the way the mind works. We first sense and then we reason why. Intuition must be allowed a free rein and be allowed to play.*[6]

Usually, we trust one intuitive sense the most and another the least. For me, I usually trust hearing the most and vision the least. You might get an answer in the first 30 seconds auditorily but then make it more complicated by doubting it, then getting your visual mode of intuition involved, which you're not as fluent in. Finally, the busy-bee mind kicks in and you get intuitively fuzzy. Trust your strongest sense the most.

Interpret

Intuitive symbols condense information in a highly sophisticated way. The symbols that you receive can be literal or figurative. How do you learn to trust that you understand your own intuitive symbols correctly . . . that you are interpreting them correctly?

First, notice if you are discounting or contaminating the information you have received. For example, have you detached from your expectations, wishes, hopes, and fears? Ask your intuition if an interpretation is right. Notice themes and see if a symbol means the same thing for you over time.

Integrate

The best decisions integrate intuitive information with other data, experience, and knowledge; each provides its own unique facet of wisdom. Use intuition to gain information you might not normally acquire. Then integrate that information and make decisions based on:

- What you know (knowledge and memories)
- How you feel (emotions and feelings)
- What you intuit (intuition)
- What you think (judgments and interpretations)

When Allen Neuharth decided to launch *USA Today*, he had printing plants in thirty-eight states operating only a few hours per day. Eighty separate reporter staffs pounded out many stories. He foresaw that satellite transmission could merge all this into a network for a national paper. The unanswered question was "Will there be a market for this?" Results of a market survey of 40,000 households indicated only "Maybe." The decision he made to launch *USA Today* was not based on logic alone.

Act

At first, implementing an intuitive decision may seem risky. With experience, curiosity, and feedback, you'll gain more confidence. Initially, keep intuitive information separate from other information so you can test and become equally skilled at each. With hindsight, you can identify decisions you've made that worked out badly because you overrode or misunderstood your intuition—maybe you didn't ask the right questions, pay attention to insights and hunches, or blend intuition with other things you knew. I keep track of my intuitive cues about which lines of cars at the tollbooths will be fastest. My wife practices with her calendar: She asks her intuition if a meeting is really going to happen or be time well spent. By looking at the results, she gets better at scheduling meetings that really happen and produce what they intend.

In this context of acting on an intuition, research is more of a confirmation tool than a discovery tool. By paying attention to your intuition, you can open up to new information that will aid you in living your personal purpose. Remember that feedback supports you in fine-tuning your ability to gain and interpret intuitive information. From a *learning* perspective, however, the experiment of acting on your intuition is always a success, even if the results are unwanted.

PROMOTING INFORMAL COMMUNITIES OF PRACTICE

Creativity sometimes involves combining information, ideas, technologies, or systems in new ways. Unanticipated exchanges with people you don't normally meet at work enable you to identify and self-organize new projects. Your ability to form networks with people gives you rich interconnections to generate better ideas and a flexible structure to make good use of them.

Informal communities of practice form around common interests for sharing information and putting what you learn to work. In chapter 6, you read about a Fortune 100 telecommunications company where key people took on the risky entrepreneurial role of (a) finding suitable business partners in emerging countries and (b) "cracking the code" of what it takes to do business in certain "emerging" conditions. In one case they cut the time-to-profitability from three years to only six months. Their success grew from translating the lessons from one region of the world to another. That's one goal of communities of practice: Through your experiments, successes, and errors, your learning can make the next assignment more efficient and effective for everyone.

These communities of practice have different tasks, depending on where their members are in their own Creative Journey (innovation process):

Innovation Process	Task for Communities of Practice
CHALLENGE	Target specific, important knowledge-creation goals
FOCUS	Stimulate robust relationships, communication, and information management
CREATIVE SOLUTIONS	Originate new insights through creative collaboration
COMPLETION	Identify and transfer new learning, to get people up to speed

Every *unexpected* creative act begins with a periods of *unofficial* activity. This provides a safe haven for the new and different, because it doesn't recognize boundaries and doesn't require massive resources (e.g., more employee time requiring higher salary). Bureaucracy fails at stimulating creativity because its rules of communication keep things separate and won't tolerate creative changes to the boundaries of power.

The intelligent organizations of the future will encourage "idea brokers" who see the value of new interconnections and find ways to bring disparate parts of the organization together. You can formally recognize and even give a little funding to support these communities of practice, but never make the mistake of formalizing them with promises of concrete deliverables. Communities of practice gain their power and value from being organic, fluid communities of people who come together from their own shared interests. Control them, and they die.

Communities of practice foster greater pluralism, choice, and equality. They create a hunger for new ideas and promote less fearful, more honest dialogue. The network is thus more likely to pursue, learn from, and act on new information and new ideas. Networks learn faster because of the following qualities:[7]

QUALITIES	EFFECTS
Broad representation (across functions and/or departments)	Breaking down isolation and opening up communication
Equal participation	Developing nonhierarchical relationships with flexible knowledge- and skill-based leadership
"Network" power	Creating new coalitions and a spirit of collaboration
New norms and values	Influencing by example rather than authority
Win-win problem solving	Diminishing turf battles

When you operate in communities of practice, you "bootleg" resources from everywhere. You seek to find leverage points for exercising power through new alliances. Free of traditional barriers and constraints, you actively seek support from—and give support to— nontraditional sources anywhere in your organization.

Should communities of practice be encouraged only for the so-called knowledge worker? Verna Allee says, "There is no typical knowledge worker. Knowledge is everywhere. All employees deserve the same 'special treatment' the literature reserves for knowledge workers."[8] As stated by Jan Carlzon, former Chairman of Scandinavian Airlines, "An individual without information cannot take responsibility; an individual who is given information cannot help but take responsibility."

FORMALIZING KNOWLEDGE MANAGEMENT

Knowledge management and corporate strategy depend on each other. Knowledge management must function in alignment with corporate initiatives that foster innovation. And corporate strategies cannot work without the focus, motivation, vision, and collaboration that knowledge management provides. You can formalize knowledge management in three ways:

- Create a knowledge management group.
- Embed knowledge management in the business and organizational structures.
- Focus knowledge management activities through internal venture teams.

Create a Knowledge Management Group

At one chemical company, they have appointed a director of knowledge management from their information technology group. His group's objectives are to stimulate, collect, and facilitate the creation, storage ("memory"), and dissemination of knowledge. The essence of their work is to promote stimulating dialogues and facilitate people's finding the right software and hardware. The director is heavily involved in networking his group to others worldwide to gain new knowledge about how to manage knowledge itself.

I participated in a study of the best practices for retaining, and producing new, intellectual capital. It involved three dozen major corporations and consulting firms, and was conducted by Ian Rose of IBR Consulting Services Ltd. in Vancouver. To form the most viable "knowledge management groups," he recommends the following ten measures:[9]

1. *Construct a strong business case*: Emphasize the importance of years of expertise to running a successful enterprise (an organization that offered early retirement to 1,000 employees, each with a quarter century of experience, has theoretically forfeited 25,000 years of institutional memory).
2. *Provide specific resources*: To get the benefits of knowledge transfer, invest in it like any other venture that may transform an organization.
3. *Appoint a chief knowledge officer*: You cannot depend just on line management to make the system work. Put a "can-do" person in charge. Knowledge management systems are like exercise; sometimes somebody has to prod you and remind you to keep

at it or you lose the benefit. You need a champion with the power to design the knowledge architecture, to set up the processes and disciplines for control, to harness the resources needed to establish and maintain the system, and to promote its benefits throughout the organization.

4. *Limit the group's role*: A knowledge management group should: (a) direct those activities best controlled from a central point and (b) support those activities best handled from decentralized locations, where each business unit remains responsible for managing their own knowledge. Too often, knowledge management groups impose themselves on an organization and attempt to dictate what the learning processes should be.

5. *Identify the most critical knowledge*: You could get crushed under the weight of all the know-how in most companies. Concentrate on, and be clear about, what is really important.

6. *Eliminate redundant information*: All the material in your system needs to have a "sell by" date. Knowledge atrophies. Its half-life is often relatively short.

7. *Do not devalue old knowledge*: Some companies may be *too* innovative. If the culture is strongly infused with leaders who value innovation and the creation of new intellectual capital, they may chase the new concepts without effectively supporting the legacy ideas and ideals that built the business.

8. *Be cautious of technology*: A sobering reality is overtaking our naive fascination with computers. As we understand their limitations, we begin to appreciate human capabilities even more. Technology is critical, but knowledge management focuses more on how people work, share information, and create value. Technology enables change but doesn't drive it.

> **Technology is critical, but knowledge management focuses more on how people work, share information, and create value.**

9. *Involve and empower more employees*: Knowledge transfer cannot be the burden of just one department. Corporate success depends on "a company of leaders"—people at all levels who embody the skills needed to lead the corporation to success. Successful knowledge management groups build a shared vision and develop the skills of those natural leaders, wherever they may be found.

10. *Eliminate the group as soon as possible*: Knowledge management should be an *integrated* part of the business rather than an *applied* part, implemented by a separate functional unit.

Embed Knowledge Management in the Business and Organizational Structures

In one biotech organization, members of the senior management of the product development group recently took a leap . . . not off a cliff, but a creative leap. As they restructured their entire organization, they wanted to go beyond the normal considerations of who reports to whom, who evaluates and makes decisions over whom, and so forth. How the new structure could enhance the growth of intellectual capital was a primary consideration. As I worked with them, we designed a solution that involved three core groups for new product development:

NEW PRODUCT DEVELOPMENT

Business Development <<<<< >>>>> Market Development
(first-stage technology)   (second-stage technology)
<<<<<<<<< Intellectual Capital Development >>>>>>>>>

Senior management and the core staff members (information technology, human resources, etc.) comprised the Intellectual Capital Development (ICD) group, but their new jobs in ICD were *not* to manage the actual work of new product development! In the new, process-based structure, the executives were to be primarily responsible for developing the human capital that contributes to intellectual capital. For example: In a functionally based organization, the head of engineering "manages engineering work" as well as develops a highly skilled staff. In a process-based organization, the head of engineering develops a highly skilled staff and then "farms them out" to process managers, who then manage the engineering work.

This change in focus for executives—from "managing work" to "developing people and knowledge"—can be a difficult internal shift for some. One's self-esteem can be challenged, and worries about job security can arise: "Am I as valuable to the company in this role, rather than overseeing the 'actual work'?" As tough as this might be, process-based organizational structures depend on this essential transition to work optimally.

Knowledge leaders—who can have this role formally or informally—have different roles they can play to support people during each stage of the Creative Journey innovation process:

Innovation Process	Roles of Business/Knowledge Leaders
CHALLENGE	*Establish stretch goals and knowledge targets.* Take time to examine and question the purpose of things, and what you don't know (but need to). Develop a sense of urgency; nowadays, learning is revolutionary rather than evolutionary, as we rapidly discard the old ways and shift quickly to the new.
FOCUS	*Stimulate people renewal, collaborative linkages, and information tools.* Spur conversations of all kinds: Learners need to talk to make sense of new ideas for themselves. This is not idle conversation; it is inventive conversation. Keep asking: "How could we have done it better?" and "Who could benefit from our learnings?"
CREATIVE SOLUTIONS	*Promote creative/diverse ideas, wise criteria, and shared decision power.* Demand intellectual respect: People care about whether their ideas are valued. We often are better at tearing down each other's ideas than building them up. Appreciation will bear the fruit of more and more ideas.
COMPLETION	*Ensure solid agreements, "full value" appraisals, and group-based wins.* Promote team learning and apply positive reinforcement: Remind team members of what they knew when they were young—that learning can be fun and rewarding! Emphasize that the more you learn, the better and quicker you learn.

Focus Knowledge Management Activities Through Internal Venture Teams

Many companies are setting up internal ventures in which a project team is put to a task outside of the normal reporting structures, or even outside of the normal compensation guidelines. These "intrapreneurial" structures have advantages, particularly when there's a need to respond to market and technological changes as quickly as smaller competitive companies can. IBM's PC was developed this way. All of their venture teams are headed by what they call *true believers*. Internal ventures are also often instituted when the normal structures have simply become too unwieldy.

At 3M, to foster deep, personal pride and ownership in ideas, the divisions created even smaller companies specifically for developing new products. Whole teams in these business-development units are responsible for seeing a product through from development to introduction. The team is evaluated as a whole; if marketing screws up, that's the engineer's problem too. 3M's goal is to produce products that meet customer needs quickly and more accurately.

An overall principle to guide venture teams is the promotion of what Rosabeth Moss Kanter calls *integrative* rather than *segmentalist* interactions among people. As she puts it, integrativeness is "the willingness to move beyond received wisdom, to combine ideas from unconnected sources, to embrace change as an opportunity to test limits." Segmentalism is "concerned with compartmentalizing actions, events, and problems and keeping each piece isolated from the others."[10]

Integrative thinking is necessary for innovation and is more likely found where there are integrative structures: few boundaries between units, mechanisms to exchange information, multiple functions involved in decisions, and so forth. Segmentalist structures, which reinforce anticreative thinking, have a large number of units walled off from each other; problems are carved into pieces for specialists who work in isolation. "Even innovation itself can become a specialty in segmentalist systems—something given to the R&D department to take care of so that no one else has to worry about it."

Segmentalist organizations also tend to value the logical, linear modes of problem solving to the exclusion of the intuitive. The integrative organization values fluency in both modes.

ACCESSING "OUTSIDE" INFORMATION

The vitality and renewal of any business depends on learning as the "inhaling" and innovation as the "exhaling" of organizational life. That is, without a rhythm and flow of learning and innovation, at a pace that leads or matches the rate of product turnover in the industry, an organization runs the risk of extinction.

In order to promote innovation, you must pay attention to the different ways that ideas for significant innovations get introduced into the corporate development system. A compilation of many research studies reveals that 50 percent of significant new ideas—ones that turn into important, profitable innovations—come from outside sources. But more revealing is the fact that only 25 percent of significant innovations come from the formal business planning process; 75 percent come in more opportunistic ways, such as listening to a customer suggestion or responding to a sudden move by a competitor. In addition, 50 percent of the ideas come from employees (internally), and 50 percent come from external sources, such as customers and suppliers.

To set appropriate strategic direction, we all need to combine purpose and vision with understanding the external environment: the gusts and waves of changing social, economic, competitor, technological, environmental, political, and human conditions.

Strategic issues most often named by CEOs include:

- Fierce competition—domestic, international, and cross-industry restructuring
- Deregulation of industries—competition, changing markets, and industry
- Changing markets—market segmentation, consumer values, and offshore markets
- Economic/financial uncertainty—growth/stability, inflation/ interest rates, capital availability, and the international monetary system
- Government policies/uncertainty—taxation, regulation, trade, and political risk
- Technological impacts on business—tracking and timing of investments
- Changing workforce—productivity, education/training, and succession planning

Gathering and disseminating information about these issues, in usable form, provide the greatest stimulus for innovation at all levels. This frequent stimulus keeps us thinking, feeling fresh, and on our creative toes. Since it is often the case that the nonexpert on a subject can most easily see the nonobvious question or insight, it makes sense to distribute condensed monitoring information widely throughout the organization and provide a means for new ideas to surface.

Widespread distribution of this information can broaden your sources of new ideas. In fast-moving markets, this broad participation in innovation can be the primary competitive advantage of your organization. On the whole, monitoring the environment and distributing the information widely can:

- Provide early notice of threats or opportunities.
- Increase personnel's awareness of the changing environment and the implications for their own work.
- Increase interdepartmental cooperation as well as bottom-up communication.
- Assist early identification of promising, innovative industrials.

There are two approaches to gathering information about the external environment: scanning and monitoring. Scanning is an early warning system used to detect signals of new trends of potential importance to the organization. Monitoring is the detailed tracking of events and trends of known importance to the organization.

A system for scanning and monitoring not only ensures that an organization has up-to-date information about trends of known importance, but also keeps it from being surprised by new trends. By using this information to develop alternative scenarios about the future, organizations can develop appropriate business strategies and hone internal operations.

Scanning Systems

A scanning system analyzes disparate events in the environment to identify an emerging trend of significance for your organization. Such a system is not a luxury but a necessity. It provides you with security from surprise threats as well as insights into potential competitive advantages.

There are some good models for formal scanning systems. For example, organizations such as the U.S. Congress, Bell Canada, and SRI International have all used a Trend Evaluation and Monitoring (TEAM) approach to identify emerging issues and early signs of social, political, economic, and technological change that could result in threats or opportunities.

TEAM is based on three levels of participation:

1. A volunteer group of monitors regularly reviews one or more publications or Internet sites for items suggesting a change that could affect the organization.
2. Brief abstracts on those items are forwarded to a small committee chosen for their diverse backgrounds and analytical skills. Once a month they attempt to piece together various bits of information that could be important to the organization.
3. The results of the analysis committee's discussions are sent to a steering committee of senior management and to each monitor. The senior committee decides which topics to bring to the attention of specific managers or the organization as a whole.

The TEAM approach can be visualized as shown on page 227:

Monitoring Systems

Monitoring alone covers only the known driving forces affecting an organization's future. There are four central issues regarding monitoring the external environment:

1. Establishing formal and informal monitoring systems.
2. Targeting the information you want.
3. Analyzing and interpreting the information.
4. Applying the information in decisions and action.

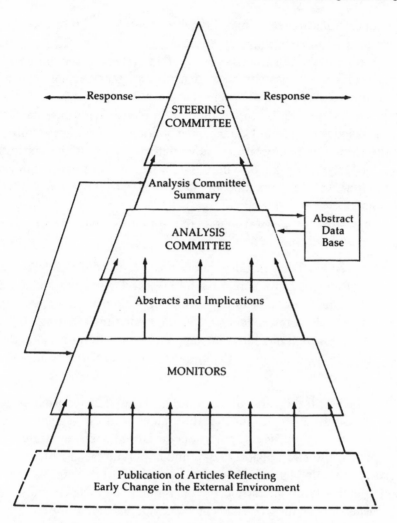

Establishing Monitoring Systems

There are both formal and informal monitoring systems. In many U.S. companies, it is difficult to find any formal monitoring system, much less one that carefully distributes information to the appropriate levels within the organization.

A formal system can be operated by a single individual, a centralized component within the organization (such as marketing research), many decentralized components, or through coordinated networking. Networking is often the most efficient and economical monitoring option. In this case, coordination is generally provided by one component in the organization. Beware: The scope of a monitoring operation is often too great for a single individual; a single component may often also lack the expertise required to properly manage it; and decentralized operations are sometimes difficult to control, and they often produce gaps or overlaps in information.

A key feature of successful monitoring systems is the presence of "gatekeepers" (see chapter 7), who act as monitors of change outside the framework of a formal system. They might communicate with their technical cohorts, for example, about technology trends. Internal technical societies might hold gatekeeping colloquia on projects going on in the various company labs. Another gatekeeping activity is exemplified by Hewlett Packard, where hardware and software engineers spend time working in retail computer stores to be more in touch with customers' wants and needs.

There are three general sources of information that should be used for monitoring:

1. External media, including public press, competitors' publications, investment analysts reports, and research companies' analyses.
2. Internal reports, including technology and market analyses and feedback from vendors, customers, trade shows.
3. Networking, including exchanging ideas within formal and informal groups (inside the organization and within professional groups).

To be worth the effort of monitoring, continuous reporting is necessary. "Continuous" means that the system produces regular reports of information, *immediately* points out deviations from key strategy assumptions, and alerts people to new and important trends. Attempts at "exceptions only" reporting erodes the usefulness of the information for updating the ongoing strategic and operational planning efforts.

Depending on the scope and complexity of the monitoring (and scanning) activity, an organization may want to computerize the information.

The combination of a formal system, gatekeepers, and other monitoring methods gives us maximum exposure to our external environment. We can experience a significant loss of valuable information if any method is missing.

Targeting the Information

There can sometimes be so much information, leading to so much confusion, that the monitoring may not seem worth the effort to us. Early on, it is important to identify the type of information that is most relevant to our organization's key factors for success.

The information also needs to be formatted and reduced into a digestible form. When using the scenario method discussed in chapter 9, key driving forces can be identified relative to a decision. Information about these key driving forces can become the focal points for monitoring activities.

For example, suppose that we were concerned about who would most likely buy some particular highly innovative new product. Defining our consumer market and knowing how market segments respond to innovation would be very important to us. Our *initial choice of market segmentation schemes* could make or break our efforts to get relevant information.

Analyzing and Interpreting Information

The wealth of available information is useless unless it is analyzed and interpreted. One application of trend information that can easily stimulate innovation is *Vulnerability Analysis*, where potential threats are examined according to the grid found below. This is a powerful tool for highlighting the need and possible directions for innovation. The basic steps of Vulnerability Analysis are as follows:

1. Identify underpinnings critical to your organization's health—resources/assets, relative costs, customer base, technologies, competition, social values, sanctions, and so on.
2. Identify forces that could damage underpinnings.
3. List potential threats.
4. Compile individuals' judgments of the potential impact from

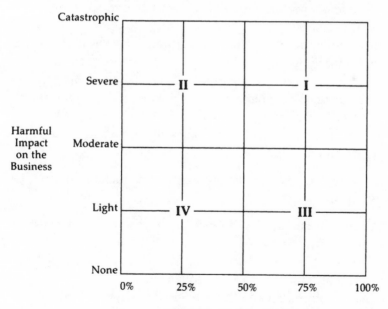

Probability That the Threatening
Event or Condition Will Occur

each threat and determine if a consensus exists.

5. Examine the overall threat pattern (How pervasive? Will it be sustained? What alternative futures can be constructed and planned for?).

USING INFORMATION TECHNOLOGY

As so beautifully put by Alan Robinson and Sam Stern,

Humans have a natural drive to explore and create. The majority of creative acts in companies are self-initiated, which explains why they are unanticipated by management. A system must reach everyone, be easy to use, have strong follow-through, document ideas, and be based on intrinsic motivation.[11]

Information technology operates at the core of almost all knowledge management processes in two ways. The first way is providing knowledge to targeted groups:

- Portions of training and career management available globally through a website.
- Customer service through the Internet or other information technologies (fax, email, etc.).
- Market development enhanced by access to internal and external product, market, financial, and technology databases.
- Product knowledge available on web pages for customers or employees.
- Storehouse for corporate-wide learnings, such as best practices, benchmarking studies, and employee expertise "yellow pages."
- Electronic "performance support" via computer applications used by service representatives to provide technical information or product information on demand.
- New author-ware tools for trainers that automate some aspects of developing multimedia training programs.

The second way is fostering spontaneous interactions between small groups of people.

- Groupware in meetings for people to respond anonymously to issues (particularly useful for culturally diverse groups).
- Remote access for working on the road or at home.
- Corporate communication through email.
- Shared information on Lotus Notes databases or Intranet websites.

I had one fast-food client that used computer networking to share crucial information needed for problem solving. For example, if there was great difficulty in negotiating a deal to place a restaurant in a certain community, that difficulty was broadcast for input and help. And when negotiations were successful, the contract language was shared worldwide within 24 hours so that similar disputed negotiations might apply the new knowledge. The crucial need for this type of information encouraged people to take the time to input it and to access it throughout the world.

The technologies that support these activities fall into four major clusters:

1. *Data management* technologies can efficiently and effectively manage huge stores of data for learning applications, especially when they include video, photographs, sound, and speech.
2. *Multimedia* technologies improve the person-machine interaction for successful learning.
3. *Network* technologies electronically link disparate databases and people for as-needed, low-effort access.
4. *Artificial intelligence* enables expert systems to package and leverage special skills and knowledge.

Although technology is useful, knowledge travels best when it travels with people. People need conversations that quickly connect them to the right people with the right information at the right time, with the information technology serving as an intelligence resource. With that in place, expertise gets tapped and knowledge gets leveraged.

The degree to which information technology (IT) plays a role in knowledge management depends in part, on the nature of the business. In financial firms such as Charles Schwab, the pioneer discount brokerage firm, the speed and sophistication of their IT is a primary feature of their products and services. IT differentiates them and what they offer to clients as an alternative to full-fee brokerage firms.

The advent of personal computers has allowed a level of empowerment and independent use of information that was unimaginable fifteen years ago. In the coming years, IT and knowledge management will cause even more dramatic changes in management and corporate structure. For example, strengthening a network between technology developers and their marketing colleagues, a new paradigm could be born, with functions called *research and marketing (R&M)* rather than *research and development (R&D)*.

The use of information systems also raises many questions regarding other issues concerning the CREATIVE climate for innovation, described in chapter 6, including:

- *Risk awareness:* Will information get wider distribution to where problems exist "locally"? Will information about the business environment get more attention and generate faster responses?
- *Collaborative learning:* Will the steps for problem solving—perceive the situation, define the problem, analyze, generate alternatives, etc.—proceed faster and more effectively, yet with broader participation?
- *Intuition and logic:* Will people develop fluency in intuition as well as logic, or will they rely on data-crunching to drive their own idea-generation and decision-making?
- *Empowered decision making:* Will a wider distribution of information processing mean more or less balance of power in departmental collaborations? Will "Lone Rangers" make decisions without collaborating by assuming that they have all the information they need?

As these questions suggest, information systems could be the greatest reinforcement—or the greatest hindrance—to our other efforts to implement a CREATIVE climate.

Information systems are often justified and designed for their impact on productivity. The savings in costs, time, and effort can generate significant competitive advantages. However, their impact on innovation can be just as significant. Many organizations suffer from a missed opportunity in not making creativity an equally urgent justification and criteria for developing information systems. Our work lives are filled with more and more information, coming to us faster and faster. How we employ information systems can dramatically affect how we employ our creativity and ultimately how we enhance our employment.

Information technology can also "mine" data and generate new knowledge across the enterprise, and then apply that information to new innovations. A sophisticated example of mining key learnings and passing them on to those who need them is Bell Canada's Electronic Performance Support System (EPSS). EPSS introduces a new user interface for new customer service reps, using graphics to deliver a series of on-line hints, prompts, coaches, and tutorials. The goal of EPSS is to significantly reduce the time in classroom training for new people in their call centers. When a rep talks to a customer, EPSS delivers learning "just-in-time" with context-sensitive hints and prompts. The reps can also access tutorials and new product updates when they're not talking directly with a customer.

Many companies still operate on the assumption that employees automatically share their knowledge. People in a *global* company must exchange information and resources on a worldwide scale. It used to be: "Do you need to know?" Now it's "Everybody needs to know." As these companies expand globally, face-to-face conversations about tacit knowledge can become less frequent, limiting new knowledge-creation. One study found two other main problems: Many people parlay their best ideas into starting their own businesses; individual contributors already "know what they know" and resist the time it takes to input their knowledge for others.

Engaging the whole organization is clearly not easy. People will share knowledge only if they see a distinct benefit. Technology has just made it easier. IT alone is necessary but insufficient for a modern knowledge-management system. Real learning depends on people's commitment to contributing valuable information (e.g., lessons learned) to a common base and getting into the habit of going to this base to find useful ideas.

IN CLOSING . . .

Knowledge management requires much more than first-rate, state-of-the-art information technology and a highly competent group leading the effort. Your personal and corporate success depend on how well you invest, renew, and leverage your *own* knowledge and creativity and *your colleagues'* creativity, since group synergy now drives personal success. This requires considerably more flexibility and courage than in the past.

The emergence of knowledge as the core corporate asset changes the nature of your relationship and career within your company. If you're like most knowledge workers, you have a stronger identity, and loyalty, to your profession than to your company: "I'm an OD specialist (or HR manager, or software engineer, or sales counselor . . .) who is currently working at _____." Your career develops not so much by moving from one position to another, but by going from one project to another (hopefully one with greater importance). Companies are saying, "We'll provide education and opportunities for your career, but you have to take the initiative with them."

True networking depends on the quality of relationships you can form. The heart and soul of knowledge management thrives by unleashing dedication, determination, collaboration, and creativity among people throughout the organization. How well you establish a CREATIVE climate for stretching, risk taking, experimenting, and celebrating will make or break your efforts.

As the poet A. R. Ammons says,[12]

Don't establish the
boundaries
first
the squares, triangles,
boxes
of preconceived
possibility,
and then
pour
life into them, trimming
off left-over edges,
ending potential:
let centers
proliferate
from
self-justifying motions!

By actively practicing core values such as authenticity, truthfulness, caring, equanimity, responsibility, and well-being, you'll elevate knowledge management to a noble quest. Mental skills are not enough. Courage and commitment come from the heart, the true seat of corporate wisdom.

CHAPTER 13

Implement *Strategic Innovation* Management

We've been working to improve the relationship between the company, the employees, and the unions who represent them. Just to get them to understand each other so they can solve their common problems together is a major undertaking. Leading through service is the key. I honor both cultures that are being represented. Their joint success is what matters to me.

I learned everything I could about them, their culture, who they are and why they see what they see as valuable . . . learning as much as I possibly could about unions, the union movement, labor law, labor relations — to really say truthfully, "I understand it, I value it, and my role here is to make sure that the unions, the company, and the people who represent them remain whole."

—ROGER, ORGANIZATIONAL CONSULTANT WITH A MAJOR UTILITY

SPONSORING INNOVATIVE TEAMS

Societies and economies have always organized themselves around the use of abundant resources and the conservation of scarce resources. Wealth and status always occur in relation to the transformation of these resources into an exchange of value. For example, from 1945 to 1985, the most abundant resource in the world was seen to be oil, and the world economy and global society grew from the production of products and services based on oil (in plastics, etc.).

As we've realized that material resources such as oil are limited in supply, we've simultaneously identified *knowledge and intelligence* as our most abundant, renewable resources. This represents a huge shift in the organizing principle of economies. To adapt and thrive, business must develop more complex and unique structures, systems, and work processes.

Mother Nature again guides us in dealing with this complexity. As one ponders the evolutionary ladder from rock to plant to reptile to mammal to human, more and more consciousness becomes clearly evident as one moves up the ladder. Teilhard de Chardin, a twentieth-century scientist and priest pointed out that consciousness exists in all matter—it simply shows up more clearly in more complex organizations of matter.[1] Consciousness increases as biological complexity increases. Similarly, as the business ecosystem evolves in complexity, organizations will require more consciousness, paralleled by more complex ways of organizing a great diversity of people and processes. The solutions will not be a lack of structure. Rather, sustainable growth will demand from us a rapid *(r)evolution in how we collaborate* to learn and innovate.

> **As the business ecosystem evolves in complexity, organizations will require more consciousness, paralleled by more complex ways of organizing . . .**

What are the keys? Mother Nature teaches us that experimentation and a great respect for diversity head the list. When this innovativeness and respect are hard to come by—for example, in a competitive situation such as union versus management—how can we bridge this critical gap? How do we sponsor innovation throughout our organization? How do we develop a corporate culture that promotes growth in consciousness and therefore in real-world effectiveness? How do we innovate flexible work processes as well as fantastic customer products or services? And how do we do all this while navigating the seas of complexity?

Valuing people is the first step. Biological growth begins with an individual cell. Consciousness growth—higher respect for experimentation and diversity—begins with an individual person. Roger James, quoted at the beginning of this chapter, personifies respect for differences, based on two of his key spiritual values: service and deep caring.

And after that? Focus on the next unit of individuation: groups and teams. Learn what it takes to establish a micro-culture of entrepreneurial skills and (r)evolutionize any tendencies toward bureaucracy in your own company culture. Bureaucracy is the enemy of innovation: It exercises too much central control and stifles the intrinsic motivation, initiative, and caring. As noted by Gifford and Elizabeth Pinchot,

> *The rules of bureaucracy forbid caring and acting on the basis of the inner values one holds dear. We find no examples of innovation where the intrapreneur did not break some bureaucratic rules. If we want to change a bureaucratic system, we can begin by liberating the self-organizing potential of people working in teams. Then the focus of change will be to provide the conditions in which this freedom leads to the most constructive results.[2]*

Even your best cross-functional team—complete with great talent, communications, vision, and values—can fall short of its potential, depending on its relationship with the rest of your organization, particularly with executive sponsors. When I was senior consultant for innovation management at SRI International, I headed a study to understand the critical success factors for corporations to integrate their entrepreneurial acquisitions. The executives I interviewed at twenty-two corporations judged less than half of their acquisitions to be long-term successes. They failed to keep alive the innovation culture and output that had made the start-up attractive in the first place.

Ultimately, I found that sixteen factors in the relationship between the parent company and the acquisition determine the life or death of innovation cultures. Further research showed that the same factors were essential in *any* relationship between *sponsors* of innovative projects and the *teams* who were actually innovating. The following table shows the key issues that sponsors and teams must satisfactorily resolve in dialogue with each other for intelligent innovation.

CULTURE ISSUES	KEY DIALOGUES "How well do sponsors and teams agree on . . ."
1. Purpose and vision	A compelling sense of vision and strategy?
2. Values and character	Personal values behind the vision?
3. Strategic knowledge	The context of risk and opportunity?
4. Risk taking	Pursuing stretch goals that offer special learning and achievement opportunities?
5. Talent development	What knowledge and skill resources are needed?
6. Staffing and empowerment	Team responsibilities equal to their talent?
7. Communications	The level of open communication?
8. "Systems" thinking	How to use IT to leverage time & effectiveness?
9. Knowledge creation	The need to challenge assumptions?
10. Innovative thinking	Using diverse approaches to generating breakthrough as well as incremental ideas?
11. Collaboration	The decision-making criteria and process?
12. Decision process	Empowerment to co-decide the best solution?
13. Resource allocation	The finances and people needed to implement?
14. Leading change	Time, performance, and budget measures?
15. Performance coaching	How to assess learning as well as achievement?
16. Motivation and rewards	Specific intrinsic & extrinsic "rewards and satisfactions?"

Significantly, these factors also align with the four stages of the team's Creative Journey process! That is, sponsors and teams must pay attention to distinctly different elements of the culture for different stages of innovation.

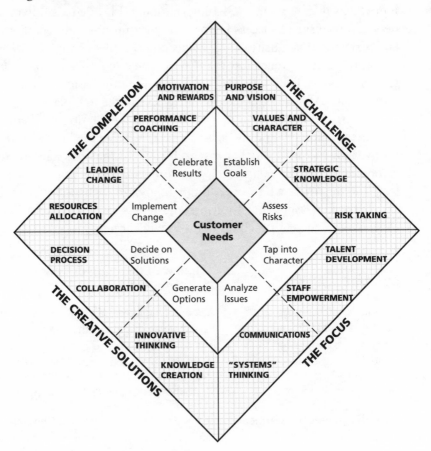

**The "Strategic Innovation Management" Culture
Supports the Creative Journey**

In the Challenge stage, leaders must address four factors based on the question, *"What's important?"* In the Focus stage, leaders must address four factors based on, *"What's empowering?"* In the Creative Solutions stage, leaders must address four factors based on, *"What's value-adding?"* In the Completion stage, leaders must address four factors based on, *"What's working?"*

Team leaders and members share the responsibility equally with sponsoring executives for creating this culture for innovation. Whatever position you're in you can take responsibility to negotiate stronger support during each stage of a team's Creative Journey. By focusing on the most critical questions, depending on the stage a team is in, you can stimulate and engage everyone's intelligence and business judgment.

MEASURING THE CULTURE FOR INNOVATION

Executives can best strategize how to develop a "systems integrity" for supporting each and every team reporting to them, making sure that the organization's policies and systems enable rather than stifle focused innovation. You can improve only what you measure, and we can measure the innovation culture for all sixteen factors.

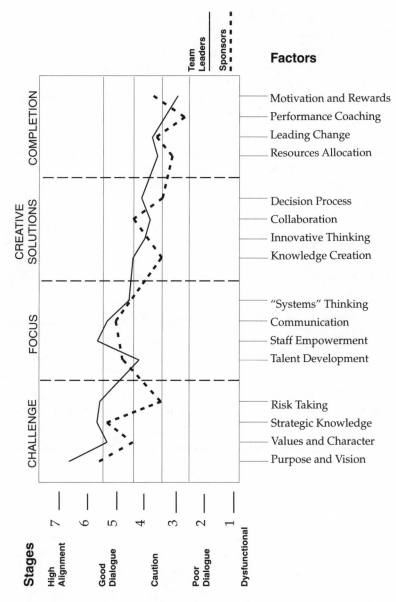

For example, the research group of a major pharmaceutical company asked forty team leaders and sixty executive sponsors to complete the *Strategic Innovation Management Assessment Profile (SIMAP)*, a survey by the Global Creativity Corporation based on the sixteen factors discussed here. The similarities and differences between these groups' responses are shown on the graph on page 239. A high score on a factor indicates high alignment between a team and its sponsoring management. Low scores indicate areas in which further dialogue between team and sponsor can improve the linkage.

You can identify leverage points for improvement by looking for:

- Agreement regarding low scores
- Agreement regarding high scores
- Different opinions about scores (gaps)
- Historical momentum of improvement (if available)

In this case, sponsors and team leaders throughout the organization have generally achieved high alignment for the early stages of the innovation process. However, their "systems integrity" breaks down in the Creative Solution and Completion stages. This pattern happens often in "early empowerment" cultures that get teams launched in the right direction but fail to provide the systems support for "follow-through" success.

At clients such as Chevron Chemicals, Marion-Merrill-Dow, and IBM, an assessment of individualized, micro-cultures for innovation has led to improvements not only for the specific participating teams but also for other teams with the same executive sponsors. They took various actions, including:

- *Talent development:* Rotating people into different functions, even every two years, to create more overlapping knowledge bases.
- *"Systems" thinking:* Establishing a multinational, multimedia computer capability to input and download key technical, customer, and competitor information.
- *Knowledge-creation:* Conducting training on how to expand intelligence and generate better ideas.
- *Resource allocation:* Establishing a fund for testing unique ideas, both locally and nationally.
- *Full value appraisal:* Including "transfer of key learnings to others parts of the organization" in performance appraisals.

At Kraft, innovation teams in one division aimed to develop breakthrough products as well as product extensions. Senior management also wanted to use these assignments to learn how to build a better culture for innovation—to optimize everyone's ability to share knowledge, collaborate on ideas, and implement faster. The senior managers and the teams were coached to dialogue on the sixteen issues, as the team progressed through the Creative Journey. This synergy produced greater alignment between sponsors and team members. The team trusted more that their efforts would not be in vain—that management would support them in testing their best ideas in the marketplace without the burdens of "bureaucratic executive meddling." The new level of collaboration had a lasting effect on the people as well as the business.

A Case in Point

We approached the development of innovation at one financial services firm by focusing on the innovative output of the broad spectrum of employees (not just a few key individuals noted for their new product ideas). We started by developing these five broad goals:

1. To make innovation the most recognized and practiced strategic initiative—seamlessly accepted and implemented, with leaders of innovation receiving the right tools.
2. To have tangible, exciting, innovative ideas for new products and services, new delivery systems, productivity improvements, and new management methods and systems.
3. To develop the collaboration, culture, and infrastructure for innovation knowledge creation, and shared learning.
4. To assist executives, managers, and team leaders in developing the knowledge, skills, and confidence to sponsor innovation challenges.
5. To integrate, where possible, the approaches used for fostering innovation in the retail organization with the strategy, organization development, and training/education efforts going on elsewhere in the company.

After assessing the culture using a customized version of the Strategic Innovation Management Assessment Profile (SIMAP), we developed the following strategy for change:

SIMAP FACTOR Action Items	OBJECTIVES	FIRST STEPS
PURPOSE and VISION Clear focuses for innovation across departments	Provide meaningful "land on the moon" missions that give a strategic focus for what types of ideas are most needed in the next months. Give more depth and comprehensiveness (and less chaos) to idea-generation.	Have the senior management group decide on a single or series of strategic purposes for innovation in a time period and actively communicate/promote the purpose(s).
RISK TAKING Better understanding of the need for new insights, ideas	Provide context and criteria for key success factors in marketplace, to help stimulate and self-screen ideas. Spark awareness of the need for new insights that add to the company's intellectual capital for competitive advantage.	Use corporate research and package it in a way that lets people determine what it means for them in their jobs (what they can do in response to the knowledge).
STAFFING and EMPOWERMENT Regionalization of innovation in products, delivery systems	Take advantage of the four "mini-companies" and their closeness to customers/each other. Provide more rapid and empowered decision making. Set up means to share across regions.	Give permission for regional testing of new products and new delivery systems; (provide budgets in that way). Set up forums for sharing and "rolling out" best ideas nationwide.
TALENT DEVELOPMENT Training on being leaders of innovation (in groups, on-line)	Develop mindset and skills for stimulating and supporting innovation, for teams, one-to-one, and the company.	Establish workshop that targets pilot branches, operations centers; include individual 360° feedback as option.
"SYSTEMS" THINKING Groupware to develop ideas across locations and share best practices	Provide means to develop, critique, and share new knowledge and new ideas, even across geographies. Maintain individual as developer of ideas, without dangers of premature "hand-off or hand-up" that could kill promising ideas.	Develop intranet site(s) and prompts for people to collaborate on developing new ideas, even across geographies; use this instead of suggestion-system for dialogue, while keeping individual ownership of ideas.
KNOWLEDGE-CREATION Idea events	Dedicate specific people ("tiger teams") to develop ideas that hold the key to present and future leadership in the industry.	Set specific strategic topics and identify people to focus on them. Involve potential idea implementers as part of team of creative thinkers.

SIMAP FACTOR Action Items	OBJECTIVES	FIRST STEPS
KNOWLEDGE-CREATION New idea channels; include person who connects idea-developers	Provide open channels for people to develop and test ideas, especially those that fall outside of their own sphere of influence and authority to implement. Stimulate ideas across and up-and-down the organization.	Set up alternative routes for new ideas to be developed, avoiding suggestion systems that "toss" ideas for others to judge and implement. Set up forums for hearing and deciding on ideas; incorporate current methods that work.
DECISION PROCESS Clearer new product development process	Streamline the product development decision process to get new ideas into the marketplace faster, with less cost and more impact.	Document process(es) as they exist today and put "tiger team" on developing more effective ways to get new products into the market.
RESOURCE ALLOCATION Prioritize projects for better timing	Enable easier choices on whether to take on an innovative idea or to maintain current project portfolio (with heavy time demands).	Assign adequate resources to all three types of projects: to be competitive; to lead today; to lead tomorrow.
RESOURCE ALLOCATION Innovation budgets as "sacred:" both financial and time budgets	Ensure the resources of time and money to test the most promising ideas, especially those that could provide present or future leadership in the industry (vs. those that just maintain competitiveness).	Set aside untouchable resources for testing ideas, at both regional and corporate levels. Include both financial resources and ability to release human resources.
PERFORMANCE COACHING Appraisals for innovation	Encourage stretch goals and risk-taking. "Farm out" and share key learning to ensure that the knowledge-economy (intellectual capital) of the company is expanded.	Include transferable learning objectives as part of annual performance appraisal process. Start documenting times of breakthrough and incremental innovations that had big impact. Document important learnings.
MOTIVATION and REWARDS Celebration of innovation at multiple milestones	Assess results and new knowledge created. Provide recognition and rewards for shared learning as well as achieved deliverables. Ensure follow-through on innovation projects. Renew energy.	Include full range of SATISFIERS and rewards, tied to full-value appraisal for individuals and groups: self-determination, advancement, training, intrinsic, social, financial, impact, environment, recognition, security.

The future belongs to organizations that are totally flexible yet totally focused on end results (both achievement and learning). To create and to anticipate and cope with chaotic change in the marketplace, we must get involved in promoting *systemic* change and fully expect that we may not even see the final outcome of the work that we do.

MANAGING QUALITY AND INNOVATION TOGETHER

Developing a culture for innovation means paying attention to both applications of innovation: *greater revenues* and *greater efficiency* in work processes. Those innovations can be either breakthrough or incremental change, as described in chapter 1:

Type of Change	"Top-Line" Innovation (Greater Revenue, Business Growth)	"Mid-Line" Innovation (Greater Effectiveness, Efficiency, Lower Costs)
Revolutionary, breakthrough change	Radical invention	Total reengineering
Evolutionary, incremental change	Product or service extensions	"Kaizen" process improvement

It's fairly easy to see the benefits of creativity for product development. But what about the role of creativity in quality improvement?

Since the 1980s, corporate programs to promote "quality improvement" have silently done a great deal to prove that *creativity* resides in everyone. These programs have challenged every employee to contribute their best ideas to make work processes better or different. That's asking them to be *creative*. At the same time, we've ignored the active role of creativity in quality improvement. One client showed me their Total Quality Management (TQM) leadership manual, detailing a ten-step process in about 200 pages. After step six, a person would thoroughly understand the customer's needs and the root causes of defects. The next page said to brainstorm possible solutions. The page after that outlined ways to decide on the best solution, implement it, and check for results. The client remarked, "What's wrong with this picture? The whole point is to find a better or different way of doing things, and we have exactly one page devoted to the creative thinking process necessary to arrive at a better or different idea!" We can no longer afford to limit employee creativity in this way, whether for process improvement or product development.

Another huge problem with the "quality" movement in the 1980s and early 1990s has been an emphasis on incremental improvements, which has resulted in a shortage of needed breakthroughs. We've limited employees by giving them tools that lead to creative ideas that are incremental rather than breakthrough (i.e., Modifying and Experimenting tools rather than Visioning and Exploring ones)—either out of ignorance or of wanting to keep the control of breakthrough changes in the hands of a few specialists. Starting in the mid-1990s however, efforts at quality improvement have shifted to a new course.

To get a feel for this shift, let's review the evolution of quality improvement, starting with the early 1900s. At that time, Frederick Taylor introduced new methods of *quality control* (QC) in production. This first paradigm emphasized inspection and measurement of results. *Quality* was defined as the absence of variation in output. John Day, DuPont's manager of its world-class manufacturing, has noted that when excellence is measured as a lack of defects, the normal approach is to add more inspection steps.[3] The second paradigm, *quality assurance* (QA), was influenced a great deal by Walter Shewhart, who emphasized statistical analysis and process improvement with his *Plan-Do-Check-Act* model. The definition of *quality* was broadened to "conformance to high standards."

In the 1980s, J. Edward Deming and Joseph Juran helped give birth to a more expansive notion of quality—*Total Quality Management (TQM)*, which emphasizes four additional dimensions beyond QC and QA: employee empowerment, team accountability, customer-supplier focus, and cycle-time speed. Thus, the definition of *quality* becomes "meeting customer expectations."

But TQM has "hit the wall," failing to deliver the results required to become and remain a world-class organization. Alcoa Aluminum's chairman, Paul H. O'Neil, eliminated the company's ten-year-old "continuous improvement" program as a "major mistake" because it was producing incremental improvements when they needed "quantum improvement."[4] It's not that TQM is poor in tools or values; it has contributed a great deal to the rejuvenation of American business from the doldrums of the 1980s. However, TQM has emphasized incremental improvements and provided few tools, or empowerment, for making the radical, breakthrough changes so many companies need.

A new paradigm for quality has emerged, called *Quantum Quality (QQ)*. It has added four additional requirements for quality breakthroughs: learning, values, creativity, and sustainability.

In this paradigm, the most inclusive definition of *quality* has become "achieving customer delight." Notice how far we have come: Quality started as a technical level of "zero defects" and has emerged as the emotional experience of a customer!

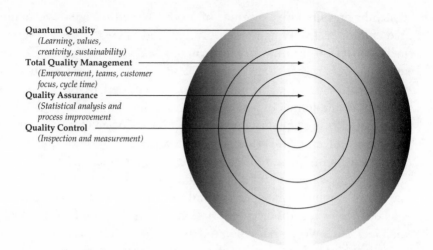

Quantum Quality
  (Learning, values,
  creativity, sustainability)
Total Quality Management
  (Empowerment, teams, customer
  focus, cycle time)
Quality Assurance
  (Statistical analysis and
  process improvement
Quality Control
  (Inspection and measurement)

QQ uses the tools and techniques of QC, QA, and TQM. In addition, you can apply all the tools and techniques for innovation to quality improvement just as easily as product development.

The *Strategic Innovation Management* model provides a common language and framework for fostering a culture for all applications of creativity, including quality improvement. You can see its direct applicability by its relation to the criteria set for the Baldrige Award, America's highest honor for quality improvement:

Baldrige Criteria (% Importance, assigned by Baldrige Committee)	Strategic Innovation Management Factors
Leadership (9.5%)	1. Purpose and vision 2. Values and character 3. Risk taking
Strategic Quality Planning (6%)	4. Strategic knowledge (of business and technical environment)
Human Resource Development and Management (15%)	5. Talent development 6. Staffing and empowerment
Information and Analysis (7.5%)	7. Communications structure 8. "Systems" thinking
Management of Process Quality (14%)	9. Knowledge-creation 10. Innovative thinking 11. Collaboration 12. Decision process
Quality and Operational Results (18%)	13. Resource allocation 14. Leading change 15. Performance coaching 16. Motivation and rewards
Customer Focus and Satisfaction (30%)	1. Purpose and vision 4. Strategic knowledge 15. Performance coaching 16. Motivation and rewards

You can take the leap into a culture that stimulates innovation across the board. Since quality improvement is innovation applied to work processes, it's no surprise that SIMAP's sixteen factors also hold the key to establishing the management practices needed to build a Baldrige Award-winning or Deming Prize-winning culture.

EMPLOYING A "SYSTEMS" APPROACH TO CHANGE

The dictionary defines *change* as "to cause to be different; alter; transform; to exchange or replace by another."[5] All organizations go through many changes—reorganizations, automation, personnel turnover, and on and on. Change often brings paradoxical feelings of excitement, fear, longing, or even anger, especially when change is introduced at work. The way the change process is managed often makes the transition more painful than necessary, prompting the perceptions that "We're falling apart!" or "Management doesn't know how to manage."

Organizational growth follows a breathing pattern of expansion and consolidation that corresponds to exhaling and inhaling. When an organization has successfully stabilized a new business with centralized decision making and functional roles (inhaling), the time eventually comes for more decentralization (exhaling). And when decentralization has succeeded in establishing a broader growth pattern for the company (exhaling), there is often a need for more consolidation (inhaling).

The very structure and culture needed to make one stage succeed can become a barrier to later growth. Not realizing this, we often hold back when the limits of one stage have been reached and the next stage is calling for a change in management practices. A typical response is, "Since our old way of managing has worked so far, we just need to do it better." This amounts to the organization "holding its breath." One the other hand, we can also exhale for too long. Change for the sake of change, or change in continual reaction to the environment, eventually diminishes productive energy at all levels. We need a point of stability during change, an anchor of constancy. This is best supplied by an organization's purpose and our commitment to fulfilling that purpose.

For us to hold our "organizational breath" and ignore the need for change means eventual unconsciousness and bare survival at best. To anticipate and embrace necessary change is to breathe long and deeply, thriving instead of merely surviving. Indeed, there is the danger of trying to minimize the task of organizational change with quick-fix solutions and overly simple programs.

The Strategic Innovation Management model helps you avoid the biggest cause of failure in changing organizational cultures: doing things too piecemeal. Without an integrated systems approach, you'll fail to gain the full commitment to the time, energy, caring, and leadership required for true transformation.

The need for change often comes when top management develops a new strategy for operating in the marketplace. The strategy is worthless unless your organization can do what's necessary to implement it: producing innovations in products, services, delivery, and operating practices.

Since the parts of our organizations are integral to the whole, we can transform the whole by affecting a critical mass of parts. This is the game of parts and wholes. Within our organizations it is the arena of innovation where we might make our most significant creative contribution.

We need to understand fully the nature of organizational change and then carefully strategize the transition process. This requires more than just a memo or presentation advising people what they're expected to do differently, as the following example illustrates.

For a nationwide insurance carrier the marketplace was dictating the need for a new, computerized claims-processing system. They developed one that could adjudicate 80 to 90 percent of the claims automatically, rather than 40 to 50 percent with the older system. The company found its strategy failing because of poor implementation. In addition to the expected system "bugs," the transition was complicated by the fact that the claims-processing jobs were so different. Performance in previous processing systems was not necessarily a good qualification for the new jobs.

Ultimately, most employees needed to attend a formal training program—at least five full weeks—to work on the new system. Special tests were formulated to determine who would likely succeed in the new jobs. (These tests needed to be validated first.) Employees became agitated because of the validated pretest and the company's use of an employment contract. If employees didn't pass the formal classroom training, they might not be placed in their old job—or even *any* job (because the old system was to be phased out). Employees complained that five to fifteen years of loyal service and good productivity weren't being acknowledged. The "you bet your job" contract also introduced an extraordinary amount of pressure into the classroom learning environment and onto the final exam.

Turnover during and after the formal training periods was twice the normal rate. Consequently, the entire employee-development process was investigated, including recruitment, pretesting, selection, formal classroom training, posttesting, on-the-job training, and on-the-job support. The feasibility of implementing the computer system was also being investigated separately, as were the work-measurement and quality-assurance programs.

Defining the problem correctly was the first major task. Defining it as strictly a morale problem or a turnover problem or a training problem or a computer systems problem or a quality assurance problem would have led to solutions with minimal overall effect. Each group that interacted in the implementation—the supervisors, the trainers, the recruiters, the computer systems people—were making decisions that made all the sense in the world given the pressures they were under. The result of all their actions was a Catch-22 reaction: The more they did to correct the problems, the more something else in the system counteracted the potential benefits.

For example, instead of fully helping to meet production pressures, the transition/employee-development process limited the potential trainee performance. As shown by the following systems flowchart, the need to increase capacity led to decisions for more trainees and more classes per time period. (These were not the only decisions that could have been made, simply the ones that *were* made.) As a result, trainers had few days between six-week courses to prepare and update materials. Given their lack of floor experience and the constant updates on the new systems, their class examples were not always up to date. On-the-job training, therefore, had a higher burden for bringing the trainees up to full production. But since the on-the-job trainers (the technical specialists) were needed to help with the production backlogs,

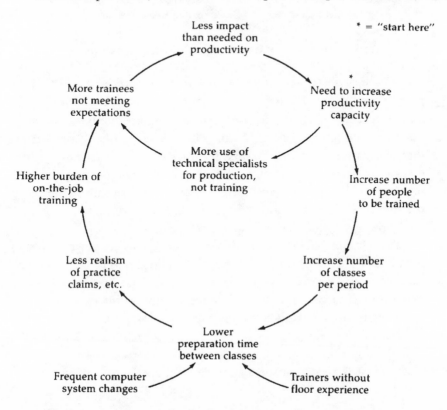

they had less time to give. Therefore, more trainees ended up not performing at the levels needed to have the desired impact on productivity.

The "solution" to not having enough trained employees, therefore, led to compounding the problem rather than diminishing it. The problem lay not in any one group not doing its job, but in the way the system of Catch-22 interactions was reinforced by previous decisions and situations.

By exploring these and three other Catch-22s, the following analogy for possible change strategies emerged.

STRATEGIC TARGETS

Imagine a fast flowing river with two landing ports and jungle in between:

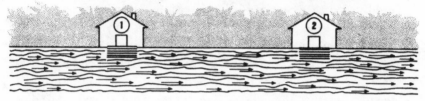

Port #1 is:

"Enhance, build, improve quality"

"Build on positive employee motivations"

"Develop high quality of trainees"

Port #2 is:

"Measures, assure, enforce quality"

"Direct policies at hard-to-motivate employees"

"Develop large quantity of trainees"

IF YOU TARGET PORT #2, IT IS VERY DIFFICULT TO GET BACK TO PORT #1.

If we aim for port 2 and land there, it is very difficult to get back to port 1! That means if we develop quality-assurance programs, for example, for the primary purpose of measuring productivity and supporting disciplinary actions, we may have a very difficult time using that program to *improve* quality. In other words, measuring performance is a necessary part of a program for improving quality, but improving quality is not necessarily a part of a program to measure performance. The insurance company was a case of aiming at port 2 *by actions* even though their stated aim was port 1.

The solution to the Catch-22s was not in changing any one factor, not even in a series of single changes. An organization is like a thermostat: It is set to regulate change around a particular "temperature" of operations. The system is set to respond to any raising or lowering of the temperature by bringing things back to a norm. Only by changing the thermostat setting itself—building a critical mass—can substantive change be sustained.

What was needed at the insurance company to transform the creative climate for adopting the innovative computer system was a package of changes. This package needed to involve *leverage points* that seemed to impact more than one of the Catch-22 cycles at the same time.

Without going into further background detail, the leverage points in the insurance company's transformation effort were: the use of pretesting and classroom tests; the collaborative roles of technical training and quality-assurance personnel; and realignment of classroom/on-the-job training cycles.

The final set of recommendations emphasized a landing at port 1. Eighty proposed actions were grouped into four packages: mandatory short-term, mandatory long-term, optional short-term, optional long-term. Each package was formulated to be implemented as a whole. We cautioned that implementing a few actions from each package might produce some short-term gains, but it wouldn't create a critical mass of substantive change; they would remain in their Catch-22 cycles.

After reading this case example, you might be thinking, "What's the use? It's beyond my influence to accomplish any real change in my organization!" You might be feeling that even more so if you're wanting to change a cultural norm (for example, to make your organization "more market-driven"). The paradox you face is that although organizational change can be formidable, it also is within your influence when you truly know your own power, love, and wisdom and when you can see your organization as a whole system!

EMBRACING "RESISTANCE" TO CHANGE

The transformation of our work groups, organizations, and larger units of society requires a *critical mass* of support, though not necessarily a majority. This transformation can emerge quite suddenly after the temperature of change has worked up (sometimes subtly) to the boiling point. It might also emerge quite slowly, in an evolutionary way that will not be hurried.

There is a dark side to change: the lack of readiness to change within the organization. People in organizations may resist change in any number of forms:

- Being unwilling to take risks
- Dwelling on internal competition
- Remaining focused on short-term goals and operations
- Assigning creativity to a single group, like R&D
- Turning rules and policies into untouchable commandments
- Emphasizing controls even where uncertainties are dominant ("Guarantee me that this will work.")

Managers and consultants often strategize about how to overcome resistance to change, how to bring about a shift in critical mass. This needs to be looked at very carefully, for there are many different reasons behind resistance, including:

- *Integrity.* You might resist a proposed change out of a sincere belief that it is not the highest good for the people or the problem. This resistance is strengthened when the status quo would be hard to reestablish if the change effort failed. You press for a solution that your heart knows is better.
- *Fear.* You might resist change when you perceive it might threaten your job, status, dignity, budgets, or relationships. You don't trust that the change is really in your best interest. Sometimes this fear may be justified. At other times it may be a "victim" mentality that doesn't like others "controlling" your life. Anger and frustration may spring from the base emotion of fear.
- *Communication.* A lack of understanding of the need for change can prevent any serious cooperation, particularly when the price seems too high. A too-forceful style of telling people what to do can offend leading to the same result.
- *History.* You might resist change if you have experienced many meaningless and poorly implemented changes or if you lack confidence in the abilities of the sponsors and change agents to make it work. This resistance is compounded by poor communications.
- *Pace.* You might resist change when you don't have enough time to grieve the passing of the way things used to be. The experience of loss and letting go heals at its own pace. Winters are a necessary time and cannot be hurried.
- *Stress.* You might resist change when there already is too much stimulation to manage. You'd rather keep problems you're familiar with than undergo possible turmoil to get to a "promised land."

What are some examples of times when you resisted change? Was your resistance based on any of the above? *The difficulties in transitions come not so much from the extent of change, but from the way change is handled!* Each type of resistance is quite natural to our human experience. We do not need either to give in to these resistances passively or to use aggressive, violent force to overcome them. When we honor the reasons for resistance by responding with compassion, we can find active means to melt their snows and create streams of commitment. These means can include education and communication, participation, facilitation and support, or negotiation. The use of manipulation and coercion can backfire and provoke more stringent resistance. Resistance evaporates when people embrace rather than just understand what would simultaneously benefit themselves and others. Because we don't always automatically know what the greatest benefit for others is, this must be co-explored. This co-exploration is the action that demonstrates proper respect for resistance.

Resistance, therefore, is not something for us to overcome but rather to befriend. (The difference is illustrated by how newspapers reported the first climb to the top of Mount Everest. A U.S. paper's headline read, "Mount Everest Conquered!" whereas a Japanese paper's headline was, "Mount Everest Befriended.") Often we have to dig deep inside ourselves to forgive ourselves and others for this resistance and promote a movement from fear to forgiveness to forging a future.

GAINING "CRITICAL MASS" SUPPORT

To leverage your time and energy for transforming your organization, you must choose which group(s) to focus on and your starting points for change. While you can address any of the sixteen SIMAP factors, there are seven easiest ways to begin fostering a culture for innovation:

STARTING POINT	CRITICAL SUCCESS FACTOR
1. Communicate the strategic importance of innovation.	Publicize the effort to the public (to gain credibility and motivation with employees, as well as shareholder credibility).
2. Facilitate/train teams on knowledge-creation and innovation—applied to specific projects	Train people on core competencies.
3. Develop "communities of practice" that turn individual learners into learning communities.	Avoid bureaucracy; foster an entrepreneurial set of critical mass activities.
4. Coach specific project teams and their sponsors on how to foster a CREATIVE climate for innovation.	Coach and train multiple groups, including executives and key teams.
5. Coach executives, as individuals and teams, with personal 360° feedback (from their peers, direct reports, customers, and managers).	Emphasize personal change, not just cultural change, from the top down.
6. Assess the culture for innovation.	Track the culture with key measures for behavior as well as outcomes.
7. Reengineer specific parts of the culture ("entrepreneurial" funding, rewards, etc.).	Install appraisal and reward systems for individuals, teams, and divisions.

Which of these points to start with depends on the level of senior executive knowledge and buy-in about the issues of creativity and innovation. In addition, *how* these actions are handled affects the culture immediately! Just choosing actions to get people focused on the need doesn't create a culture that can actually *follow through*! What is measured tends to improve almost automatically—the feedback and rewards are most likely to be there.

IN CLOSING . . .

You can help develop an organization that inspires and empowers people to exercise their talents and values. It depends on how you live as a SPIRITED person, how you undertake your Creative Journeys, and how you promote a CREATIVE climate for innovation.

Begin with a firm understanding of how the organization functions as a system, using the SIMAP model. The trick is getting the critical mass of actions, covering all aspects of the innovation process. You must have a coordinated strategy entailing all of these activities and all of the levels of executives, managers, teams, and individual contributors. Otherwise. you will unwittingly make knowledge management or innovation simply a "flavor of the month management fad" and prove that the Dilbert Effect (the mass cynicism of employees to any management initiative) is alive and well.

You can leverage your insights, skills, and commitments by supporting your colleagues and yourself to be all you can be. This is not a Pollyanna formula; the process can certainly be slow, formidable, and complex. Nurture the attitude that you have what it takes to live your purpose and values wherever you are. You can make your vision of your workplace the dominant force, rather than waiting for someone else to make the first move and change things for you. It begins with you.

Keep the *Faith*— Integrate *Profits* and *Prophets*

Our organizations are living organisms within the greater whole. Like cells in a biological system, we find meaning for our work by contributing to the whole. This contribution stimulates the flow of nourishment—revenues and profits—to and from the larger organism. Certainly, competition stimulates people and organizations to grow, to stretch, and to create, which feeds us with creative challenges. This healthy competition aims at diversity rather than dominance.

The sense of competition is based on a notion that we are separate from each other, engaged in a struggle to survive. Internal competition leads us to withhold information from each other thus reducing the growth of the core asset of any business: knowledge. External competition leads us to develop strategies for dominating one another, thus reducing the diversity that makes for a healthy industry, a vital society, and a conserved environment.

In this light, the religious and revolutionary entreaty to "love your enemy" takes on a new application. Strategic thinking is more a search for meaning than a search for advantage. Creative strategic planning envisions a higher purpose for business than attempts at dominance, and then discovers means of collaboration. The most peak-performing, knowledge-creating, and innovative organizations wholeheartedly embody this wisdom. The search for higher meaning in business must go beyond goals of dominance and envision a New Story for business strategies and corporate cultures—one built on respect, honesty, caring, and trust. As stated in India by the spiritual leader Sai Baba, "Not until man learns to value mankind will anything else find its proper value." We can discover and embrace this value, this deeper meaning for work, in the creative expression of our minds, hearts, and souls.

CHAPTER 14

Earn the Right to
Lead Innovation

> *Democracy is the idea that every individual is sacred, is a Son*
> *or Daughter of God and has inalienable rights to express that*
> *unlimited creativity. Science is the mind's understanding of the*
> *laws and processes of creation. Technology, when appropriately*
> *applied, is the capacity to cooperate with those laws to create a*
> *world beyond the limits of scarcity and separation.*
> —Barbara Marx Hubbard, A Gift of a Positive Future

HEARING THE CALL

Over the past fifteen years, I've had the wonderful opportunity to provide corporate consulting on creativity, innovation, and quality improvement in countries such as Czechoslovakia, Bulgaria, the
Netherlands, Great Britain, Italy, France, Japan, Australia, Singapore,
Malaysia, China, Canada, and the United States. Although people in
each culture are certainly different, deep down they are very much the
same in their quest for a rich quality of life— spiritually, emotionally,
and mentally as well as materially.

Yet, somehow, all around this planet, we've lost a basic feel for the
deeper, more spiritual side of this richness. We've lost touch with how
our work contribution can be an exercise of our deepest values and a
training ground for discovering more of who we are as spiritual/human
beings. By focusing so much on material growth, we actually miss the
very basis of healthy, economic prosperity—giving our best to enrich
our surroundings, our environment, and our planet.

Vaclav Havel said in his inaugural address as president of Czechoslovakia, "We have been lied to a great deal, and I don't presume you
elected me to lie to you more. We are a morally ill country." He went
on to say that unless they learned to be truthful, open, and respectful

with each other, they would never succeed in rebuilding the economy and the country.

More recently he stated,

> *We are heading irreversibly into a multicultural and multipolar world. It is necessary to restore humanity's sense of responsibility for this world, and this responsibility must have a metaphysical anchor. Humankind's only way out of this narrow pass is a far-reaching spiritual regeneration. We cannot simply copy the expansion of the European and later Euro-American spirit, values, lifestyle, and vigor. We should look for the common roots of human spirituality, undertake a new reflection of the moral order in them, and translate [them] into jointly accepted standards and rules of human coexistence.[1]*

We all must answer this call. To create this better life, we can't wait for the system to change; the system will change as a result of our creative work to build a better life. Our powers to affect the environment, and the well-being of people all over the planet, make this spiritual renewal absolutely critical to our economic and social health. We are called, by *spirit* and by *necessity*, to integrate our quest for profits into the message of prophets throughout the ages.

TRANSFORMING TECHNOLOGY WITH HUMAN VALUES

As Havel's remarks reflect, there is a widespread awakening to the importance of bringing our deepest values into our work, to make a better contribution to others' well-being while fostering our own personal growth. Native peoples throughout the world refer to the earth as "Mother," the very embodiment of love and caring. Their relationship with life has been—is—so personal! They live and work very differently, based on a sense of connection rather than an alienated "me-versus-them" world view. Imagine the frame of mind it takes to poison our own mother, yet so many business decisions do just that! Our spiritual fulfillment, and the fate of Mother Earth, are at stake—literally. If we continue as we've done in most of this century, we will drive that stake into our hearts. If we awaken to our calling, we'll stake out a new territory for human evolution. The choice is *ours*.

So much of our creative expression goes into the invention of new technologies. That is a blessing and a curse. Buckminster Fuller noted in the 1980s that over 50 percent of the world's population live at a higher standard of material living than 99 percent of the population lived in 1900. Yet for every technological advance, we seem to produce an adverse impact, socially or environmentally. We will end this millennium with complex issues and problems, as mentioned in chapter 1:

- The globalization of national economies
- The evolution to an intelligence-based economy
- The pace of technological evolution
- The super-competitive environment
- New and shifting social values and demographics
- Changes in labor force values
- Health, lifestyle, and stress awareness
- Prosperity versus human survival

As we face the challenges of the new millennium, a key question is, "Who's in charge here—people or technology, prophets or profits?" Innovative technologies are a critical resource for building a more human future. And the fostering of human values is an economic imperative for the lasting development of innovative technologies. These are perhaps bold statements—the first in light of the nuclear threat, environmental problems, and dehumanization that people have experienced in our technological world; and the second in light of the seeming polarities between some people in the business community and various subcultures in America.

> **As we face the challenges of the new millennium, a key question is, "Who's in charge here—people or technology, prophets or profits?"**

Technologies *are* a critical resource for a more human future. The fact that diphtheria, cholera, smallpox, and typhoid have been eliminated as prime causes of death is one testimony to this fact. As Gandhi, Maslow, and others have pointed out, it is hard to stretch for higher values when essentials for life are missing.

Human values *are* an economic imperative for lasting technological innovation. We must selectively *choose* what we want to develop on the basis of values that build a healthy society and economy and support long-term business and technological development. The primary causes of death—vascular diseases and cancer—are lifestyle based; and our lifestyles are shaped dramatically by our technologies and the pace of work required to produce them competitively. The flames of increasing health-care costs are being fanned, therefore, by this "technological push" on lifestyles. And the health care burden on our GNP could become fatal to individual industries and our economy as a whole. (For example, health care costs add over $1,000 to the price of the average U.S.-made automobile, giving foreign manufacturers a better competitive advantage. Our economic health will be destroyed if we continue to seek only technological solutions to problems caused to a large degree by a technology-dominated economy. A "value pull" must be added to the "technology push."

What may appear to be technological choices are really human choices. Technology is a mirror of our consciousness and our values. Development of computerized psychotherapy or human cloning isn't a *technical* choice, a system that follows irrevocably from the demands of technology; it is a human choice, a consequence of people's losing faith in human interaction and happening to have a computer available. We often still look at technology as though it were inevitable and that it dictates certain solutions. We must control technology's development, realizing that we are not just dealing with technical questions, but social, political, and moral issues.

The collective challenge for us is to employ an economics of value(s) that involves our hearts, not just our minds and bank accounts. We *can* conduct our business proactively and infuse the world with our heart's desire rather than "planning" reactively to a runaway future. We *can* steer our organizations to become more effective in meeting these challenges.

Our future will be strongly influenced by the possibilities inherent in our emerging technologies. Today we stand at the crossroads between two very different futures. One is marked by vulnerability, and the other is filled with opportunity. Technological breakthroughs in areas such as computers, biotech, and space can help create new jobs, new opportunities, and new hope. Systems that require a long-term investment in human education and sophisticated equipment will likely be the strength of information-based economies even as the less-developed nations become strong competitors in low technology fields.

Technology and human values *can* become intimate partners (and in many cases already have), for economics is most fundamentally the exchange of value—or exchange of *values*. Land, products, services, labor, and money are all exchanged in relation to the values of the people involved and the value they place on the *experience* of having those items.

This exchange of value can get seriously out of balance when "paper profits" start to dominate decision making (in takeovers, tax-shelter moves, and such) or when people remain in jobs to "survive" (i.e., have an income) without a fair return for their contributions. With such "trade deficits," employees often impose "import restrictions" on management communications and motivators. Productivity, creativity, and committed involvement of employees can shrink to bare minimums, often focused on ways to *beat* the system rather than enhance it.

Profits are a measure of an organization's *effectiveness* in producing the value it exchanges. But our inability or unwillingness to understand nonquantitative measures of success has kept us from taking charge of our technologies. Rather than making human choices, we let the numbers dictate our decisions about technology.

The partnership of business and human values requires a specific context for leadership in our organizations. For the moment at least, the window of opportunity is open, and the optimistic future is reachable. But reaching it will require changes in management behavior throughout our institutions. Questions of management controls, motivation, competition, personal power, ethics, and decision making all require redefinition.

We have created the world we live in, with its prosperities, poverties, loves, fears, services, and exploitations. We have created how our businesses function, how we compete and collaborate, and how we employ technology.

Business is a creative art, a function of our tremendous logical and intuitive capabilities. How we envision, develop, and use it is a reflection of our inner wholeness (and dividedness!). Just as "all mind and no heart" produces a barren human being, business without heart produces a barren world and lifestyle—a barrenness that cannot handle the challenges we face in the next decades.

Having "heart" and "human values" means having integrity and caring—expressing our personal and collective creativity in ways that benefit and serve others as well as ourselves—and making business decisions in light of higher spiritual and ethical values.

MASTERING YOUR OWN TRANSFORMATION

Flashes of brilliance come much more often when they're invited. We open ourselves and our organizations to rich breakthroughs when we take charge of transforming ourselves at four levels:

- *Spirit*:our purpose, values, and SPIRITED mindset for creative service in the world.
- *Style*: our personal ways of igniting the Creative Journey and tapping deep into the intuitive source of vital, new ideas.
- *Sponsorship*: our leadership of teams while deliberately fostering a CREATIVE climate.
- *Sustainability*: our ensuring the long-term renewability of resources and the just distribution of wealth throughout the planet.

All of this requires personal and organizational change. In order to qualify for, and be effective at, leading such transformation, you must

master your own personal change process first! Otherwise, as you ask others to go through change, you won't really know what you're asking them to go through, and you won't be able to lead them through their fears and resistance. This doesn't mean getting rid of your own fears; rather, it means feeling your fears, making friends with them, and asking them to come along with you for a wild ride. As the following stories illustrate, you *can* learn to master your own change process as an individual, a group, or an entire business unit.

Transforming an Individual Executive

Janice was a middle manager at a financial services company who was older than her peers (they called her "Mom"). She had gone back to school in her early thirties and she showed good people skills and leadership. However, she was rather uncreative and structured about others' new ideas. She would immediately polarize groups into the "idea people" and "real workers." Because she was so good in her people skills, she could influence a group to kill any ideas that were in any way out-of-the-box thinking. She wanted things to be predictable. She was never offensive, but you could count on not leaving a meeting with any breakthrough ideas. As a result, her career was stuck.

Her executive coach, Kate Ludeman, spent about four hours coaching her with 360-degree feedback and psychological profiling, plus another day with her team. In the private coaching sessions Janice began to see how she was wasting the tremendous assets of her staff, plus her own good ideas, and would eventually lead her group downhill, until they were behind the times. She also began to learn some new skills that honored her team's diversity and creativity, including listening, affirming, and probing. Over time, she experienced a new degree of her own creativity.

As a result, Janice's "problems"—which had been talked about behind her back—came out into the open. She looked seriously at how she could change, and enlisted the support of her peers to give her ongoing candid support and feedback.

Today, she has leapfrogged four levels to become the president of the financial firm's largest income-producing division. Over half of the company's total employees now report to her. Her demeanor has changed from what some people called "dowdy" to "very smart"; she exudes a strong executive presence in the considerable time she spends with Wall Street types each week.

This personal-change process worked due to Janice's personal motivation (partially spurred by her manager), the honest feedback from her colleagues, the guidance and encouragement of her coach, her willingness to openly solicit support from her colleagues, and her manager's reinforcement and validation of her progress.

Transforming an Executive Peer Group

From 1992–1996, I was a presenter at Motorola University's corporate Vice President Institute (VPI). Three times a year, thirty VPs who had been hired or promoted as officers in the last year were brought together for a week. Care was taken to ensure that the mix represented a variety of different nationalities, different businesses, and different roles in those businesses. The concept evolved from the realization that for Motorola to continue growing at a fast rate, they would have to help invent entire new industries, primarily at the intersection of current businesses. The culture of Motorola was known not only for its candid exchanges of opinion, but also for managers who were empowered to experiment boldly. Now, however, networking, and initiative were needed beyond anything seen at Motorola before. Therefore, the VPI was begun to promote the creative interconnections and collaboration required to sustain growth and spur new growth. My focus at the VPI was to help them create a tangible, innovative vision of Motorola for 2025 and how Motorola could get there. Bob Galvin, the former CEO, then-COO Chris Galvin, and then-CEO Gary Tooker each attended sessions for a significant amount of time, with Chris and Gary responsible for listening to the group's ideas about the future corporation on the last day.[2]

This culture and personal-change process worked due to the combination of peer interaction (including learning partners), stimulating presentations and discussions, a compelling business issue/goal, and 360-degree coaching. Each officer also went through a two-and-a-half hour coaching session based on a 360-degree assessment (filled out by 25-30 peers and other employees during the previous two months), and psychological profiling. Kate Ludeman, the executive coach mentioned in the previous story, developed the customized assessment in dialogue with the office of the CEO to represent not the leadership qualities required today, but the ones required in the next two to five years to keep Motorola growing. By now, over 300 executives have been reviewed by over 8,000 Motorola employees—employees who have thus been exposed to the top thinking about what it takes to be a successful executive at Motorola.

As a group, these vice presidents have changed enormously over the last five years: Survey categories that measured low for the early groups now consistently rank much higher with the new people, showing that the corporate culture has changed to promote and reinforce these qualities. They were exposed to new thinking—about strategic planning, creativity, and how to bridge the "white spaces" between their businesses. Over $200 million in revenue was generated on new, previously nonexistent products that crossed traditional business boundaries, just because of the connectivity. About $300 to $400 million was saved through sharing resources, using another businesses' manufacturing facility in a different country, and so forth.

Transforming an Entire Business Unit—and Corporation

By 1988, GE had already gone through massive divestiture and downsizing, long before it became a trend. Morale was at an all-time low, the company was losing good people, and there still was much of the old bureaucracy hampering change and innovation. The executive team of GE, led by Jack Welch, came up with the idea to have "GE Workouts" to get rid of unnecessary, unproductive work (like getting rid of excess weight). This was before *process management* became a buzzword, so there wasn't much process expertise as we know it today. Originally, the ongoing goal was to put a critical mass of employees through the process, perhaps one-third to one-half of GE employees.

None of the early program designs (from teams all over the country), were very successful in engaging people, eliciting action-oriented ideas, or overcoming resistance from managers and executives (who thought their authority was being undermined). Therefore, GE added Steve Kerr from USC to lead the design, and his team brought in Kate Ludeman. They developed a newer concept and design and piloted it three to four times. It ultimately became the model for the rest of the company.

The business unit that eventually became the landmark of success—nuclear power generation—had not sold a new system for five years and had downsized from 8,000 to 3,000 people. In addition it faced huge competition from the high-end consulting services in nuclear engineering. The general manager of the unit was extremely resistant to the Workout concept: He was fear- and control-oriented and had long used a very traditional direct-reporting system. In addition, there was general cynicism because of the failure of the program designs produced by the original trial of the Workout concept.

Workout sessions were often conducted in groups of 100 or more from one business unit. The first day's session focused on personal insights and skills for handling change. This personal growth gave people insights into their own change patterns and their own resistance to shifting. Then teams of 25 to 40 from the same department within the business unit got together; levels were skipped, so that one group might have clerical people along with directors of science. For one-and-a-half days each team examined what their department was doing and identified what they could get rid of. Then all the teams came together to comment liberally on each other's work, using flip charts to record their comments.

On the last day, the head of the business unit (general manager) and his key staff came in. Each team was to present its ideas for what they should stop doing, both big and little stuff; each team was also to present what they thought should be done in the business unit as a whole. The general manager (GM) was supposed to respond "yes," "no", or "need more study" (with a definite due date). When the time came to show up to hear the team reports, the resistant GM of the nuclear unit was thirty minutes late and sat tensely with his arms folded. However, the energy, enthusiasm, and quality of work were so high, and the entire process was so energizing, that it kindled great hope and enthusiasm in him, which eventually spread throughout his unit. The process created *space* for new thinking and taking personal responsibility for change. The originally "by the book," control-oriented GM formed a much closer connection to his people and became a top role model for change and innovation at GE.

In the preceding three stories, what factors can we identify that *worked* to bring about the transformation that occurred?

Janice's personal transformation worked due to:

- Her own motivation (partially spurred by her manager)
- The honest feedback from her colleagues
- The guidance and encouragement of her executive coach
- Her willingness to openly solicit support from her colleagues
- Her manager's reinforcement and validation of her progress

Motorola's VPI group process worked due to a combination of:

- Peer interaction, including learning partners
- Stimulating group presentations and discussions
- A compelling business issue and a specific goal
- New approaches to creative visioning
- 360-degree coaching

GE's culture and personal change process (Workouts) worked due to:

- Starting the process with an engaging personal growth orientation designed to quickly get people out of a denial and resistance mode
- Emphasis on collaboration for the generation of creative ideas
- Instant response from executive management

When you personally choose these types of experiences, you earn the right to lead others to greater learning, innovation, and change. Without personal transformation, you cannot be as effective as you can be when you sponsor(or react to) change at work.

Your courage to look within your own soul will most surely be tested. Often we perceive ourselves as victims of our technologies, our work environment, our economic structure, and our managers. We then strive to get these "causes" of our ennui to change so that we can feel powerful rather than victimized. But even if that works, we still perceive ourselves as victims because we believe the environment causes our feelings.

Several years ago I listened to a nun, who had just returned from a memorial service in Hiroshima, speak about eliminating the nuclear threat to the world. She reminded us not to fall into the trap of "them versus us"—those who want bombs versus those who don't—because that same consciousness gives rise to war in any form. Instead, she suggested we remember that we have our own "departments of defense" between ourselves and others, that we have our own "security councils" keeping us safe, that we have our own "departments of energy" determining how we use our energies. The departments in Washington are but a reflection of our own values and tendencies. She concluded that from a spirit of union and with a sense of personal responsibility we can rise together to accomplish goals of safety, security, and energy management.

Substantive change—transformation or evolution—occurs with less effort when we have an inner sense of power and responsibility for events *first,* then take action that has a chance of making a difference. The power enables our actions to be more effective. A victim's actions, with an underlying, self-perceived powerlessness, usually produce self-fulfilling prophecies of little real change.

For many of us the source of this inner power comes from our spiritual experiences and ethical principles. From that basis in integrity we are more willing to share each other's weaknesses and burdens and climb toward higher values and prosperity (in all meanings of the word) together. We therefore accept more responsibility for contributing to our organizations and society. We realize that as we share each problem together, we achieve together.

IN CLOSING . . .

Our work is an expression of our souls, our deepest being, the creative spirit working through us. We are the composers, playing the melodies and harmonies of purpose and vision. We need not be limited by poor instruments—instruments that dictate the melody.

For each of us the music comes from within. For our organizations the music comes from the alignment and attunement of all who work there. Can you hear it? The thoughts of Kabir can help us listen more closely.[3]

> *The flute of the Infinite is played without ceasing, and its sound is love: When love renounces all limits, it reaches truth.*
> *How widely the fragrance spreads! It has no end, nothing stands in its way.*
> *The form of this melody is bright like a million suns.*

Into this wondrous, mysterious world, we are all born and we all die. The measure of our lives is what we create with our time on earth and what character we bring to bear on our creations. Spirituality is immanently present in all creation, including ourselves, our planet, even our corporate competitors. Bold as it may seem to make the claim, I have found that the richest purpose of life is to fully experience our relationship with the divine and, from that experience, to creatively serve others. Said in another

> **The measure of our lives is what we create and what character we bring to bear on our creations.**

way on the menus and above the food- service areas in Hard Rock Cafes around the world, life's call is to *"Love all, Serve all. "*

It's too late to argue about whether spirituality belongs in the workplace or doesn't. Our spiritual values go to work with us, and it's time to express them consciously. The technological advances of this world have so outstripped our own human development that we are in mortal danger of destroying our planet if we do not find a way to bring our inner spiritual life into balance with what we have created on the material plane. We need both the material and the spiritual, but not separately. We *have* to take our spiritual values to work. It is more urgent than ever before. We *have* to stop working six days and worshipping for a half hour on one day. We *have* to give what we do a *context* that is real and alive for each one of us, a context that serves mankind.

We hesitate, perhaps for good reason, to bring the subject of spirituality into business. For many, spirituality is the last bastion of personal life, and we fear the "corporate takeover" and exploitation of our values and souls. History too displays the tendency to make religious differences the excuse for conflict and warfare, the last thing we need in corporate life. Yet the spiritual underpinnings of the world's religions have a great deal in common: fundamental human values based on deep human needs that provide a true and solid foundation for business success (to replace greed and exploitation).

Be clear—genuine spirituality is not ethereal. It is not empty ethers and wispy shadows. Spirituality is gutsy, primal, essential. It connects us to all we hold sacred and informs our creativity. So for us to speak of creativity in the workplace—or anywhere else—without considering spirituality, is already to cut the potential of what we can do or achieve to less than half.

We are an integral part of creation. When we awaken the creator within, we merge with the creative force infusing all of our life. When we express our creative potential with a noble purpose, we give ourselves not only to each other, but back to the Source. With that link to the all-loving power of the universe, only good will come.

This book is dedicated to a New World beyond scarcity and separation—to a world where each person prospers materially and spiritually. Ultimately, the value of this book is not in what it says, but in what people like you do with it.

Who you are, and what you achieve, is your gift and blessing to us all. Thank you.

Suggested Reading

Adams, J. *Conceptual Blockbusting*. Reading, Mass: Addison-Wesley, 1986.

Adams, J. *Transforming Work*. Alexandria, Virginia: Miles River Press, 1984.

Allee, V. *The Knowledge Evolution*. Boston: Butterworth-Heinemann, 1997.

Bandrowski, J. *Creative Planning Throughout the Organization*. New York: AMACOM, 1986.

Bennis, W.G., K.D. Benne, R. Chin, and K.E. Corey. *The Planning of Change*, 3rd ed. New York: Holt, Rinehart & Winston, 1976.

Bernbaum, E. *The Way to Shambhala*. New York: Anchor Books, 1980.

Block, P. *Stewardship*. San Francisco: Berrett-Koehler Publishers, 1993.

Briskin, A. *The Stirring of Soul in the Workplace*. San Francisco, Jossey-Bass, 1996.

Buzan, T. *Use Both Sides of Your Brain*. New York: Dutton, 1983.

Cameron, J. *The Artist's Way*. New York: Jeremy P. Tarcher/Putnam, 1992.

Chakraborty, S. *Managerial Effectiveness and Quality of Worklife*. New Delhi: Tata McGraw-Hill Publishing Co. Ltd., 1991.

Conger, J. and Associates. *Spirit at Work*. San Francisco: Jossey-Bass Publishers, 1994.

Couger, J. *Creative Problem Solving and Opportunity Finding*. Danvers, Mass: International Thomson Publishing, Inc./boyd & fraser publishing company,1995.

Crandall, R., ed. *Break-Out Creativity: Bringing Creativity to the Workplace*. Corte Madera, California: Select Press, 1998.

Creativity and Innovation: Learning from Practice. Report of the Second European Conference on Creativity, and Innovation, Noordwijk aan Zee, 10–13 December 1989, organized by the Netherlands Organization for Applied Scientific Research TNO, The Netherlands, Innovation Consulting Group TNO, 1991.

The Dalai Lama and Jean-Claude Carriere. *Violence and Compassion*. New York: Doubleday, 1994.

Deal, T. and A. Kennedy. *Corporate Cultures*. Reading, Mass: Addison-Wesley, 1982.

Deal, T. and M.K. Key. *Corporate Celebration*. San Francisco: Berrett-Koehler Publishers, 1998.

de Bono, E. *Eureka: An Illustrated History of Inventions from the Wheel to the Computer*. New York: Holt, Rinehart & Winston, 1974.

de Bono, E. *Lateral Thinking: Creativity Step by Step*. New York: Harper & Row, 1970.

de Bono, E. *Lateral Thinking for Management*. New York, McGraw-Hill, 1971.

de Chardin, T. *The Phenomenon of Man*. New York: Harper Torch, 1955/1959.

Doyle M., and David Straus. *How to Make Meetings Work*. New York: Berkeley Publishing Group, 1976.

Drucker, Peter F. *Innovation and Entrepreneurship*. New York: Harper-Business, 1985.

Drucker, Peter F. *Post Capitalist Society*. New York: HarperBusiness, 1993.

Drucker, Peter F. *The New Realities*. New York: HarperBusiness, 1989.

Edvinsson, L. and M. Malone. *Intellectual Capital*. New York: Harper-Collins Publishers, Inc., 1997.

Fletcher, J. *Patterns of High Performance*. San Francisco: Berrett-Koehler Publishers, 1993.

Fromm, Erich: *The Art of Loving*. New York: Harper, 1956.

Garfield, P. *Creative Dreaming*. New York, Ballantine, 1974.

Gawain, S. *Creative Visualization*. Mill Valley, California: Whatever Publishing, 1978.

Gibran. K. *The Prophet*. New York: Alfred A. Knopf, 1958.

Goldberg, P. *The Intuitive Edge: Understanding and Developing Intuition*. Los Angeles: Tarcher Publishing, 1983.

Goldberg, P. and C. Hegarty. *How to Manage Your Boss*, New York: Rawson Associates, 1981.

Gordon, W.J.J. *Synectics—The Development of Creative Capacity*. New York: Harper & Row, 1961.

Grove, A. *Only the Paranoid Survive*. New York: Currency Doubleday, 1996.

Hanks, K. and J. Parry. *Wake Up Your Creative Genius*. Los Angeles: Kaufmann, 1983.

Harman, W. *Creativity and Intuition in Business*, Menlo Park, California: SRI International, 1985

Harman, W. and M. Porter. *The New Business of Business*. San Francisco: Berrett-Koehler Publishers, 1997.

Harmon, W. and H. Rheingold. *Higher Creativity: Liberating the Unconscious for Breakthrough Insights*. Los Angeles: Tarcher Publishing, 1984.

Hawley, J. *Reawakening the Spirit in Work*. New York: Fireside, 1993.

Henderson, H. *Building a Win-Win World*. San Francisco: Berrett-Koehler Publishers, 1996.

Hendricks, G. and K. Ludeman. *The Corporate Mystic*. New York: Bantam Books, 1996.

Jaffe, D., C. Scott and G. Tobe. *Rekindling Commitment*. San Francisco: Jossey-Bass Publishers, 1994.

Jagadeesan, J. *Everyday Human Values*. Malaysia:Federalb Publications SDN.BHD., 1995.

Joy, W.B. *Joy's Way*. Los Angeles: Tarcher Publishing, 1979.

Kanter, R. M. *The Change Masters*. New York: Simon & Schuster, 1983.

Kaufman, R. *Identifying and Solving Problems: A System Approach*, 3rd ed. San Diego: University Associates, 1982.

Kelly, K. *The Home Planet*. Reading Mass: Addison-Wesley, 1988.

Kelley, R. *The Gold Collar Worker*. Reading Mass: Addison-Wesley, 1985.

Kidder, R. *Shared Values for a Troubled World*. San Francisco: Jossey-Bass Publishers., 1994.

King, U. *Spirit of Fire: The Life and Vision of Teilhard de Chardin*. Maryknoll, NY: Orbis Books, 1996.

Krishnamurti, J. *Beyond Violence*. New York: Harper & Row, 1973.

Kuhn, R. *Handbook for Creative and Innovative Managers*. New York: McGraw-Hill Book Company, 1988.

Lao Tsu. *Tao Te Ching*. Translated by Gia-Fu Feng and Jane English, New York: Alfred A. Knopf, 1972.

Ludeman, Kate. *The Worth Ethic*. New York: E.P. Dutton, 1989.

Maps, J.J. *Quantum Leap Thinking*. Beverly Hills: Dove Books, 1996.

Marcic, D. *Managing with the Wisdom of Love*. San Francisco: Jossey-Bass Publishers, 1997.

Marquardt, M. and A. Reynolds. *The Global Learning Organization*. New York: Irwin Professional Publishing, 1994.

Maslow, A. *The Farther Reaches of Human Nature*. New York: Viking Press, 1974.

Maturana, H. and F.J. Varela. *The Tree of Knowledge: The Biological Roots of Human Understanding*. Boston: Shambhala, 1992.

McMaster, Michael D. *The Intelligence Advantage, Organising for Complexity*. London: Knowledge Based Development Co. Ltd., 1995.

Meyer, P. *Quantum Creativity*. Chicago: yeZand Press, 1997.

Miller, William C., *Fostering Creativity: The VALS Perspective*. Menlo Park, CA: SRI International, 1987.

Miller, W. *Quantum Quality*. New York: Quality Resources, 1993.

Miller, W., *The Creative Edge*. Reading, Mass: Addison-Wesley, 1987.

Miller, W. C. and N. Terry Pearce. "Synergizing Total Quality and Innovation." *National Productivity Review*, (Winter, 1987).

Miller, W. *Creativity, The Eight Master Keys to Discover, Unlock, and Fulfill Your Creative Potential*. Pleasanton, CA: SyberVision Systems, Inc., 1989.

Mooney, R.L. and T.A. Razik, eds. *Explorations in Creativity*. New York: Harper & Row, 1967.

Nonaka, I. And H. Takeuchi. *The Knowledge-Creating Company*. New York: Oxford University Press, 1995.

One Hundred Poems of Kabir. Translated by Rabindranath Tagore, London: MacMillan Publishers Ltd., 1961.

Ornstein, R. *The Roots of the Self*. New York: HarperCollins Publishers, 1995.

Osborn, A.F. *Applied Imagination: Principles and Procedures of Creative Problem-Solving.* New York: Scribner's, 1963.

Parnes, S.J. *The Magic of Your Mind.* Buffalo, N.Y.: Creative Education Foundation, 1981.

Pearce, J. P. *The Bond of Power.* New York: Dutton, 1981.

Pelletier, K.R. *Toward a Science of Consiousness.* New York: Delta Books, 1977.

Perkins, D. *Outsmarting IQ.* New York: The Free Press, 1995.

Peters, T. *The Circle of Innovation.* New York: Alfred A. Knopf, 1997.

Peters, T. and R. Waterman, Jr., *In Search of Excellence,* New York: Warner Books, 1982.

Pinchot, G. and E. Pinchot. *The Intelligent Organization.* San Francisco: Berrett-Koehler Publishers, 1994.

Quinn, R. *Deep Change.* San Francisco: Jossey-Bass Publishers, 1996.

Raudsepp, E. *How Creative Are You?,* New York: Perigee Books, 1981.

Ray, M. and J. Renesch. *The New Entrepreneurs.* San Francisco: New Leaders Press, 1994.

Ray, Paul. "The Integral Culture Survey," Research Report 96-A, Institute of Noetic Scientists in partnership with Fetzer Institute, 1996.

Rickards, T., P. Coleman, P. Groholt, M. Parker, and H. Smeekes. *Creativity and Innovation: Learning from Practice.* The Netherlands: Innovation Consulting Group TNO, 1991.

Renesch, J., ed. *Leadership in a New Era.* San Francisco: New Leaders Press, 1994.

Renesch, J., ed. *New Traditions in Business.* San Francisco: Sterling & Stone, Inc., 1991.

Renesch, J. and B. DeFoore, ed. *The New Bottom Line.* San Francisco: New Leaders Press, 1996.

Renesch, J. and B. DeFoore, ed. *Rediscovering the Soul of Business.* San Francisco: New Leaders Press, 1995.

Robinson, A.G., and S. Stern. *Corporate Creativity.* San Francisco: Berrett-Koehler Publishers, 1997.

Rogers, C. *Freedom to Learn.* Columbus, Ohio: Merrill, 1979.

Rogers, E.M. *Diffusion of Innovations,* 3rd. ed. New York: Free Press, 1983.

Rothenberg, A. and C.R. Hausman. *The Creativity Question.* Durham N.C: Duke University Press, 1976.

Roszak, T. *The Voice of the Earth.* New York: Touchstone, 1993.

Rowan, R. *The Intuitive Manager.* Boston: Little, Brown and Company, 1986.

Rubin, I., W. Fry, and J. Plovnik. *Task-Oriented Team Development.* New York: McGraw-Hill, 1978.

Russell, P. and R. Evans. *The Creative Manager*. San Francisco: Jossey-Bass Publishers, 1992.

Sakaiya, T. *The Knowledge-Value Revolution*. New York: Kodansha International, 1991.

Schultz, R. *Unconventional Wisdom*. New York: HarperCollins, 1994.

Schwartz. P. *The Art of the Long View*. New York: Doubleday/Currency, 1991.

Senge, P. *The Fifth Discipline*. New York: Doubleday/Currency, 1990.

Shoff, J., J. Connella, P. Robin, and G. Sobel. *Imagery—Its Many Dimensions and Applications*. New York: Plenum Press, 1980.

Smith, A. *The Powers of Mind*. New York: Summit Books, 1982.

Stacey, R. *Complexity and Creativity in Organizations*. San Francisco: Berrett-Koehler Publishers, 1996.

Stewart, T. *Intellectual Capital*. London: Nicholas Brealey Publishing, 1997.

Sturner, W. *Mystic in the Marketplace*. New York: Creative Education Foundation Press, 1994.

Swimme, B. *The Universe is a Green Dragon*. Santa Fe, N.M: Bear & Company, 1985.

Talbot, M. *The Holographic Universe*. New York: HarperCollins, 1991.

Vaughan, F. and R. Von Oech. *How to Unlock Your Mind for Innovation: A Whack on the Side of the Head*. Menlo Park: Creative Think, 1982.

Watson, T., Jr. *A Business and Its Beliefs: The Ideas That Helped Build IBM*. New York: McGraw-Hill, 1963.

Wheatley, Margaret J. and Myron Kellner-Rogers. *A Simpler Way*. San Francisco: Berrett-Koehler Publishers Inc., 1997.

Youngblood, M. *Life at the Edge of Chaos*. Dallas: Perceval Publishing, 1997.

Zdenek, M. *The Right-Brain Experience*. Santa Barbara: Two Roads Publishing, 1983.

Zohar, D. *ReWiring the Corporate Brain*. San Francisco: Berrett-Koehler Publishers., 1997.

Notes

INTRODUCTION

1. Peter M. Senge. "The Knowledge Era." *Executive Excellence*, (January 1998) : 15.
2. Leif Edvinsson and Michael S. Malone. *Intellectual Capital*. New York: HarperCollins, 1997
3. Thomas A. Stewart, *Intellectual Capital*. London: Nicholas Brealey Publishing, 1997; Thomas A. Stewart, "Your Company's Most Valuable Asset: Intellectual Capital." *Fortune Magazine*, (October 3 1994): 68–74); and "Brain Power, Who Owns It . . . How They Profit From It." *Fortune Magazine*, (March 1997).
4. Ikujiro Nonaka and Hirotaka Takeuchi. *The Knowledge-Creating Company*. New York: Oxford University Press, 1995, pp. 56–93.
5. Margaret J. Wheatley. "The New Story is Ours to Tell." *World Business Academy Perspectives*, (June 1997); San Francisco: World Business Academy and Berrett-Koehler, Vol. II, Number 2, pp. 21–34; and Margaret J. Wheatley. "Goodbye, Command and Control." *Executive Forum*, Leader to Leader, (Summer 1997) pp. 21–28.
6. Michael Talbot. *The Holographic Universe*. New York: HarperCollins, 1991.
7. Gifford and Elizabeth Pinchot. *The Intelligent Organization, Engaging the Talent and Initiative of Everyone*. San Francisco: Berrett-Koehler, 1996. (Previously published in 1994 as *The End of Bureaucracy & The Rise of the Intelligent Organization*.)
8. Michael D. McMaster. *The Intelligence Advantage, Organising for Complexity*. London: Knowledge Based Development Co. Ltd., 1995.
9. Verna Allee. *The Knowledge Evolution*. Boston: Butterworth-Heinemann, 1977.
10. cf. Tom Peters' endorsement quote on book jacket for Dorothy Marcic's *Managing with the Wisdom of Love*. San Francisco: Jossey-Bass, 1997.

CHAPTER 1 *Put Your Creativity and Spirituality to Work*

1. Joseph Chilton Pearce. *The Bond of Power*. New York: Dutton, 1981.
2. Humberto R. Maturana and F.J. Varela. *The Tree of Knowledge: The Biological Roots of Human Understanding*. Boston: Shambhala, 1992.
3. Alan Watts, who played such a pivotal role in bringing Eastern spirituality to the West, once said that even an act of violence is a grossly miseducated attempt to get life to conform to what that person believes it can then love and be at peace with.

4. The Dalai Lama and Jean-Claude Carriere. *Violence and Compassion*. New York: Doubleday, 1994.

5. St. Augustine. *The Confessions*. New York: Oxford University Press, 1991.

6. Leo Tolstoy. *What is Art?* New York: Penguin USA, 1996.

7. *The American Heritage Dictionary of the English Language*, New College Ed. Boston: Houghton Mifflin Co., 1991.

8. Landor Associates is based in San Francisco, California.

9. "Values Congruence and Differences Between the Interplay of Personal and Organizational Value Systems." *Journal of Business Ethics*. (December 1993) :174

10. Harlan Cleveland. "Information as a Resource." *The Futurist*. (December 1982) :35.

11. From a speech before the American Society of Newspaper Editors, April 16, 1953.

12. Willis Harman. *Global Mind Change*. Indianapolis: Knowledge Systems Inc., 1988, p. 132.

CHAPTER 2 *Develop Yourself as a Creative Spirit*

1. Brian Swimme. *The Universe is a Green Dragon*. Santa Fe, N.M: Bear & Company, 1985, p.117.

2. Kahlil Gibran. *The Prophet*. New York: Alfred A. Knopf, 1958, p. 28.

3. Abraham Maslow. *The Farther Reaches of Human Nature*. New York: Viking Press, 1974

4. Eric Adams. "Electric Pets." *American Way*, (March 18, 1986): 70–72.

5. Erich Fromm. *The Art of Loving*. New York: Harper, 1956.

6. *One Hundred Poems of Kabir*. Translated by Rabindranath Tagore. London: MacMillan Publishers Ltd., 1961.

CHAPTER 3 *Embark on Your Creative Journey*

1. Excerpted from William C. Miller. *Creativity, The Eight Master Keys to Discover, Unlock, and Fulfill Your Creative Potential*. Pleasanton, CA: SyberVision Systems, Inc., 1989, tape # 4.

2. Edwin Bernbaum. *The Way to Shambhala*. New York: Anchor Books, 1980.

3. Thanks to Lorna Catford and Cathy DeForest, Ph.D., for their contributions to this model.

4. Thanks to Cathy DeForest, Ph.D., for sharing her article, "The Art of Conscious Celebration: A New Concept for Today's Leaders." ©1985. Published in *Transforming Leadership: from Vision to Results*. John D. Adams, General Editor. Alexandria, VA: Miles River Press, 1986, p.4.

5. Ibid., p.11.

6. Terence E. Deal and M.K. Key. *Corporate Celebrations*. San Francisco: Berrett-Koehler, 1998.

7. DeForest, p. 12.

8. "Leader as Storyteller." *Executive Excellence*, (October 1996).
9. Alexander Pope. "An Essay on Criticism." *A Treasury of the World's Best Loved Poems*. New York: Avenue Books, 1961, pp. 21–22.

CHAPTER 4 *Employ Innovation Styles as Your Compass*

1. Michael J. Kirton. "Have Adaptors and Innovators Equal Levels of Creativity?." *Psychological Reports*, (Vol. 42, 1978) :695–98 and "Adaptors and Innovators: Why New Initiatives Get Blocked." *Long Range Planning*, (Vol. 52, 1984) :137–43.
2. William C. Miller. *Fostering Creativity: The VALS Perspective*. Menlo Park, CA: SRI International, 1987.
3. The Innovation Styles ® Profile is available from the Global Creativity Corporation 4210 Spicewood Springs Road, Suite 205, Austin, TX 78759. Visit the website at www.globalcreativity.com for more information.
4. Patricia Garfield. *Creative Dreaming*. New York: Ballantine, 1974, p.44.
5. Kurt Hanks and Jay Parry.*Wake Up Your Creative Genius,*. Los Angeles: Kaufman Inc., 1983, p. 55.
6. Roy Rowan.*The Intuitive Manager*. Boston: Little Brown and Company, 1986, p.11.
7. Ibid., p.122.
8. Ibid., p.115.
9. William Wordsworth. "The Recluse, Part First, Book First—Home at Grasmere." *The Complete Poetical Works . . .*, London, Macmillan and Co., 1888.
10. Kevin Kelly. *The Home Planet*. Reading MA: Addison Wesley, 1988, p. 95.

CHAPTER 5 *Transform Blocks to Your Creativity*

1. Thanks to Werner Erhard for his telling of this story.
2. Maya Pines. "Psychological Hardiness: The Role of Challenging Health." *Pyschology Today*, (December 1980) :34.
3. Adam Smith. *The Powers of the Mind*. New York: Summit Books, 1982, p. 188.
4. James Adams. *Conceptual Blockbusting*, 3d ed. Reading, MA: Addison-Wesley, 1986. p.4.
5. Lao Tsu. *Tao Te Ching*. Translated by Gia-Fu Feng and Jane English. New York: Alfred A. Knopf, 1972, p. 63.

CHAPTER 6 *Stimulate a "CREATIVE" Climate for Innovation*

1. Ralph D. Stacey. *Creativity and Complexity in Organizations*. San Francisco: Berrett Koehler, 1996, p.13.
2. Simon Caulkin. "Chaos, Inc." *Across the Board*, pp. 33–36.
3. Based on a summary by Verna Allee. *The Knowledge Evolution*. op.cit., p. 98.
4. Kate Ludeman. *The Worth Ethic*. New York: E.P. Dutton, 1989.

CHAPTER 7 *Align and Attune Innovative Teams*

1. Robert Staubli as conference keynote speaker for "Human Development: A Crucial Prerequisite for the Efficiency of a Company in a Changing Environment." Fourth European Symposium on Long Term Questions of the Future. GDI Institute, Ruschlikon, Switzerland, July 3–5, 1986.

CHAPTER 8 *Take the Lead in Innovative Meetings*

1. Michael Doyle and David Straus. *How to Make Meetings Work*. New York: Berkeley Publishing Group, 1976.
2. Hoffman. *Albert Einstein*, p. 124–25.
3. Michael Ray. "The New Entrepreneurship: A Heroic Path in a Time of Transition." *The New Entrepreneurs*, edited by Michael Ray and John Renesch. San Francisco: New Leaders Press, 1994, p.243.

CHAPTER 9 *Generate Ideas by Modifying and Experimenting*

1. Thanks to Scott Isaksen, former Director of Creative Studies, State University College at Buffalo, for this list.
2. Two "classic" articles on scenario-based planning are: Pierre Wack. "Scenarios: Uncharted Waters Ahead." *Harvard Business Review*, (September/October 1985) :72–89 ;and "Shooting the Rapids," op.cit., (November-December 1985) :139–150.
3. Used with permission of the company

CHAPTER 10 *Generate Ideas by Visioning and Exploring*

1. Thanks to Sharon Jeffrey-Lehrer for this example.
2. Thanks to Chuck McConnell for this drawing.
3. Thanks to Jennifer Hammond for this chart.

PART III

1. Thanks to Juanita Brown for coining this term.

CHAPTER 11 *Inspire Growth with Purpose, Vision, and Values*

1. Thomas Watson, Jr. *A Business and Its Beliefs: The Ideas That Helped Build IBM*. New York: McGraw-Hill, 1963, pp. 4–6.
2. Thomas Peters and Robert Waterman, Jr. *In Search of Excellence*. New York: Warner Books, 1982, p. 279.
3. James Bandrowski. *Creative Planning Throughout the Organization*. New York: Amacom, 1986, p. 17.
4. Thanks to Dave Morley, Strategic Planning Executive at Monsanto Corporation, for this model.
5. Tom Peters. *The Circle of Innovation*. New York: Alfred A. Knopf, 1997, p.22.

6. "Where Do New Ideas Come From?" 1995 Hot Wired Ventures LLC, 1995 Wired Ventures Ltd. Message 31, 1-1-96 From <nicholas@media.mit.edu> To <Ir@Wired.com>.
7. Terrence Deal and Allen Kennedy. *Corporate Cultures.* Reading, MA: Addison-Wesley, 1982, pp. 37, 43.
8. Peter Russell and Roger Evans. *The Creative Manager*, San Francisco: Jossey-Bass, 1992, p.125.
9. Robert Quinn. *Deep Change*, San Francisco:Jossey-Bass,1996, pp. 203–204.
10. Roy Rowan, op. cit., p.130.
11. Ibid., p.43.

CHAPTER 12 *Create and Manage Knowledge*

1. Ikujiro Nonaka and Hirotaka Takeuchi. *The Knowledge Creating Company.* New York: Oxford University Press, 1995, Chapters 3–4.
2. cf. Gene Youngblood on Creative Conversation and work done for Electronic Café for Los Angeles Olympics.
3. "Where Do New Ideas Come From?" op.cit.
4. Rowan, op.cit., p.167.
5. Ibid., pp. 143–44.
6. Ibid., p.120.
7. Thanks to Dennis Jaffe for this formulation.
8. Verna Allee. *The Knowledge Evolution.* Boston: Butterworth-Heinemann, 1997, p.215.
9. cf. report published by Ian Rose, IBR Consulting, 5110 Meadfeild Road, West Vancouver, BC, Canada V7W 3G2, IBRConsulting@compuserve.com.
10. Rosabeth Moss Kanter. *The Change Masters.* New York: Simon & Schuster, 1983, pp. 28–35.
11. Alan G. Robinson and Sam Stern. *Corporate Creativity*, San Francisco: Berrett Koehler,1997, p.148.
12. A. R. Ammons. *Tape for the Turn of the Year.* New York: W.W. Norton, 1965.

CHAPTER 13 *Implement Strategic Innovation Management*

1. Teilhard de Chardin. *Phenomenon of Man.* New York: Harper Torchbooks, 1955/59 cf. also Ursula King. *Spirit of Fire: The Life and Vision of Teilhard de Chardin.* Maryknoll NY: Orbis Books, 1996.
2. Gifford and Elizabeth Pinchot. *The Intelligent Organization, Engaging the Talent and Initiative of Everyone in the Workplace.* San Francisco: Berrett Koehler, 1994, p.32.
3. "The Quality Imperative," *Business Week*, (Oct. 25, 1991) :10–14.
4. "The Quality Imperative." op.cit., p. 14
5. *Webster's New World Dictionary*, Third College Edition. Cleveland & New York, Simon & Schuster, 1991.

CHAPTER 14 *Earn the Right to Lead Innovation*

1. Vaclav Havel. "A Revolution in the Human Mind." A speech delivered before the Latin American Parliament in Sao Paolo, Brazil in September 1996 and reprinted with permission in *Perspectives on Business and Global Change*, (Vol. 11 No. 2, June 1997). Palo Alto: World Business Academy.

2. Chris Galvin is now CEO and Gary Tooker is now Chairman.

3. *One Hundred Poems of Kabir.* translated by Rabindranath Tagore. London: MacMillan Publishers Ltd., 1961.

Permissions Acknowledgments

Grateful acknowledgment is made to the following for permission to use copyrighted material:

Addison Wesley Longman: For an excerpt from James L. Adams, *Conceptual Blockbusting* (excerpted from page 4). © 1986 by James L. Adams. Reprinted with permission.

John Grimes: For the cartoon on page 256. ©1998 by John Grimes.

Alfred A. Knopf, Inc.: For the excerpt from Poem #63 from *Tao Te Ching*, by Lao Tsu, translated by Gia-Fu Feng and Jane English. Copyright © 1972 by Gia-Fu Feng and Jane English. Reprinted with permission.

Little, Brown and Company: For excerpts from *The Intuitive Manager* by Roy Rowan. Coyright © 1986 by Roy Rowan. Reprinted with permission.

Simon & Schuster: For the use of excerpts from poems L: I.126 and LXXIII: III.26 from *One Hundred Poems of Kabir* translated by Rabindranath Tagore. (New York: Macmillan, 1961). Reprinted with permission.

Miles River Press: for the excerpt from the article by Cathy DeForest, "The Art of Conscious Celebration: A New Concept for Today's Leaders." Copyright © 1985 by Cathy DeForest. From *Transforming Leadership: from Vision to Results*, John D. Adams, General Editor. Alexandria, VA: Miles River Press, 1986. Reprinted with permission.

The New Yorker Magazine for the following cartoons:

"I didn't actually build it, but it was based on my idea." © The New Yorker Collection 1984. Charles Addams from cartoonbank.com. All rights reserved.

"Just how fresh are these insights?" © The New Yorker Collection 1984. Lee Lorenz from cartoonbank.com. All rights reserved.

"You know what I'd like to do, Caslow? I'd like to . . ." © The New Yorker Collection 1984. James Stevenson from cartoonbank.com. All rights reserved.

W.W. Norton & Company: for an excerpt from *Tape for the Turn of the Year* by A. R. Ammons. Copyright ©1965 by A. R. Ammons. Reprinted with permission.

Index

Full Value Appraisals, 107, 240
Full Value Satisfactions, 109
Fuller, Buckminster, 260
Future annual report, 167–168
Fuzzy thinking, 213

G

Galvin, Bob, 16, 265
Galvin, Chris, 265
Gandhi, Mohandas, 261
Gatekeepers, 130
GE, transformation of, 266–267, 268
Georgescu, Peter, 194
Gibran, Khalil, 26
Gingrich, Newt, 45
Global Creativity Corporation, 240
Global economy, 19
    issues in, 20–22
Global Mind Change (Harman), 22
Goal
    establishing, 48, 50, 139–140
    mixing long- and short-term, 194
Goal statement, 140
Gooden, John, 68
Gore, W.L. and Associates, 132–133
Green, Ron, 61
Grove, Andrew, 146–147
Gubrud, Bob, 15–16
Guided imagery, 171–174, 181–182
Guilt, as block, 91
Gutenberg, Johannes, 66

H

Harman, Willis, 22
Havel, Vaclav, 259–260
Health, modern improvements in,
    21, 261
Health care, future of, 261
Hewlett Packard, information
    management at, 228

Hock, Dee, 102
Hot-stove method, of transforming
    blocks, 88–89
How to Make Meetings Work
    (Doyle and Straus), 135
Howe, Elias, 76
HP Labs, 106, 190
Hubbard, Barbara Marx, 259
Humor, as aspect of celebration, 60
Hypercompetition, 20
Hypothetical situations, 161

I

IBM, innovative climate at, 240
Ice cream cone, invention of, 31
Idea brokers, 219
Idea-generation matrix, 182–185
Ideas
    collecting, 182
    generating, 29–30, 51–52, 146,
        151–164, 165–185. *See also*
        Experimenting; Exploring;
        Modifying; Visioning
Illusion, recognizing, 87
Imagery, guided, 171–174, 181–182
Imagination
    defined, 96
    importance of, 96–97
Impatience, as block, 92
Implicit knowledge, 211
In Search of Excellence (Peters and
    Waterman), 190
Incisiveness, as aspect of creativity,
    38
Information
    centralized, xiv, xv
    exchange of, 101
    See also Outside information
Information gathering
    accessing, 216
    acting, 217–218
    asking, 215–216